THIS BOOK BELONGS TO

Jadon D. McKee

♡
Mom

Bible Promises for Life
for Teens

The Ultimate Handbook for Your Every Need

BroadStreet
PUBLISHING

Published by BroadStreet Publishing® Group, LLC
Savage, Minnesota, USA
BroadStreetPublishing.com

© 2019 by BroadStreet Publishing

Bible Promises for Life for Teens
The Ultimate Handbook for Your Every Need

978-1-4245-5635-9 (faux leather)
978-1-4245-5724-0 (e-book)

All rights reserved. No part of this book may be reproduced in any form, except for brief quotations in printed reviews, without permission in writing from the publisher.

Scripture quotations marked TPT are taken from *The Psalms: Poetry on Fire, Proverbs: Wisdom from Above, Matthew: Our Loving King, Luke and Acts: To the Lovers of God, John: Eternal Love, Romans: Grace and Glory, Letters from Heaven by the Apostle Paul,* or *Hebrews and James: Faith Works,* The Passion Translation®, copyright © 2014. Used by permission of BroadStreet Publishing Group, LLC, Racine, Wisconsin, USA. All rights reserved. Scripture quotations marked NIV are from the Holy Bible, NEW INTERNATIONAL VERSION®, NIV® Copyright © 1973, 1978, 1984, 2011 by Biblica, Inc.® Used by permission. All rights reserved worldwide. Scripture quotations marked ESV are from the ESV® Bible (The Holy Bible, English Standard Version®), copyright © 2001 by Crossway, a publishing ministry of Good News Publishers. Used by permission. All rights reserved. Scripture quotations marked NLT are from the Holy Bible, New Living Translation, copyright ©1996, 2004, 2007, 2013 by Tyndale House Foundation. Used by permission of Tyndale House Publishers, Inc., Carol Stream, Illinois 60188. All rights reserved. Scripture quotations marked MSG are from THE MESSAGE. Copyright © by Eugene H. Peterson 1993, 1994, 1995, 1996, 2000, 2001, 2002. Used by permission of Tyndale House Publishers, Inc. Scripture quotations marked NKJV are from the New King James Version®. Copyright © 1982 by Thomas Nelson. Used by permission. All rights reserved. Scripture quotations marked HCSB are taken from the Holman Christian Standard Bible®, Copyright © 1999, 2000, 2002, 2003, 2009 by Holman Bible Publishers. Used by permission. HCSB® is a federally registered trademark of Holman Bible Publishers.

Stock or custom editions of BroadStreet Publishing titles may be purchased in bulk for educational, business, ministry, fundraising, or sales promotional use. For information, please e-mail info@broadstreetpublishing.com.

Compiled by Jeremy Bouma at www.jeremybouma.com
Design by Chris Garborg at www.garborgdesign.com

Printed in China
19 20 21 22 23   5 4 3 2 1

Promise Themes

Abandonment	7
Abundance	8
Acceptance	12
Adoption	13
Anger	14
Anxiety	15
Assurance	16
Atonement	17
Authority	18
Belief	19
Belonging	21
Blessing	22
Brokenhearted	28
Calling	29
Care	31
Chosen	34
Church	37
Comfort	38
Companionship	40
Compassion	42
Condemnation	45
Confession	47
Confidence	48
Contentment	49
Courage	50
Covenant	51
Creation	56
Death	58
Defense	61
Deliverance	63
Depression	68
Discipleship	69
Discipline	73
Disobedience	74
Enemies	77
Eternal Life	80
Fairness	83
Faith	84
Faithfulness	87
Family	92
Fear	96
Forgiveness	101
Freedom	109
Friendship	111
Fruit	112
Fulfillment	113
Future	114
Generosity	118
Glory	120
God	121
Goodness	127
Gospel	129
Grace	130
Guidance	133
Healing	139
Heaven	142
Help	143
Holiness	155
Holy Spirit	156
Hope	159
Humility	162
Hunger	163
Identity	164
Idolatry	169
Jesus	170
Joy	173
Judgment	175
Justice	177

Justification	180
Kindness	181
Kingdom	182
Leadership	184
Liberation	186
Life	187
Loneliness	192
Love	193
Mercy	199
New Birth	203
Obedience	204
Patience	213
Peace	215
Persecution	219
Perseverance	221
Plans	223
Poverty	225
Power	226
Prayer	228
Presence	234
Prophecy	237
Prosperity	239
Protection	243
Provision	249
Punishment	261
Purity	267
Purpose	269
Reconciliation	272
Redemption	273
Refuge	275
Relationship	278
Religion	279
Remembrance	280
Renewal	281
Repentance	285
Rescue	288
Rest	295
Restoration	297
Resurrection	305
Revelation	307
Reward	310
Righteousness	313
Sacrifice	315
Sadness	316
Safety	317
Salvation	321
Satisfaction	330
Savior	332
Scripture	335
Security	336
Self-Control	338
Shame	339
Sin	340
Sovereignty	343
Spiritual Gifts	345
Stability	346
Strength	347
Success	352
Suffering	354
Support	357
Temptation	358
Testing	359
The Law	360
Transformation	361
Trust	364
Truth	366
Understanding	367
Unity	368
Victory	369
Weariness	373
Wickedness	374
Wisdom	376
Wonders	380
Work	381
Worry	382
Worship	383

How to Use this Book of God's Promises

God's Word declares, "The earth and sky will wear out and fade away before one word I speak loses its power or fails to accomplish its purpose" (Matthew 24:35 TPT). What a wonderful promise, one of many that God has spoken over your life. Did you know there are hundreds of similar guarantees from God for every one of your needs?

From compassion to confidence, provision to protection, and forgiveness to freedom, these promises don't change. They are for all people, for all time. They reflect the character of God and his ultimate purpose. Keep this in mind as you explore this handbook. Let it guide your life.

Who are God's promises meant for, and which of them still matter today? General promises are given to every one of God's people. Many promises in the Bible are general promises. Specific promises were made to individuals or groups of people—mainly the children of Israel. To help discern how to apply the hundreds of guarantees found in God's Word

1. **Check the context.** Often a promise is part of a bigger story. Referencing your Bible will help you determine the background of a promise.
2. **Look for "if."** Some of God's promises are conditional. *If* you do something, *then* God will do something. Many of God's promises help us yield to his will.
3. **Seek God's character.** Whether a promise is general or specific, the character of God will be evident. This will help you know when God's assurances are relevant to your life.

What you are holding is the ultimate handbook to every one of your needs because it brings you the personal guarantees God has given in his Word. There are more than 2,100 promises arranged in 144 relevant topics, in alphabetical order. You can use this book in a number of ways. Here are some suggestions:

- *Flip to the topic that describes your current situation* if you need encouragement or are searching for a reminder of who God is and what he has promised. Speak truth over your circumstances.
- *Start at the front and work your way to the back* to learn more about God's assurances and his character.
- *Open the book randomly* to see how God's promises apply to you in the moment. God often highlights Scriptures as we read.
- *Read a verse or two from different topics.* Pray and listen. This book

intentionally only includes Scripture because God's Word is powerful enough to speak to you on its own.

• *Use a section as a journaling tool.* Write down your thoughts as you ponder how God's promises apply to your life.

Be ready for God to reveal himself through the promises in this book. Expect to feel his unconditional love. Allow yourself to be challenged, corrected, and changed. Each of God's promises are about his character and his divine purpose. You can stand on his promises because he is fiercely loyal, overly gracious, quick to show compassion, and slow to anger. The Scriptures are also your sure defense for any occasion.

God's promises will never lose their power or fail to accomplish their purpose in your life!

Abandonment

God answered, "I will be with you. And this is your sign that I am the one who has sent you: When you have brought the people out of Egypt, you will worship God at this very mountain."
EXODUS 3:12 NLT

My father and mother walked out and left me,
but GOD took me in.
PSALM 27:10 MSG

GOD will never walk away from his people,
never desert his precious people.
PSALM 94:14 MSG

For no one is abandoned
by the Lord forever.
LAMENTATIONS 3:31 NLT

We are hunted down, but never abandoned by God. We get knocked down, but we are not destroyed.
2 CORINTHIANS 4:9 NLT

Abundance

"You may ask, 'What will we eat in the seventh year if we do not plant or harvest our crops?' I will send you such a blessing in the sixth year that the land will yield enough for three years."
LEVITICUS 25:20-21 NIV

How beautiful are your tents, Jacob,
your dwellings, Israel.
They stretch out like river valleys,
like gardens beside a stream,
like aloes the LORD has planted,
like cedars beside the water.
Water will flow from his buckets,
and his seed will be by abundant water.
His king will be greater than Agag,
and his kingdom will be exalted.
NUMBERS 24:5-7 HCSB

So it shall be, when the LORD your God brings you into the land of which He swore to your fathers, to Abraham, Isaac, and Jacob, to give you large and beautiful cities which you did not build, houses full of all good things, which you did not fill, hewn-out wells which you did not dig, vineyards and olive trees which you did not plant—when you have eaten and are full.
DEUTERONOMY 6:10-11 NKJV

GOD is about to bring you into a good land, a land with brooks and rivers, springs and lakes, streams out of the hills and through the valleys. It's a land of wheat and barley, of vines and figs and pomegranates, of olives, oil, and honey. It's a land where you'll never go hungry—always food on the table and a roof over your head. It's a land where you'll get iron out of rocks and mine copper from the hills.
DEUTERONOMY 8:7-9 MSG

But the land that you are going over to possess is a land of hills and valleys, which drinks water by the rain from heaven, a land that the LORD your God cares for. The eyes of the LORD your God are always upon it, from the beginning of the year to the end of the year.
DEUTERONOMY 11:11-12 ESV

The LORD will send a blessing on your barns and on everything you put your hand to. The LORD your God will bless you in the land he is giving you.
DEUTERONOMY 28:8 NIV

The LORD will grant you abundant prosperity—in the fruit of your womb, the young of your livestock and the crops of your ground—in the land he swore to your ancestors to give you.
DEUTERONOMY 28:11 NIV

GOD will throw open the doors of his sky vaults and pour rain on your land on schedule and bless the work you take in hand. You will lend to many nations but you yourself won't have to take out a loan. GOD will make you the head, not the tail; you'll always be the top dog, never the bottom dog, as you obediently listen to and diligently keep the commands of GOD, your God, that I am commanding you today.
DEUTERONOMY 28:12-13 MSG

All may drink of the anointing from the abundance of your house!
All may drink their fill from the delightful springs of Eden.
PSALM 36:8 TPT

Your visitations of glory bless the earth;
the rivers of God overflow and enrich it.
You paint the wheat fields golden as you provide rich harvests.
PSALM 65:9 TPT

Honor the LORD with your wealth
and with the best part of everything you produce.
Then he will fill your barns with grain,
and your vats will overflow with good wine.
PROVERBS 3:9-10 NLT

Those who work their land will have abundant food,
but those who chase fantasies have no sense.
> PROVERBS 12:11 NIV

The lovers of God will have more than enough,
but the wicked will always lack what they crave.
> PROVERBS 13:25 TPT

Yes, there will be an abundance of flowers
and singing and joy!
The deserts will become as green as the mountains of Lebanon,
as lovely as Mount Carmel or the plain of Sharon.
There the LORD will display his glory,
the splendor of our God.
> ISAIAH 35:2 NLT

"In those days people will live in the houses they build
and eat the fruit of their own vineyards."
> ISAIAH 65:21 NLT

This is what the LORD says:
"I will give Jerusalem a river of peace and prosperity.
The wealth of the nations will flow to her.
Her children will be nursed at her breasts,
carried in her arms, and held on her lap."
> ISAIAH 66:12 NLT

"I will satisfy the priests with abundance,
and my people will be filled with my bounty,"
declares the LORD.
> JEREMIAH 31:14 NIV

The threshing floors will be full of grain,
and the vats will overflow
with new wine and olive oil.
> JOEL 2:24 HCSB

I always thank my God for you because of his grace given you in Christ Jesus. For in him you have been enriched in every way—with all kinds of speech and with all knowledge
>   1 CORINTHIANS 1:5 NIV

For God is the one who provides seed for the farmer and then bread to eat. In the same way, he will provide and increase your resources and then produce a great harvest of generosity in you.
>   2 CORINTHIANS 9:10 NLT

Everything heaven contains has already been lavished upon us as a love gift from our wonderful heavenly Father, the Father of our Lord Jesus—all because he sees us wrapped into Christ. This is why we celebrate him with all our hearts!
>   EPHESIANS 1:3 TPT

Acceptance

The LORD is a friend to those who fear him.
He teaches them his covenant.
> PSALM 25:14 NLT

"For a brief moment I abandoned you,
but with great compassion I will take you back."
> ISAIAH 54:7 NLT

And you did not receive the "spirit of religious duty," leading you back into the fear of never being good enough. But you have received the "Spirit of Full Acceptance," enfolding you into the family of God. And you will never feel orphaned, for as he rises up within us, our spirits join him in saying the words of tender affection, "Beloved Father, Abba!"
> ROMANS 8:15 TPT

Remember the prophecy God gave in Hosea:
"To those who were rejected and not my people,
I will say to them: 'You are mine.'
And to those who were unloved I will say:
'You are my darling.'"
> ROMANS 9:25 TPT

Now you are no longer a slave but God's own child. And since you are his child, God has made you his heir.
> GALATIANS 4:7 NLT

Adoption

For all who are led by the Spirit of God are children of God.
ROMANS 8:14 NLT

The Spirit Himself testifies together with our spirit that we are God's children, and if children, also heirs—heirs of God and co-heirs with Christ—seeing that we suffer with Him so that we may also be glorified with Him.
ROMANS 8:16-17 HCSB

It is not merely the natural offspring of Abraham who are considered the children of God; rather, the children born because of God's promise are counted as descendants.
ROMANS 9:8 TPT

"I will be a Father to you,
And you shall be My sons and daughters,
Says the LORD Almighty."
2 CORINTHIANS 6:18 NKJV

But when that era came to an end and the time of fulfillment had come, God sent his Son, born of a woman, born under the written law. Yet all of this was so that he would redeem and set free all those held hostage to the written law so that we would receive our freedom and a full legal adoption as his children.
GALATIANS 4:4-5 TPT

God decided in advance to adopt us into his own family by bringing us to himself through Jesus Christ. This is what he wanted to do, and it gave him great pleasure.
EPHESIANS 1:5 NLT

But Christ is faithful as the Son over God's house. And we are his house, if indeed we hold firmly to our confidence and the hoped in which we glory.
HEBREWS 3:6 NIV

What marvelous love the Father has extended to us! Just look at it—we're called children of God! That's who we really are. But that's also why the world doesn't recognize us or take us seriously, because it has no idea who he is or what he's up to.
1 JOHN 3:1 MSG

Anger

A gentle answer deflects anger,
but harsh words make tempers flare.
> PROVERBS 15:1 NLT

Good sense makes one slow to anger,
and it is his glory to overlook an offense.
> PROVERBS 19:11 ESV

Human anger does not produce the righteousness God desires.
> JAMES 1:20 NLT

Anxiety

Surrender your anxiety!
Be silent and stop your striving
and you will see that I am God.
I am the God above all the nations,
and I will be exalted throughout the whole earth.
   PSALM 46:11 TPT

"So don't worry, saying, 'What will we eat?' or 'What will we drink?' or 'What will we wear?' For the idolaters eagerly seek all these things, and your heavenly Father knows that you need them."
   MATTHEW 6:31-32 HCSB

"Listen to me. Never let anxiety enter your hearts. Never worry about any of your needs, such as food or clothing. For your life is infinitely more than just food or the clothing you wear."
   LUKE 12:22-23 TPT

Cast all your anxiety on him because he cares for you.
   1 PETER 5:7 NIV

Assurance

"Is anything too hard for the LORD? I will return to you at the appointed time next year, and Sarah will have a son."
GENESIS 18:14 NIV

GOD said, "And who do you think made the human mouth? And who makes some mute, some deaf, some sighted, some blind? Isn't it I, GOD? So, get going. I'll be right there with you—with your mouth! I'll be right there to teach you what to say."
EXODUS 4:11-12 MSG

The LORD replied, "My Presence will go with you, and I will give you rest."
EXODUS 33:14 NIV

The LORD answered Moses, "Is the LORD's power limited? You will see whether or not what I have promised will happen to you."
NUMBERS 11:23 HCSB

God is not man, that he should lie,
or a son of man, that he should change his mind.
Has he said, and will he not do it?
Or has he spoken, and will he not fulfill it?
NUMBERS 23:19 ESV

"No misfortune is seen in Jacob,
no misery observed in Israel.
The LORD their God is with them;
the shout of the King is among them."
NUMBERS 23:21 NIV

"No magic spells can bind Jacob,
no incantations can hold back Israel.
People will look at Jacob and Israel and say,
'What a great thing has God done!'"
NUMBERS 23:23 MSG

Atonement

"For the life of a creature is in the blood, and I have given it to you to make atonement for yourselves on the altar; it is the blood that makes atonement for one's life."
LEVITICUS 17:11 NIV

"The priest is to make atonement for the whole Israelite community, and they will be forgiven, for it was not intentional and they have presented to the LORD for their wrong a food offering and a sin offering. The whole Israelite community and the foreigners residing among them will be forgiven, because all the people were involved in the unintentional wrong."
NUMBERS 15:25-26 NIV

"I will establish My covenant with you, and you will know that I am Yahweh, so that when I make atonement for all you have done, you will remember and be ashamed, and never open your mouth again because of your disgrace." This is the declaration of the Lord GOD.
EZEKIEL 16:62-63 HCSB

My dear children, I write this to you so that you will not sin. But if anybody does sin, we have an advocate with the Father—Jesus Christ, the Righteous One. He is the atoning sacrifice for our sins, and not only for ours but also for the sins of the whole world.
1 JOHN 2:1-2 NIV

Authority

"I will raise up for them a prophet like you from among their brothers. And I will put my words in his mouth, and he shall speak to them all that I command him. And whoever will not listen to my words that he shall speak in my name, I myself will require it of him."

DEUTERONOMY 18:18-19 ESV

So the LORD said to Moses, "Take Joshua son of Nun, a man in whom is the spirit of leadership, and lay your hand on him. Have him stand before Eleazar the priest and the entire assembly and commission him in their presence. Give him some of your authority so the whole Israelite community will obey him. He is to stand before Eleazar the priest, who will obtain decisions for him by inquiring of the Urim before the LORD. At his command he and the entire community of the Israelites will go out, and at his command they will come in."

NUMBERS 27:18-21 NIV

All Israel came together to David at Hebron and said, "We are your own flesh and blood. In the past, even while Saul was king, you were the one who led Israel on their military campaigns. And the LORD your God said to you, 'You will shepherd my people Israel, and you will become their ruler.'"

1 CHRONICLES 11:1-2 NIV

Belief

Therefore the Lord GOD said:
"Look, I have laid a stone in Zion,
a tested stone,
a precious cornerstone, a sure foundation;
the one who believes will be unshakable."
ISAIAH 28:16 HCSB

Jesus said to him, "If you can believe,
all things are possible to him who believes."
MARK 9:23 NKJV

Jesus shouted out passionately, "To believe in me is to believe in God who sent me. For when you look at me you are seeing the One who sent me. I have come as a light to shine in this dark world so that all who trust in me will no longer wander in darkness."
JOHN 12:44-46 TPT

"Because you have seen me, you have believed; blessed are those who have not seen and yet have believed."
JOHN 20:29 NIV

Jesus ordered us to preach and warn the people that God had appointed him to be the judge of the living and the dead. And not only us, but all of the prophets agree in their writings that everyone who believes in him receives complete forgiveness of sins through the power of his name.
ACTS 10:42-43 TPT

But to the one who does not work, but believes on Him who declares the ungodly to be righteous, his faith is credited for righteousness.
ROMANS 4:5 HCSB

"See, I lay in Zion a stone that causes people to stumble
and a rock that makes them fall,
and the one who believes in him will never be put to shame."
ROMANS 9:33 NIV

For the Scriptures encourage us with these words:
"Everyone who believes in him will never be disappointed."
ROMANS 10:11 TPT

Since God in his wisdom saw to it that the world would never know him through human wisdom, he has used our foolish preaching to save those who believe.
1 CORINTHIANS 1:21 NLT

I have written these things to you who believe in the name of the Son of God, so that you may know that you have eternal life.
1 JOHN 5:13 HCSB

Belonging

"You will be My people,
and I will be your God."
JEREMIAH 30:22 HCSB

"However, your real source of joy isn't merely that these spirits submit to your authority, but that your names are written in the journals of heaven and that you belong to God's kingdom. This is the true source of your authority."
LUKE 10:20 TPT

Jesus, the Holy One, makes us holy. And as sons and daughters, we now belong to his same Father, so he is not ashamed or embarrassed to introduce us as his brothers and sisters!
HEBREWS 2:11 TPT

Blessing

"And I will make of you a great nation, and I will bless you and make your name great, so that you will be a blessing. I will bless those who bless you, and him who dishonors you I will curse, and in you all the families of the earth shall be blessed."

GENESIS 12:2-3 ESV

"I will certainly bless you. I will multiply your descendants beyond number, like the stars in the sky and the sand on the seashore. Your descendants will conquer the cities of their enemies. And through your descendants all the nations of the earth will be blessed—all because you have obeyed me."

GENESIS 22:17-18 NLT

From the time he put him in charge of his household and of all that he owned, the LORD blessed the household of the Egyptian because of Joseph. The blessing of the LORD was on everything Potiphar had, both in the house and in the field.

GENESIS 39:5 NIV

Then [Israel] blessed Joseph and said:
"The God before whom my fathers Abraham and Isaac walked,
the God who has been my shepherd all my life to this day,
the Angel who has redeemed me from all harm—
may He bless these boys.
And may they be called by my name
and the names of my fathers Abraham and Isaac,
and may they grow to be numerous within the land."

GENESIS 48:15-16 HCSB

"You must make an earthen altar for Me and sacrifice on it your burnt offerings and fellowship offerings, your sheep and goats, as well as your cattle. I will come to you and bless you in every place where I cause My name to be remembered."

EXODUS 20:24 HCSB

"The LORD bless you and keep you;
The LORD make His face shine upon you,
And be gracious to you."

NUMBERS 6:24-25 NKJV

"The LORD your God has multiplied you, and here you are today, as the stars of heaven in multitude. May the LORD God of your fathers make you a thousand times more numerous than you are, and bless you as He has promised you!"
DEUTERONOMY 1:10–11 NKJV

GOD, your God, has blessed you in everything you have done. He has guarded you in your travels through this immense wilderness. For forty years now, GOD, your God, has been right here with you. You haven't lacked one thing.
DEUTERONOMY 2:7 MSG

He will love you, bless you, and multiply you. He will bless your descendants, and the produce of your land—your grain, new wine, and oil—the young of your herds, and the newborn of your flocks, in the land He swore to your fathers that He would give you.
DEUTERONOMY 7:13 HCSB

You will be blessed above all peoples; there will be no infertile male or female among you or your livestock.
DEUTERONOMY 7:14 HCSB

See, I am setting before you today a blessing and a curse: the blessing, if you obey the commandments of the LORD your God, which I command you today, and the curse, if you do not obey the commandments of the LORD your God, but turn aside from the way that I am commanding you today, to go after other gods that you have not known.
DEUTERONOMY 11:26–28 ESV

There will be no poor among you, however, because the LORD is certain to bless you in the land the LORD your God is giving you to possess as an inheritance.
DEUTERONOMY 15:4 HCSB

Oh yes—GOD, your God, will bless you just as he promised. You will lend to many nations but won't borrow from any; you'll rule over many nations but none will rule over you.
DEUTERONOMY 15:6 MSG

You are to hold a seven-day festival for the LORD your God in the place He chooses, because the LORD your God will bless you in all your produce and in all the work of your hands, and you will have abundant joy.
DEUTERONOMY 16:15 HCSB

You will be blessed in the city and blessed in the country.
DEUTERONOMY 28:3 HCSB

Your children and your crops will be blessed.
The offspring of your herds and flocks will be blessed.
DEUTERONOMY 28:4 NLT

Your basket and kneading bowl will be blessed.
DEUTERONOMY 28:5 HCSB

GOD'S blessing in your coming in, GOD'S blessing in your going out.
DEUTERONOMY 28:6 MSG

"Now listen! Today I am giving you a choice between life and death, between prosperity and disaster. For I command you this day to love the LORD your God and to keep his commands, decrees, and regulations by walking in his ways. If you do this, you will live and multiply, and the LORD your God will bless you and the land you are about to enter and occupy."
DEUTERONOMY 30:15-16 NLT

Blessed is the one whom God corrects;
so do not despise the discipline of the Almighty.
For he wounds, but he also binds up;
he injures, but his hands also heal.
JOB 5:17-18 NIV

Blessed is the one
who does not walk in step with the wicked
or stand in the way that sinners take
or sit in the company of mockers,
but whose delight is in the law of the LORD,
and who meditates on his law day and night.
PSALM 1:1-2 NIV

For You, LORD, bless the righteous one;
You surround him with favor like a shield.
PSALM 5:12 HCSB

You prepare a feast for me
in the presence of my enemies.
You honor me by anointing my head with oil.
My cup overflows with blessings.
> PSALM 23:5 NLT

He will receive blessing from the LORD,
and righteousness from the God of his salvation.
> PSALM 24:5 HCSB

For those blessed by Him shall inherit the earth,
But those cursed by Him shall be cut off.
> PSALM 37:22 NKJV

Blessed is the one
who trusts in the LORD,
who does not look to the proud,
to those who turn aside to false gods.
> PSALM 40:4 NIV

God always blesses those who are
kind to the poor and helpless.
They're the first ones God helps
when they find themselves in any trouble.
> PSALM 41:1 TPT

Praise the LORD!
Blessed is the man who fears the LORD,
Who delights greatly in His commandments.
> PSALM 112:1 NKJV

Yes! He will bless his lovers who bow before him,
no matter who they are.
> PSALM 115:13 TPT

He strengthens the bars of your gates
and blesses your people within you.
> PSALM 147:13 NIV

You're blessed when you meet Lady Wisdom,
when you make friends with Madame Insight.
PROVERBS 3:13 MSG

The wicked walk under God's constant curse.
But godly lovers walk under a stream of his blessing
for they seek to do what is right.
PROVERBS 3:33 TPT

The blessing of the LORD makes a person rich,
and he adds no sorrow with it.
PROVERBS 10:22 NLT

The one who blesses others is abundantly blessed;
those who help others are helped.
PROVERBS 11:25 MSG

Good people obtain favor from the LORD,
but he condemns those who devise wicked schemes.
PROVERBS 12:2 NIV

Blessed is the one who fears the LORD always,
but whoever hardens his heart will fall into calamity.
PROVERBS 28:14 ESV

"I will make them and the places all around My hill a blessing; and I will cause showers to come down in their season; there shall be showers of blessing."
EZEKIEL 34:26 NKJV

Jesus replied, "Go back and report to John what you hear and see: The blind receive sight, the lame walk, those who have leprosy are cleansed, the deaf hear, the dead are raised, and the good news is proclaimed to the poor. Blessed is anyone who does not stumble on account of me."
MATTHEW 11:4-6 NIV

Jesus replied, "Blessed are you, Simon son of Jonah, for this was not revealed to you by flesh and blood, but by my Father in heaven."
MATTHEW 16:17 NIV

"For he set his tender gaze upon me, his lowly servant girl.
And from here on, everyone will know that I have been favored and blessed.
The Mighty One has worked a mighty miracle for me; holy is his name!"
LUKE 1:48-49 TPT

"Now go back and tell John what you have just seen and heard here today. The blind are now seeing. The crippled are now walking. Those who were lepers are now cured. Those who were deaf are now hearing. Those who were dead are now raised back to life. The poor and broken are given the hope of salvation. And tell John these words: 'The blessing of heaven comes upon those who never lose their faith in me no matter what happens.'"
LUKE 7:22-23 TPT

"Very truly I tell you, no servant is greater than his master, nor is a messenger greater than the one who sent him. Now that you know these things, you will be blessed if you do them."
JOHN 13:16-17 NIV

Finally, all of you be of one mind, having compassion for one another; love as brothers, be tenderhearted, be courteous; not returning evil for evil or reviling for reviling, but on the contrary blessing, knowing that you were called to this, that you may inherit a blessing.
1 PETER 3:8-9 NKJV

Blessed is the one who reads aloud the words of this prophecy, and blessed are those who hear it and take to heart what is written in it, because the time is near.
REVELATION 1:3 NIV

"Look, I will come as unexpectedly as a thief! Blessed are all who are watching for me, who keep their clothing ready so they will not have to walk around naked and ashamed."
REVELATION 16:15 NLT

"Write: 'Blessed are those who are called to the marriage supper of the Lamb!'" And he said to me, "These are the true sayings of God."
REVELATION 19:9 NKJV

Brokenhearted

He heals the brokenhearted
and binds up their wounds.
> PSALM 147:3 NIV

The Spirit of the Sovereign LORD is upon me,
for the LORD has anointed me
to bring good news to the poor.
He has sent me to comfort the brokenhearted
and proclaim that captives will be released
and prisoners will be freed.
He has sent me to tell those who mourn
that the time of the LORD's favor has come,
and with it, the day of God's anger against their enemies.
> ISAIAH 61:1-2 NLT

Calling

"I, the LORD, have called you to demonstrate my righteousness.
I will take you by the hand and guard you,
and I will give you to my people, Israel,
as a symbol of my covenant with them."

ISAIAH 42:6 NLT

"And you will be a light to guide the nations.
You will open the eyes of the blind.
You will free the captives from prison,
releasing those who sit in dark dungeons."

ISAIAH 42:6-7 NLT

Listen to me, all you in distant lands!
Pay attention, you who are far away!
The LORD called me before my birth;
from within the womb he called me by name.

ISAIAH 49:1 NLT

But the LORD said to me, "Do not say, 'I am too young.' You must go to everyone I send you to and say whatever I command you."

JEREMIAH 1:7 NIV

"God authorized and commanded me to commission you: Go out and train everyone you meet, far and near, in this way of life, marking them by baptism in the threefold name: Father, Son, and Holy Spirit."

MATTHEW 28:18-19 MSG

Jesus called out to them, "Come, follow me, and I will show you how to fish for people!"

MARK 1:17 NLT

"Do not yield to your fear, Simon Peter. From now on you will catch men for salvation!"

LUKE 5:10 TPT

"From everyone who has been given much, much will be demanded; and from the one who has been entrusted with much, much more will be asked."
LUKE 12:48 NIV

"I bestow on you a kingdom, just as My Father bestowed one on Me, so that you may eat and drink at My table in My kingdom. And you will sit on thrones judging the 12 tribes of Israel."
LUKE 22:29-30 HCSB

"I tell you the truth, anyone who believes in me will do the same works I have done, and even greater works, because I am going to be with the Father."
JOHN 14:12 NLT

Jesus repeated his greeting, "Peace to you!" And he told them, "Just as the Father has sent me, I'm now sending you."
JOHN 20:21 TPT

A spiritual gift is given to each of us so we can help each other.
1 CORINTHIANS 12:7 NLT

And he has appointed some with grace to be apostles, and some with grace to be prophets, and some with grace to be evangelists, and some with grace to be pastors, and some with grace to be teachers. And their calling is to nurture and prepare all the holy believers to do their own works of ministry, and as they do this they will enlarge and build up the body of Christ.
EPHESIANS 4:11-12 TPT

My dear brothers and sisters, don't be so eager to become a teacher in the church since you know that we who teach are held to a higher standard of judgment.
JAMES 3:1 TPT

Then Samuel took a flask of olive oil and poured it on Saul's head and kissed him, saying, "Has not the LORD anointed you ruler over his inheritance?"
1 SAMUEL 10:1 NIV

Care

The LORD answered Moses, "Go on ahead of the people and take some of the elders of Israel with you. Take the staff you struck the Nile with in your hand and go. I am going to stand there in front of you on the rock at Horeb; when you hit the rock, water will come out of it and the people will drink."
EXODUS 17:5-6 NIV

"I'll take care of you. You'll have a quiet death and be buried in peace. You won't be around to see the doom that I'm going to bring upon this place."
2 KINGS 23:27 MSG

Day by day the LORD takes care of the innocent,
and they will receive an inheritance that lasts forever.
PSALM 37:18 NLT

The faithful lovers of God will inherit the earth
and enjoy every promise of God's care,
dwelling in peace forever.
PSALM 37:29 TPT

What a glorious God!
He gives us salvation over and over,
then daily he carries our burdens!
PSALM 68:19 TPT

Yes, you have been with me from birth;
from my mother's womb you have cared for me
No wonder I am always praising you!
PSALM 71:6 NLT

He cares for the orphans and widows,
but he frustrates the plans of the wicked.
PSALM 146:9B NLT

For the LORD is our judge,
our lawgiver, and our king.
He will care for us and save us.
ISAIAH 33:22 NLT

I will be your God throughout your lifetime—
until your hair is white with age.
I made you, and I will care for you.
I will carry you along and save you.
ISAIAH 46:4 NLT

"In an outburst of anger I turned my back on you—
but only for a moment.
It's with lasting love
that I'm tenderly caring for you."
ISAIAH 54:8 MSG

"Return, O faithless children,
declares the LORD;
for I am your master;
I will take you, one from a city and two from a family,
and I will bring you to Zion.
And I will give you shepherds after my own heart, who will feed you with
knowledge and understanding."
JEREMIAH 3:14–15 ESV

"I'll take care of your orphans.
Your widows can depend on me."
JEREMIAH 49:11 MSG

I will place over them one shepherd, my servant David, and he will tend them; he will tend them and be their shepherd. I the LORD will be their God, and my servant David will be prince among them. I the LORD have spoken.
EZEKIEL 34:23–24 NIV

The LORD is good,
a refuge in times of trouble.
He cares for those who trust in him.
NAHUM 1:7 NIV

"Aren't five sparrows sold for two pennies? Yet not one of them is forgotten in God's sight. Indeed, the hairs of your head are all counted. Don't be afraid; you are worth more than many sparrows!"
LUKE 12:6-7 HCSB

"Look at the lilies and how they grow. They don't work or make their clothing, yet Solomon in all his glory was not dressed as beautifully as they are. And if God cares so wonderfully for flowers that are here today and thrown into the fire tomorrow, he will certainly care for you. Why do you have so little faith?"
LUKE 12:27-28 NLT

Don't run roughshod over the concerns of your brothers and sisters. Their concerns are God's concerns, and he will take care of them. We've warned you about this before.
1 THESSALONIANS 4:6 MSG

Chosen

"Abraham is to become a great and powerful nation, and all the nations of the earth will be blessed through him. For I have chosen him so that he will command his children and his house after him to keep the way of the LORD by doing what is right and just. This is how the LORD will fulfill to Abraham what He promised him."
GENESIS 18:18-19 HCSB

GOD spoke to Moses: "See what I've done; I've personally chosen Bezalel son of Uri, son of Hur of the tribe of Judah. I've filled him with the Spirit of God, giving him skill and know-how and expertise in every kind of craft."
EXODUS 31:1-3 MSG

"Your job is to take care of the Sanctuary and the Altar so that there will be no more outbreaks of anger on the People of Israel. I personally have picked your brothers, the Levites, from Israel as a whole. I'm giving them to you as a gift, a gift of GOD, to help with the work of the Tent of Meeting. But only you and your sons may serve as priests, working around the Altar and inside the curtain. The work of the priesthood is my exclusive gift to you; it cannot be delegated—anyone else who invades the Sanctuary will be executed."
NUMBERS 18:5-7 MSG

And because He loved your fathers, therefore He chose their descendants after them; and He brought you out of Egypt with His Presence, with His mighty power, driving out from before you nations greater and mightier than you, to bring you in, to give you their land as an inheritance, as it is this day.
DEUTERONOMY 4:39-40 NKJV

For you are a people holy to the LORD your God. The LORD your God has chosen you to be a people for his treasured possession, out of all the peoples who are on the face of the earth.
DEUTERONOMY 7:6 ESV

But it was your ancestors that GOD fell in love with; he picked their children— that's you!—out of all the other peoples. That's where we are right now.
DEUTERONOMY 10:15 MSG

And the LORD has declared today that you are a people for his treasured possession, as he has promised you, and that you are to keep all his commandments, and that he will set you in praise and in fame and in honor high above all nations that he has made, and that you shall be a people holy to the LORD your God, as he promised.

DEUTERONOMY 26:18-19 ESV

And of all my sons (for the LORD has given me many sons) He has chosen my son Solomon to sit on the throne of the kingdom of the LORD over Israel. Now He said to me, "It is your son Solomon who shall build My house and My courts; for I have chosen him to be My son, and I will be his Father."

1 CHRONICLES 28:5-6 NKJV

Be careful now, for the LORD has chosen you to build a house for the sanctuary; be strong and do it.

1 CHRONICLES 28:10 ESV

For God knew his people in advance, and he chose them to become like his Son, so that his Son would be the firstborn among many brothers and sisters.

ROMANS 8:29 NLT

Even before he made the world, God loved us and chose us in Christ to be holy and without fault in his eyes.

EPHESIANS 1:4 NLT

For we know, brothers and sisters loved by God, that he has chosen you, because our gospel came to you not simply with words but also with power, with the Holy Spirit and deep conviction.

1 THESSALONIANS 1:4-5 NIV

But we ought always to thank God for you, brothers and sisters loved by the Lord, because God chose you as firstfruits to be saved through the sanctifying work of the Spirit and through belief in the truth. He called you to this through our gospel, that you might share in the glory of our Lord Jesus Christ.

2 THESSALONIANS 2:13-14 NIV

Listen, my beloved brethren: Has God not chosen the poor of this world to be rich in faith and heirs of the kingdom which He promised to those who love Him?
JAMES 2:5 NKJV

But you are a chosen people, a royal priesthood, a holy nation, God's special possession, that you may declare the praises of him who called you out of darkness into his wonderful light.
1 PETER 2:9 NIV

So, dear brothers and sisters, work hard to prove that you really are among those God has called and chosen. Do these things, and you will never fall away. Then God will give you a grand entrance into the eternal Kingdom of our Lord and Savior Jesus Christ.
2 PETER 1:10-11 NLT

Church

What we have is one body with many parts, each its proper size and in its proper place. No part is important on its own.
1 CORINTHIANS 12:20 MSG

Now you are the body of Christ, and each one of you is a part of it.
1 CORINTHIANS 12:27 NIV

His intent was that now, through the church, the manifold wisdom of God should be made known to the rulers and authorities in the heavenly realms, according to his eternal purpose that he accomplished in Christ Jesus our Lord.
EPHESIANS 3:10-11 NIV

Comfort

LORD, you know the hopes of the helpless.
Surely you will hear their cries and comfort them.
> PSALM 10:17 NLT

Your rod and your staff,
they comfort me.
> PSALM 23:4 NIV

The LORD will comfort Israel again
and have pity on her ruins.
Her desert will blossom like Eden,
her barren wilderness like the garden of the LORD.
Joy and gladness will be found there.
Songs of thanksgiving will fill the air.
> ISAIAH 51:3 NLT

"I have seen what they do,
but I will heal them anyway!
I will lead them.
I will comfort those who mourn."
> ISAIAH 57:18 NLT

To all who mourn in Israel,
he will give a crown of beauty for ashes,
a joyous blessing instead of mourning,
festive praise instead of despair.
In their righteousness, they will be like great oaks
that the LORD has planted for his own glory.
> ISAIAH 61:3 NLT

"As a mother comforts her son,
so I will comfort you,
and you will be comforted in Jerusalem."
> ISAIAH 66:13 HCSB

"Then young women will dance and be glad,
young men and old as well.
I will turn their mourning into gladness;
I will give them comfort and joy instead of sorrow."
> JEREMIAH 31:13 NIV

Should you talk that way, O family of Israel?
Will the LORD's Spirit have patience with such behavior?
If you would do what is right,
you would find my words comforting.
> MICAH 2:7 NLT

Praise the God and Father of our Lord Jesus Christ, the Father of mercies and the God of all comfort
> 2 CORINTHIANS 1:3 HCSB

Companionship

Then the Lord God said, "It is not good for the man to be alone. I will make a helper who is just right for him."
GENESIS 2:18 NLT

When the angel of the LORD appeared to Gideon, he said, "The LORD is with you, mighty warrior."
JUDGES 6:12 NIV

And the LORD said to him, "Surely I will be with you, and you shall defeat the Midianites as one man."
JUDGES 6:16 NKJV

The LORD is with you when you are with Him. If you seek Him, He will be found by you, but if you abandon Him, He will abandon you.
2 CHRONICLES 15:2 HCSB

There they are in great terror,
for God is with the generation of the righteous.
PSALM 14:5 ESV

I know the LORD is always with me.
I will not be shaken, for he is right beside me.
PSALM 16:8 NLT

The LORD Almighty is with us;
the God of Jacob is our fortress.
PSALM 46:7 NIV

Nevertheless, I am continually with you;
you hold my right hand.
PSALM 73:23 ESV

"Do not be afraid, Jacob, my servant,
for I am with you," says the LORD.
"I will completely destroy the nations to which I have exiled you,
but I will not completely destroy you.
I will discipline you, but with justice;
I cannot let you go unpunished."
   JEREMIAH 46:28 NLT

Though he brings grief, he will show compassion,
so great is his unfailing love.
For he does not willingly bring affliction
or grief to anyone.
   LAMENTATIONS 3:32-33 NIV

"Thus they shall know that I, the LORD their God, am with them, and they, the house of Israel, are My people," says the Lord GOD.
   EZEKIEL 34:30 NKJV

"You will know that I am present in Israel
and that I am Yahweh your God,
and there is no other.
My people will never again be put to shame."
   JOEL 2:27 HCSB

"Teach these new disciples to obey all the commands I have given you. And be sure of this: I am with you always, even to the end of the age."
   MATTHEW 28:20 NLT

"Every person the Father gives me eventually comes running to me. And once that person is with me, I hold on and don't let go."
   JOHN 6:37 MSG

Jesus answered and said to him, "If anyone loves Me, he will keep My word; and My Father will love him, and We will come to him and make Our home with him."
   JOHN 14:23 NKJV

Compassion

The LORD will indeed vindicate His people
and have compassion on His servants
when He sees that their strength is gone
and no one is left—slave or free.
   DEUTERONOMY 32:36 HCSB

"Even after they had cast an image of a calf
for themselves and said,
'This is your God who brought you out of Egypt,'
and they had committed terrible blasphemies,
You did not abandon them in the wilderness
because of Your great compassion."
   NEHEMIAH 9:18-19 HCSB

But You, Lord, are a compassionate and gracious God,
slow to anger and rich in faithful love and truth.
   PSALM 86:15 HCSB

The LORD is compassionate and gracious,
slow to anger, abounding in love.
   PSALM 103:8 NIV

The LORD is good to all;
he has compassion on all he has made.
   PSALM 145:9 NIV

For the LORD will have compassion on Jacob and will again choose Israel,
and will set them in their own land, and sojourners will join them and will attach
themselves to the house of Jacob.
   ISAIAH 14:1 ESV

Thus says the LORD: "Against all My evil neighbors who touch the inheritance which I have caused My people Israel to inherit—behold, I will pluck them out of their land and pluck out the house of Judah from among them. Then it shall be, after I have plucked them out, that I will return and have compassion on them and bring them back, everyone to his heritage and everyone to his land. And it shall be, if they will learn carefully the ways of My people, to swear by My name, 'As the LORD lives,' as they taught My people to swear by Baal, then they shall be established in the midst of My people."

JEREMIAH 12:14-16 NKJV

This is what the LORD says:
"I will restore the fortunes of Jacob's tents
and have compassion on his dwellings;
the city will be rebuilt on her ruins,
and the palace will stand in its proper place."

JEREMIAH 30:18 NIV

"But now I will return Jacob back from exile, I'll be compassionate with all the people of Israel, and I'll be zealous for my holy name. Eventually the memory will fade, the memory of their shame over their betrayals of me when they lived securely in their own land, safe and unafraid."

EZEKIEL 39:25-26 MSG

"You are a merciful and compassionate God, slow to become angry, rich in faithful love, and One who relents from sending disaster."

JONAH 4:2 HCSB

He will again have compassion on us,
And will subdue our iniquities.
You will cast all our sins
Into the depths of the sea.

MICAH 7:19 NKJV

"Because of our God's merciful compassion,
the Dawn from on high will visit us
to shine on those who live in darkness
and the shadow of death,
to guide our feet into the way of peace."
LUKE 1:78-79 HCSB

"Show mercy and compassion for others, just as your heavenly Father overflows with mercy and compassion for all."
LUKE 6:36 TPT

As you know, we count as blessed those who have persevered. You have heard of Job's perseverance and have seen what the Lord finally brought about. The Lord is full of compassion and mercy.
JAMES 5:11 NIV

Condemnation

So now there is no longer any condemnation for those who believe in him, but the unbeliever already lives under condemnation because they do not believe in the name of God's beloved Son.
JOHN 3:18 TPT

"I speak to you an eternal truth: if you embrace my message and believe in the One who sent me, you will never face condemnation, for in me, you have already passed from the realm of death into the realm of eternal life!"
JOHN 5:24 TPT

Jesus was left alone with the woman still standing there in front of him. So he stood back up and said to her, "Dear woman, where are your accusers? Is there no one here to condemn you?"
Looking around, she replied, "I see no one, Lord."
Jesus said, "Then I certainly don't condemn you either. Go, and from now on, be free from a life of sin."
JOHN 8:10-11 TPT

And this free-flowing gift imparts to us much more than what was given to us through the one who sinned. For because of one transgression, we are all facing a death sentence with a verdict of "Guilty!" But this gracious gift leaves us free from our many failures and brings us into the perfect righteousness of God—acquitted with the words "Not guilty!"
ROMANS 5:16 TPT

So now there is no condemnation for those who belong to Christ Jesus.
ROMANS 8:1 NLT

Who then is left to condemn us? Certainly not Jesus, the Anointed One! For he gave his life for us, and even more than that, he has conquered death and is now risen, exalted, and enthroned by God at his right hand. So how could he possibly condemn us since he is continually praying for our triumph?

ROMANS 8:34 TPT

Our actions will show that we belong to the truth, so we will be confident when we stand before God. Even if we feel guilty, God is greater than our feelings, and he knows everything.

1 JOHN 3:19-20 NLT

Confession

"But if they confess their iniquity and the iniquity of their fathers in their treachery that they committed against me, and also in walking contrary to me, so that I walked contrary to them and brought them into the land of their enemies—if then their uncircumcised heart is humbled and they make amends for their iniquity, then I will remember my covenant with Jacob, and I will remember my covenant with Isaac and my covenant with Abraham, and I will remember the land."
LEVITICUS 26:40-42 ESV

This is what I've learned through it all:
Every believer should confess their sins to God;
do it every time God has uncovered you in the time of exposing.
For if you do this, when sudden storms of life overwhelm,
you'll be kept safe.
PSALM 32:6 TPT

Whoever conceals his transgressions will not prosper,
but he who confesses and forsakes them will obtain mercy.
PROVERBS 28:13 ESV

If we claim to be without sin, we deceive ourselves and the truth is not in us. If we confess our sins, he is faithful and just and will forgive us our sins and purify us from all unrighteousness.
1 JOHN 1:8-9 NIV

Confidence

Then the LORD turned to him and said, "Go with the strength you have, and rescue Israel from the Midianites. I am sending you!"
JUDGES 6:14 NLT

[The righteous] are confident and fearless
and can face their foes triumphantly.
PSALM 112:8 NLT

And so, dear brothers and sisters, we can boldly enter heaven's Most Holy Place because of the blood of Jesus. By his death, Jesus opened a new and life-giving way through the curtain into the Most Holy Place.
HEBREWS 10:19-20 NLT

Contentment

"You're blessed when you're content with just who you are—no more, no less. That's the moment you find yourselves proud owners of everything that can't be bought."
MATTHEW 5:5 MSG

Now godliness with contentment is great gain. For we brought nothing into this world, and it is certain we can carry nothing out. And having food and clothing, with these we shall be content.
1 TIMOTHY 6:6-8 NKJV

Don't be obsessed with money but live content with what you have, for you always have God's presence. For hasn't he promised you,
"I will never leave you alone, never!
And I will not loosen my grip on your life!"
HEBREWS 13:5 TPT

Courage

"Look! He has placed the land in front of you. Go and occupy it as the LORD, the God of your ancestors, has promised you. Don't be afraid! Don't be discouraged!"
DEUTERONOMY 1:21 NLT

Then Moses called Joshua and said to him in the sight of all Israel, "Be strong and of good courage, for you must go with this people to the land which the LORD has sworn to their fathers to give them, and you shall cause them to inherit it."
DEUTERONOMY 31:7 NKJV

"Be strong and courageous, for you will distribute the land I swore to their fathers to give them as an inheritance."
JOSHUA 1:6 HCSB

"Do not be afraid or discouraged because of this vast army. For the battle is not yours, but God's."
2 CHRONICLES 20:15 NIV

Then David said to Solomon his son, "Be strong and courageous and do it. Do not be afraid and do not be dismayed, for the LORD God, even my God, is with you. He will not leave you or forsake you, until all the work for the service of the house of the LORD is finished."
1 CHRONICLES 28:20 ESV

"For this night an angel of the God I belong to and serve stood by me, and said, 'Don't be afraid, Paul. You must stand before Caesar. And, look! God has graciously given you all those who are sailing with you.' Therefore, take courage, men, because I believe God that it will be just the way it was told to me."
ACTS 27:23-25 HCSB

Don't lose your bold, courageous faith, for you are destined for a great reward!
HEBREWS 10:35 TPT

Covenant

Then God spoke to Noah and his sons: "I'm setting up my covenant with you including your children who will come after you, along with everything alive around you—birds, farm animals, wild animals—that came out of the ship with you. I'm setting up my covenant with you that never again will everything living be destroyed by floodwaters; no, never again will a flood destroy the Earth."
GENESIS 9:8-11 MSG

And God said, "This is the sign of the covenant I am making between Me and you and every living creature with you, a covenant for all future generations: I have placed My bow in the clouds, and it will be a sign of the covenant between Me and the earth. Whenever I form clouds over the earth and the bow appears in the clouds, I will remember My covenant between Me and you and all the living creatures: water will never again become a flood to destroy every creature. The bow will be in the clouds, and I will look at it and remember the everlasting covenant between God and all the living creatures on earth."
GENESIS 9:12-16 HCSB

"I will confirm my covenant with you and your descendants after you, from generation to generation. This is the everlasting covenant: I will always be your God and the God of your descendants after you. And I will give the entire land of Canaan, where you now live as a foreigner, to you and your descendants. It will be their possession forever, and I will be their God."
GENESIS 17:7-8 NLT

And he said, "Behold, I am making a covenant. Before all your people I will do marvels, such as have not been created in all the earth or in any nation. And all the people among whom you are shall see the work of the LORD, for it is an awesome thing that I will do with you."
EXODUS 34:10 ESV

"If you pay attention to these laws and are careful to follow them, then the LORD your God will keep his covenant of love with you, as he swore to your ancestors."
DEUTERONOMY 7:12 NIV

"But you are not the only ones with whom I am making this covenant with its curses. I am making this covenant both with you who stand here today in the presence of the LORD our God, and also with the future generations who are not standing here today."
DEUTERONOMY 29:14-15 NLT

For You have made Your people Israel Your very own people forever; and You, LORD, have become their God.
2 SAMUEL 7:24 NKJV

But the LORD was gracious to them and had compassion on them, and he turned toward them, because of his covenant with Abraham, Isaac, and Jacob, and would not destroy them, nor has he cast them from his presence until now.
2 KINGS 13:23 ESV

He remembers his covenant forever,
the promise he made, for a thousand generations,
the covenant he made with Abraham,
the oath he swore to Isaac.
1 CHRONICLES 16:15-16 NIV

And you made your people Israel to be your people forever, and you, O LORD, became their God.
1 CHRONICLES 17:22 ESV

Yet the LORD would not destroy the house of David, because of the covenant that He had made with David, and since He had promised to give a lamp to him and to his sons forever.
2 CHRONICLES 21:7 NKJV

O LORD, God of heaven, the great and awesome God who keeps his covenant of unfailing love with those who love him and obey his commands, listen to my prayer!
NEHEMIAH 1:6 NLT

You are the LORD God,
Who chose Abram,
And brought him out of Ur of the Chaldeans,
And gave him the name Abraham;
You found his heart faithful before You,
And made a covenant with him
To give the land of the Canaanites,
The Hittites, the Amorites,
The Perizzites, the Jebusites,
And the Girgashites—
To give it to his descendants.
You have performed Your words,
For You are righteous.

NEHEMIAH 9:7-8 NKJV

He said to me, "You are my son;
today I have become your father.
Ask me,
and I will make the nations your inheritance,
the ends of the earth your possession."

PSALM 2:7-8 NIV

You said, "I have made a covenant with my chosen one,
I have sworn to David my servant,
'I will establish your line forever
and make your throne firm through all generations.'"

PSALM 89:3-4 NIV

And he will come before me, saying—
"You truly are my Father, my only God, and my strong Savior!
I am setting him apart, favoring him as my firstborn son.
I will make him like unto me, the most high king in all the earth!
I will love him forever and always show him kindness.
My covenant with him will never be broken."

PSALM 89:26-28 TPT

He remembers his covenant forever,
the word that he commanded, for a thousand generations,
the covenant that he made with Abraham,
his sworn promise to Isaac,
which he confirmed to Jacob as a statute,
to Israel as an everlasting covenant.
>   PSALM 105:8-10 ESV

"As for Me, this is My covenant with them," says the LORD: "My Spirit who is on you, and My words that I have put in your mouth, will not depart from your mouth, or from the mouth of your children, or from the mouth of your children's children, from now on and forever," says the LORD.
>   ISAIAH 59:21 HCSB

"The day is coming," says the LORD, "when I will make a new covenant with the people of Israel and Judah. This covenant will not be like the one I made with their ancestors when I took them by the hand and brought them out of the land of Egypt. They broke that covenant, though I loved them as a husband loves his wife," says the LORD.
>   JEREMIAH 31:31-32 NLT

"I will make an everlasting covenant with them: I will never turn away from doing good to them, and I will put fear of Me in their hearts so they will never again turn away from Me. I will take delight in them to do what is good for them, and with all My heart and mind I will faithfully plant them in this land."
>   JEREMIAH 32:40-41 HCSB

"O Lord, great and awesome God, who keeps His covenant and mercy with those who love Him, and with those who keep His commandments,"
>   DANIEL 9:4 NKJV

At the same time I'll make a peace treaty between you
and wild animals and birds and reptiles,
And get rid of all weapons of war.
Think of it! Safe from beasts and bullies!
And then I'll marry you for good—forever!
I'll marry you true and proper, in love and tenderness.
Yes, I'll marry you and neither leave you nor let you go.
You'll know me, GOD, for who I really am.
>   HOSEA 2:18-20 MSG

My beloved brothers and sisters, I want to share with you a mystery concerning Israel's future. For understanding this mystery will keep you from thinking you already know everything. A partial and temporary hardening to the gospel has come over Israel, which will last until the full number of non-Jews has come into God's family. And then God will bring all of Israel to salvation! The prophecy will be fulfilled that says:

"Coming from Zion will be the Savior,
and he will turn Jacob away from evil.
For this is my covenant promise with them."

ROMANS 11:25-27 TPT

But Jesus has now obtained a superior ministry, and to that degree He is the mediator of a better covenant, which has been legally enacted on better promises.

HEBREWS 8:6 HCSB

"For here is the covenant I will one day establish with the people of Israel: I will embed my laws within their thoughts and fasten them onto their hearts. I will be their loyal God and they will be my loyal people."

HEBREWS 8:10 TPT

So Jesus is the One who has enacted a new covenant with a new relationship with God so that those who accept the invitation will receive the eternal inheritance he has promised to his heirs. For he died to release us from the guilt of the violations committed under the first covenant.

HEBREWS 9:15 TPT

"I will make a covenant of peace with them; it will be an everlasting covenant. I will establish them and increase their numbers, and I will put my sanctuary among them forever."

EZEKIEL 37:26 NIV

Creation

In the beginning God created the heavens and the earth.
   GENESIS 1:1 NIV

Great is the LORD! He is most worthy of praise!
He is to be feared above all gods.
The gods of other nations are mere idols,
but the LORD made the heavens!
   1 CHRONICLES 16:25-26 NLT

The world also is firmly established,
It shall not be moved.
   1 CHRONICLES 16:30 NKJV

You're the one,
GOD, you alone;
You made the heavens,
the heavens of heavens, and all angels;
The earth and everything on it,
the seas and everything in them;
You keep them all alive;
heaven's angels worship you!
   NEHEMIAH 9:6 MSG

The heavens declare the glory of God;
the skies proclaim the work of his hands.
Day after day they pour forth speech;
night after night they reveal knowledge.
   PSALM 19:1-2 NIV

GOD claims Earth and everything in it,
God claims World and all who live on it.
He built it on Ocean foundations,
laid it out on River girders.
   PSALM 24:1-2 MSG

The LORD merely spoke,
and the heavens were created.
He breathed the word,
and all the stars were born.
He assigned the sea its boundaries
and locked the oceans in vast reservoirs.
PSALM 33:6-7 NLT

For since the creation of the world God's invisible qualities—his eternal power and divine nature—have been clearly seen, being understood from what has been made, so that people are without excuse.
ROMANS 1:20 NIV

Everything God created is good, and to be received with thanks. Nothing is to be sneered at and thrown out. God's Word and our prayers make every item in creation holy.
1 TIMOTHY 4:4-5 ESV

"You are worthy, O Lord our God,
to receive glory and honor and power.
For you created all things,
and they exist because you created what you pleased."
REVELATION 4:11 NLT

Death

But the Lord God warned him, "You may freely eat the fruit of every tree in the garden-except the tree of the knowledge of good and evil. If you eat its fruit, you are sure to die."
GENESIS 2:16-17 NLT

You shall come to your grave in ripe old age,
like a sheaf gathered up in its season.
JOB 5:26 ESV

But as for me, God will redeem my life.
He will snatch me from the power of the grave.
PSALM 49:15 NLT

When one of God's holy lovers dies,
it is costly to the Lord, touching his heart.
PSALM 116:15 TPT

The wicked are crushed by every calamity,
but the lovers of God find a strong hope
even in the time of death.
PROVERBS 14:32 TPT

He will destroy death forever.
ISAIAH 25:8A HCSB

"No longer will babies die when only a few days old.
No longer will adults die before they have lived a full life.
No longer will people be considered old at one hundred!
Only the cursed will die that young!"
ISAIAH 65:20 NLT

"I will deliver this people from the power of the grave;
I will redeem them from death.
Where, O death, are your plagues?
Where, O grave, is your destruction?"
HOSEA 13:14 NIV

"I speak to you eternal truth: Soon the dead will hear the voice of the Son of God, and those who listen will arise with life!"
JOHN 5:25 TPT

"I speak to you this eternal truth: whoever cherishes my words and keeps them will never experience death."
JOHN 8:51 TPT

"I am the Resurrection, and I am Life Eternal. Anyone who clings to me in faith, even though he dies, will live forever. And the one who lives by believing in me will never die. Do you believe this?"
JOHN 11:25-26 TPT

We know that when Jesus was raised from the dead it was a signal of the end of death-as-the-end. Never again will death have the last word.
ROMANS 6:9 MSG

But the truth is that Christ has been raised up, the first in a long legacy of those who are going to leave the cemeteries.
1 CORINTHIANS 15:20 MSG

For our dying bodies must be transformed into bodies that will never die; our mortal bodies must be transformed into immortal bodies. Then, when our dying bodies have been transformed into bodies that will never die, this Scripture will be fulfilled:
"Death is swallowed up in victory.
O death, where is your victory?
O death, where is your sting?"
1 CORINTHIANS 15:53-55 NLT

For me, living is Christ and dying is gain.
PHILIPPIANS 1:21 HCSB

Brothers and sisters, we do not want you to be uninformed about those who sleep in death, so that you do not grieve like the rest of mankind, who have no hope. For we believe that Jesus died and rose again, and so we believe that God will bring with Jesus those who have fallen asleep in him.

1 THESSALONIANS 4:13-14 NIV

And now he has made all of this plain to us by the appearing of Christ Jesus, our Savior. He broke the power of death and illuminated the way to life and immortality through the Good News.

2 TIMOTHY 1:10 NLT

Since all his "children" have flesh and blood, so Jesus became human to fully identify with us. He did this, so that he could experience death and annihilate the effects of the intimidating accuser who holds against us the power of death. By embracing death Jesus sets free those who live their entire lives in bondage to the tormenting dread of death.

HEBREWS 2:14-15 TPT

And I heard a voice from heaven saying, "Write this down: Blessed are those who die in the Lord from now on. Yes, says the Spirit, they are blessed indeed, for they will rest from their hard work; for their good deeds follow them!"

REVELATION 14:13 NLT

Defense

"He will protect his faithful ones,
but the wicked will disappear in darkness.
No one will succeed by strength alone."
   1 SAMUEL 2:9 NLT

"You protect me with salvation-armor;
you touch me and I feel ten feet tall."
   2 SAMUEL 22:36 MSG

But You, O LORD, are a shield for me,
My glory and the One who lifts up my head.
I cried to the LORD with my voice,
And He heard me from His holy hill.
   PSALM 3:3-4 NKJV

I'll never turn back and run,
for Lord, you surround and protect me.
   PSALM 27:1 TPT

Everything inside of me will shout it out:
"There's just no one like you, Lord!"
For look at how you protect the weak and helpless
from the strong and heartless who oppress them.
   PSALM 35:10 TPT

His huge outstretched arms protect you—
under them you're perfectly safe;
his arms fend off all harm.
   PSALM 91:4 MSG

God sends angels with special orders
to protect you wherever you go,
defending you from all harm.
   PSALM 91:11 TPT

Don't rob the poor just because you can,
or exploit the needy in court.
For the LORD is their defender.
He will ruin anyone who ruins them.
> PROVERBS 22:22–23 NLT

And this is what the LORD says about the king of Assyria:
"His armies will not enter Jerusalem.
They will not even shoot an arrow at it.
They will not march outside its gates with their shields
nor build banks of earth against its walls.
The king will return to his own country
by the same road on which he came.
He will not enter this city,"
says the LORD.
"For my own honor and for the sake of my servant David,
I will defend this city and protect it."
> ISAIAH 37:33–35 NLT

But the LORD is with me like a violent warrior.
Therefore, my persecutors will stumble and not prevail.
Since they have not succeeded, they will be utterly shamed,
an everlasting humiliation that will never be forgotten.
> JEREMIAH 20:11 HCSB

The other angel said, "Hurry, and say to that young man, 'Jerusalem will someday be so full of people and livestock that there won't be room enough for everyone! Many will live outside the city walls. Then I, myself, will be a protective wall of fire around Jerusalem, says the LORD. And I will be the glory inside the city!'"
> ZECHARIAH 2:4–5 NLT

Deliverance

Then the LORD said to Moses, "Tell the Israelites to turn back and encamp near Pi Hahiroth, between Migdol and the sea. They are to encamp by the sea, directly opposite Baal Zephon. Pharaoh will think, 'The Israelites are wandering around the land in confusion, hemmed in by the desert.' And I will harden Pharaoh's heart, and he will pursue them. But I will gain glory for myself through Pharaoh and all his army, and the Egyptians will know that I am the LORD." So the Israelites did this.
EXODUS 14:1-4 NIV

"You will bring them in and plant them on your own mountain—
the place, O LORD, reserved for your own dwelling,
the sanctuary, O Lord, that your hands have established."
EXODUS 15:17 NLT

Remember the great terrors the LORD your God sent against them. You saw it all with your own eyes! And remember the miraculous signs and wonders, and the strong hand and powerful arm with which he brought you out of Egypt. The LORD your God will use this same power against all the people you fear.
DEUTERONOMY 7:19 NLT

And Samuel said to all the house of Israel, "If you are returning to the LORD with all your heart, then put away the foreign gods and the Ashtaroth from among you and direct your heart to the LORD and serve him only, and he will deliver you out of the hand of the Philistines."
1 SAMUEL 7:3 ESV

"The LORD is my rock, my fortress and my deliverer."
2 SAMUEL 22:2 NIV

"He is the God who avenges me,
who puts the nations under me,
who sets me free from my enemies."
2 SAMUEL 22:48 NIV

But the LORD your God you shall fear; and He will deliver you from the hand of all your enemies.
2 KINGS 17:39 NKJV

"If disaster comes on us—sword or judgment, pestilence or famine—we will stand before this temple and before You, for Your name is in this temple. We will cry out to You because of our distress, and You will hear and deliver."
2 CHRONICLES 20:9 HCSB

He will deliver even one who is not innocent,
who will be delivered through the cleanness of your hands.
JOB 22:30 NIV

But those who suffer he delivers in their suffering;
he speaks to them in their affliction.
JOB 36:15 NIV

From the LORD comes deliverance.
May your blessing be on your people.
PSALM 3:8 NIV

Our fathers trusted in You;
They trusted, and You delivered them.
They cried to You, and were delivered;
They trusted in You, and were not ashamed.
PSALM 22:4-5 NKJV

The righteous person may have many troubles,
but the LORD delivers him from them all.
PSALM 34:19 NIV

The LORD helps [the righteous] and delivers them;
he delivers them from the wicked and saves them,
because they take refuge in him.
PSALM 37:40 NIV

He will rescue you from every hidden trap of the enemy,
and he will protect you from false accusation
and any deadly curse.
   PSALM 91:3 TPT

He is my faithful love and my fortress,
my stronghold and my deliverer.
   PSALM 144:2 HCSB

The LORD is gracious and compassionate,
slow to anger and rich in love.
   PSALM 145:8 NIV

The godly are rescued from trouble,
and it falls on the wicked instead.
   PROVERBS 11:8 NLT

I'll deliver you from the grip of the wicked.
I'll get you out of the clutch of the ruthless.
   JEREMIAH 15:21 MSG

For the LORD will deliver Jacob
and redeem them from the hand of those stronger than they.
   JEREMIAH 31:11 NIV

"Indeed, I will certainly deliver you so that you do not fall by the sword. Because you have trusted in Me, you will keep your life like the spoils of war." This is the LORD's declaration.
   JEREMIAH 39:18 HCSB

Then the trees of the field shall yield their fruit, and the earth shall yield her increase. They shall be safe in their land; and they shall know that I am the LORD, when I have broken the bands of their yoke and delivered them from the hand of those who enslaved them.
   EZEKIEL 34:27 NKJV

"For He is the living God,
and He endures forever;
His kingdom will never be destroyed,
and His dominion has no end.
He rescues and delivers;
He performs signs and wonders
in the heavens and on the earth,
for He has rescued Daniel
from the power of the lions."

DANIEL 6:26B-27 HCSB

"I'm still your GOD,
the God who saved you out of Egypt.
I'm the only real God you've ever known.
I'm the one and only God who delivers."

HOSEA 13:4 MSG

"And everyone who calls
on the name of the LORD will be saved;
for on Mount Zion and in Jerusalem
there will be deliverance,
as the LORD has said,
even among the survivors
whom the LORD calls."

JOEL 2:32 NIV

But on Mount Zion there shall be deliverance,
And there shall be holiness;
The house of Jacob shall possess their possessions.

OBADIAH 17 NKJV

"And you will be hated by everyone because of My name. But the one who endures to the end will be delivered."

MARK 13:13 HCSB

"You can expect betrayal even by your parents, your brothers, your relatives and friends—and yes, some of you will die as martyrs. You will be hated by all because of my life in you. But don't worry. My grace will never desert you or depart from your life. And by standing firm with patient endurance you will find your souls' deliverance."

LUKE 21:16-19 TPT

Jesus replied, "I tell you the truth, everyone who sins is a slave of sin. A slave is not a permanent member of the family, but a son is part of the family forever. So if the Son sets you free, you are truly free."

JOHN 8:34-36 NLT

He has delivered us from such a terrible death, and He will deliver us. We have put our hope in Him that He will deliver us again.

2 CORINTHIANS 1:10 HCSB

And my Lord will continue to deliver me from every form of evil and give me life in his heavenly kingdom. May all the glory go to him alone for all the ages of eternity!

2 TIMOTHY 4:18 TPT

Depression

"Thanksgivings will pour out of the windows;
laughter will spill through the doors.
Things will get better and better.
Depression days are over.
They'll thrive, they'll flourish.
The days of contempt will be over."
JEREMIAH 30:19 MSG

"So fear no more, Jacob, dear servant.
Don't despair, Israel.
Look up! I'll save you out of faraway places,
I'll bring your children back from exile.
Jacob will come back and find life good,
safe and secure."
JEREMIAH 30:10 MSG

We are pressed on every side by troubles, but we are not crushed. We are perplexed, but not driven to despair.
2 CORINTHIANS 4:8 NLT

Discipleship

Then He said to them, "Follow Me, and I will make you fishers of men."
MATTHEW 4:19 NKJV

"Whoever finds their life will lose it, and whoever loses their life for my sake will find it."
MATTHEW 10:39 NIV

Then Jesus said to his disciples, "If any of you wants to be my follower, you must turn from your selfish ways, take up your cross, and follow me."
MATTHEW 16:24 NLT

"When you receive the childlike on my account, it's the same as receiving me."
MATTHEW 18:5 NLT

"Why are you critical of this woman? She has done a beautiful act of kindness for me. You will always have someone poor that you can help, but you will not always have me! When she poured the fragrant oil over me she was preparing my body for burial. I promise you this: as this wonderful gospel spreads all over the world, the story of her lavish devotion to me will also be mentioned in her memory."
MATTHEW 26:10-13 TPT

"Who are my mother and my brothers?" he asked. Then he looked at those seated in a circle around him and said, "Here are my mother and my brothers! Whoever does God's will is my brother and sister and mother."
MARK 3:33-35 NIV

Summoning the crowd along with His disciples, He said to them, "If anyone wants to be My follower, he must deny himself, take up his cross, and follow Me. For whoever wants to save his life will lose it, but whoever loses his life because of Me and the gospel will save it."
MARK 8:34-35 HCSB

Then he put a little child among them. Taking the child in his arms, he said to them, "Anyone who welcomes a little child like this on my behalf welcomes me, and anyone who welcomes me welcomes not only me but also my Father who sent me."
MARK 9:36-37 NLT

"No one who does a miracle in my name can in the next moment say anything bad about me, for whoever is not against us is for us. Truly I tell you, anyone who gives you a cup of water in my name because you belong to the Messiah will certainly not lose their reward."
MARK 9:39-41 NIV

"I'd say it's easier for a camel to go through a needle's eye than for the rich to get into God's kingdom." That set the disciples back on their heels. "Then who has any chance at all?" they asked. Jesus was blunt: "No chance at all if you think you can pull it off by yourself. Every chance in the world if you let God do it."
MARK 10:24-27 MSG

"If you tenderly care for this little child on my behalf, you are tenderly caring for me. And if you care for me, you are honoring my Father who sent me. For the one who is least important in your eyes is actually the most important one of all."
LUKE 9:48 TPT

Jesus concluded his instructions to the seventy with these words:
"Remember this: Whoever listens to your message is actually listening to me. And anyone who rejects you is rejecting me, and not only me but the one who sent me."
LUKE 10:16 TPT

"If you want to be my disciple, follow me and you will go where I am going. And if you truly follow me as my disciple, the Father will shower his favor upon your life."
JOHN 12:26 TPT

If anyone builds on that foundation with gold, silver, costly stones, wood, hay, or straw, each one's work will become obvious, for the day will disclose it, because it will be revealed by fire; the fire will test the quality of each one's work.
1 CORINTHIANS 3:12-13 HCSB

Each person should do as he has decided in his heart—not reluctantly or out of necessity, for God loves a cheerful giver.
2 CORINTHIANS 9:7 HCSB

So let's not get tired of doing what is good. At just the right time we will reap a harvest of blessing if we don't give up.
GALATIANS 6:9 NLT

Our immaturity will end! And we will not be easily shaken by trouble, nor led astray by novel teachings or by the false doctrines of deceivers who teach clever lies that sound like the truth—only to pull us into their "flock." But instead we will remain strong and always sincere in our love as we express the truth. All our direction and ministries will flow from Christ and lead us deeper into him, the anointed Head of his body, the church.
EPHESIANS 4:14–15 TPT

Therefore, my dear friends, as you have always obeyed—not only in my presence, but now much more in my absence—continue to work out your salvation with fear and trembling, for it is God who works in you to will and to act in order to fulfill his good purpose.
PHILIPPIANS 2:12–13 NIV

For physical training is of some value, but godliness has value for all things, holding promise for both the present life and the life to come. This is a trustworthy saying that deserves full acceptance.
1 TIMOTHY 4:8–9 NIV

Watch your life and doctrine closely. Persevere in them, because if you do, you will save both yourself and your hearers.
1 TIMOTHY 4:16 NIV

Speak and act as those who will be judged by the law of freedom.
JAMES 2:12 NKJV

Be careful to live properly among your unbelieving neighbors. Then even if they accuse you of doing wrong, they will see your honorable behavior, and they will give honor to God when he judges the world.
1 PETER 2:12 NLT

Since everything around us is going to be destroyed like this, what holy and godly lives you should live, looking forward to the day of God and hurrying it along. On that day, he will set the heavens on fire, and the elements will melt away in the flames.
2 PETER 3:11-12 NLT

If anyone claims, "I am living in the light," but hates a Christian brother or sister, that person is still living in darkness. Anyone who loves another brother or sister is living in the light and does not cause others to stumble.
1 JOHN 2:9-10 NLT

This is how we know who the children of God are and who the children of the devil are: Anyone who does not do what is right is not God's child, nor is anyone who does not love their brother and sister.
1 JOHN 3:10 NIV

This is how we know that we love the children of God: by loving God and carrying out his commands.
1 JOHN 5:2 NIV

Dear friend, do not imitate what is evil but what is good. Anyone who does what is good is from God. Anyone who does what is evil has not seen God.
3 JOHN 11 NIV

Discipline

My child, when the Lord God speaks to you,
never take his words lightly
and never be upset when he corrects you.
For the Father's discipline comes only
from his passionate love and pleasure for you.
And even when it seems like his correction is harsh,
it's still better than any father on earth gives to his child.
PROVERBS 3:11-12 TPT

As you endure this divine discipline, remember that God is treating you as his own children. Who ever heard of a child who is never disciplined by its father? If God doesn't discipline you as he does all of his children, it means that you are illegitimate and are not really his children at all. Since we respected our earthly fathers who disciplined us, shouldn't we submit even more to the discipline of the Father of our spirits, and live forever?
HEBREWS 12:7-9 NIV

For our earthly fathers disciplined us for a few years, doing the best they knew how. But God's discipline is always good for us, so that we might share in his holiness. No discipline is enjoyable while it is happening—it's painful! But afterward there will be a peaceful harvest of right living for those who are trained in this way.
HEBREWS 12:10-11 NLT

"Those whom I love I rebuke and discipline. So be earnest and repent."
REVELATION 3:19 NLT

Disobedience

"And here you are, a brood of sinners, standing in the place of your fathers and making the LORD even more angry with Israel. If you turn away from following him, he will again leave all this people in the wilderness, and you will be the cause of their destruction."

NUMBERS 32:14-15 NIV

When GOD heard what you said, he exploded in anger. He swore, "Not a single person of this evil generation is going to get so much as a look at the good land that I promised to give to your parents. Not one—except for Caleb son of Jephunneh. He'll see it. I'll give him and his descendants the land he walked on because he was all for following GOD, heart and soul."

DEUTERONOMY 1:34-36 MSG

"If you ever forget the LORD your God and follow other gods and worship and bow down to them, I testify against you today that you will surely be destroyed. Like the nations the LORD destroyed before you, so you will be destroyed for not obeying the LORD your God."

DEUTERONOMY 8:19-20 NIV

"The LORD will send on you curses, confusion and rebuke in everything you put your hand to, until you are destroyed and come to sudden ruin because of the evil you have done in forsaking him."

DEUTERONOMY 28:20 NIV

All these curses are going to come on you. They're going to hunt you down and get you until there's nothing left of you because you didn't obediently listen to the Voice of GOD, your God, and diligently keep his commandments and guidelines that I commanded you. The curses will serve as signposts, warnings to your children ever after.

DEUTERONOMY 28:45-46 MSG

"If you are not careful to do all the words of this law that are written in this book, that you may fear this glorious and awesome name, the LORD your God, then the LORD will bring on you and your offspring extraordinary afflictions, afflictions severe and lasting, and sicknesses grievous and lasting. And he will bring upon you again all the diseases of Egypt, of which you were afraid, and they shall cling to you. Every sickness also and every affliction that is not recorded in the book of this law, the LORD will bring upon you, until you are destroyed. Whereas you were as numerous as the stars of heaven, you shall be left few in number, because you did not obey the voice of the LORD your God."

DEUTERONOMY 28:58-62 ESV

But I warn you: If you have a change of heart, refuse to listen obediently, and willfully go off to serve and worship other gods, you will most certainly die. You won't last long in the land that you are crossing the Jordan to enter and possess.

DEUTERONOMY 30:17-18 MSG

"Since every good thing the LORD your God promised you has come about, so He will bring on you every bad thing until He has annihilated you from this good land the LORD your God has given you. If you break the covenant of the LORD your God, which He commanded you, and go and worship other gods, and bow down to them, the LORD's anger will burn against you, and you will quickly disappear from this good land He has given you."

JOSHUA 23:15-16 HCSB

"But if you or your sons at all turn from following Me, and do not keep My commandments and My statutes which I have set before you, but go and serve other gods and worship them, then I will cut off Israel from the land which I have given them; and this house which I have consecrated for My name I will cast out of My sight. Israel will be a proverb and a byword among all peoples."

1 KINGS 9:6-7 NKJV

He will hit Israel hard, as a storm slaps reeds about; he'll pull them up by the roots from this good land of their inheritance, weeding them out, and then scatter them to the four winds. And why? Because they made GOD so angry with Asherah sex-and-religion shrines. He'll wash his hands of Israel because of Jeroboam's sins, which have led Israel into a life of sin.

1 KINGS 14:15-16 MSG

People of Israel, do not fight against the LORD, the God of your ancestors, for you will not succeed.

2 CHRONICLES 13:12 NIV

Then the Spirit of God came on Zechariah son of Jehoiada the priest. He stood before the people and said, "This is what God says: 'Why do you disobey the LORD'S commands? You will not prosper. Because you have forsaken the LORD, he has forsaken you.'"

2 CHRONICLES 24:20 NIV

The face of the LORD is set
against those who do what is evil,
to erase all memory of them from the earth.

PSALM 34:16 HCSB

You rebuke the proud—the cursed,
Who stray from Your commandments.

PSALM 119:21 NKJV

"Listen, all the earth!
I will bring disaster on my people.
It is the fruit of their own schemes,
because they refuse to listen to me.
They have rejected my word."

JEREMIAH 6:19 NLT

"For has not Moses told us:
'The Lord your God will raise up
a prophet from among you who is like me.
Listen to him and follow everything he tells you.
Every person who disobeys that prophet
will be cut off and completely destroyed.'"

ACTS 3:22-23 TPT

Enemies

"I will send my terror ahead of you and create panic among all the people whose lands you invade. I will make all your enemies turn and run. I will send terror ahead of you to drive out the Hivites, Canaanites, and Hittites."

EXODUS 23:27-30 NLT

You'll make mincemeat of all the peoples that GOD, your God, hands over to you. Don't feel sorry for them. And don't worship their gods—they'll trap you for sure.

DEUTERONOMY 7:16 MSG

The LORD your God will clear away these nations before you little by little.

DEUTERONOMY 7:22 ESV

"But the LORD your God will give them over to you and throw them into great confusion, until they are destroyed. And he will give their kings into your hand, and you shall make their name perish from under heaven. No one shall be able to stand against you until you have destroyed them."

DEUTERONOMY 7:23-24 ESV

"The LORD will cause the enemies who rise up against you to be defeated before you. They will march out against you from one direction but flee from you in seven directions."

DEUTERONOMY 28:7 HCSB

"The LORD your God will put all these curses on your enemies who hate and persecute you."

DEUTERONOMY 30:7 HCSB

Stay alert: I have assigned to you by lot these nations that remain as an inheritance to your tribes—these in addition to the nations I have already cut down—from the Jordan to the Great Sea in the west. GOD, your God, will drive them out of your path until there's nothing left of them and you'll take over their land just as GOD, your God, promised you.

JOSHUA 23:4-5 MSG

"I'm going to give you peace from all your enemies."
2 SAMUEL 7:11 MSG

"Evildoers will not continue to oppress them as they formerly have ever since the day I ordered judges to be over My people Israel. I will also subdue all your enemies."
1 CHRONICLES 17:9-10 HCSB

Your enemies will be clothed in shame,
and the tents of the wicked will be no more.
JOB 8:22 ESV

All my enemies will be ashamed and shake with terror;
they will turn back and suddenly be disgraced.
PSALM 6:10 HCSB

My enemies turn back;
they stumble and perish before you.
For you have upheld my right and my cause,
sitting enthroned as the righteous judge.
PSALM 9:3-4 NIV

Your hand will find all Your enemies;
Your right hand will find those who hate You.
You shall make them as a fiery oven in the time of Your anger;
The LORD shall swallow them up in His wrath,
And the fire shall devour them.
PSALM 21:8-9 NKJV

God will crush every enemy, shattering their strength.
He will make heads roll,
for they refuse to repent of their stubborn, sinful ways.
PSALM 68:21 TPT

"Get out of Babylon as fast as you can.
Run for your lives! Save your necks!
Don't linger and lose your lives to my vengeance on her
as I pay her back for her sins."
JEREMIAH 51:6 MSG

"But love your enemies, do good to them, and lend to them without expecting to get anything back. Then your reward will be great, and you will be children of the Most High, because he is kind to the ungrateful and wicked."
LUKE 6:35 TPT

"Look, I will force those who belong to Satan's synagogue—those liars who say they are Jews but are not—to come and bow down at your feet. They will acknowledge that you are the ones I love."
REVELATION 3:9 NLT

Eternal Life

"Truly I tell you," Jesus said to them, "no one who has left home or wife or brothers or sisters or parents or children for the sake of the kingdom of God will fail to receive many times as much in this age, and in the age to come eternal life."

LUKE 18:29-30 NIV

Then he said, "Jesus, remember me when you enter your kingdom."
He said, "Don't worry, I will. Today you will join me in paradise."

LUKE 23:42-43 MSG

For this is how much God loved the world—he gave his uniquely conceived Son as a gift. So now everyone who believes in him will never perish but experience everlasting life.

JOHN 3:16 TPT

"Whoever believes in the Son has eternal life, but whoever rejects the Son will not see life, for God's wrath remains on them."

JOHN 3:36 NIV

"This is what my Father wants: that anyone who sees the Son and trusts who he is and what he does and then aligns with him will enter real life, eternal life. My part is to put them on their feet alive and whole at the completion of time."

JOHN 6:40 MSG

"I give them eternal life, and they will never perish. No one can snatch them away from me, for my Father has given them to me, and he is more powerful than anyone else. No one can snatch them from the Father's hand."

JOHN 10:28-29 NLT

"I assure you: Unless a grain of wheat falls to the ground and dies, it remains by itself. But if it dies, it produces a large crop. The one who loves his life will lose it, and the one who hates his life in this world will keep it for eternal life."

JOHN 12:24-25 HCSB

"When everything is ready, I will come and get you, so that you will always be with me where I am. And you know the way to where I am going."
JOHN 14:3-4 NLT

"He will give to each one in return for what he has done."
For those living in constant goodness and doing what pleases him, seeking an unfading glory and honor and imperishable virtue, will experience eternal life.
ROMANS 2:6-7 TPT

But now that you have been set free from sin and have become slaves of God, the benefit you reap leads to holiness, and the result is eternal life. For the wages of sin is death, but the gift of God is eternal life in Christ Jesus our Lord.
ROMANS 6:22-23 NIV

Don't you realize that in a race everyone runs, but only one person gets the prize? So run to win! All athletes are disciplined in their training. They do it to win a prize that will fade away, but we do it for an eternal prize.
1 CORINTHIANS 9:24-25 NLT

Then, together with them, we who are still alive and remain on the earth will be caught up in the clouds to meet the Lord in the air. Then we will be with the Lord forever.
1 THESSALONIANS 4:17 NLT

He died for us so that, whether we are awake or asleep, we may live together with him.
1 THESSALONIANS 5:10 NIV

Now may our Lord Jesus Christ himself, and God our Father, who loved us and gave us eternal comfort and good hope through grace, comfort your hearts and establish them in every good work and word.
2 THESSALONIANS 2:16-17 ESV

Let them do good, that they be rich in good works, ready to give, willing to share, storing up for themselves a good foundation for the time to come, that they may lay hold on eternal life.
1 TIMOTHY 6:18-19 NKJV

The promise of "arrival" and "rest" is still there for God's people. God himself is at rest. And at the end of the journey we'll surely rest with God. So let's keep at it and eventually arrive at the place of rest, not drop out through some sort of disobedience.

HEBREWS 4:9-11 MSG

As for you, see that what you have heard from the beginning remains in you. If it does, you also will remain in the Son and in the Father. And this is what he promised us—eternal life.

1 JOHN 2:24-25 NIV

And this is the testimony: that God has given us eternal life, and this life is in His Son. He who has the Son has life; he who does not have the Son of God does not have life.

1 JOHN 5:11-12 NKJV

But you, dear friends, must build each other up in your most holy faith, pray in the power of the Holy Spirit, and await the mercy of our Lord Jesus Christ, who will bring you eternal life. In this way, you will keep yourselves safe in God's love.

JUDE 20-21 NLT

Fairness

Do you know what I want?
I want justice—oceans of it.
I want fairness—rivers of it.
That's what I want. That's all I want.
AMOS 5:24 MSG

Peter said, "Now I know for certain that God doesn't show favoritism with people but treats everyone on the same basis. It makes no difference what race of people one belongs to. If they show deep reverence for God, and are committed to doing what's right, they are acceptable before him."
ACTS 10:34-35 TPT

Anyone who does evil can expect tribulation and distress—to the Jew first and also to the non-Jew. But when we do what pleases God, we can expect unfading glory, true honor, and a continual peace—to the Jew first and also to the non-Jew, for God sees us all without partiality.
ROMANS 2:9-11 TPT

And masters, treat your slaves the same way, without threatening them, because you know that both their Master and yours is in heaven, and there is no favoritism with Him.
EPHESIANS 6:9 HCSB

Faith

And he believed! Believed God! God declared him "Set-Right-with-God."
GENESIS 15:6 MSG

Listen to me, Judah and people of Jerusalem! Have faith in the LORD your God and you will be upheld; have faith in his prophets and you will be successful.
2 CHRONICLES 20:20 NIV

"I assure you: If you have faith the size of a mustard seed, you will tell this mountain, 'Move from here to there,' and it will move. Nothing will be impossible for you."
MATTHEW 17:20 HCSB

But the woman, fearing and trembling, knowing what had happened to her, came and fell down before Him and told Him the whole truth. And He said to her, "Daughter, your faith has made you well. Go in peace, and be healed of your affliction."
MARK 5:33-34 NKJV

"Have faith in God. I tell you the truth, you can say to this mountain, 'May you be lifted up and thrown into the sea,' and it will happen. But you must really believe it will happen and have no doubt in your heart."
MARK 11:22-23 NLT

When Jesus heard this, he said, "Jairus, don't yield to your fear. Have faith in me and she will live again."
LUKE 8:50 TPT

Jesus responded, "If you have even the smallest measure of authentic faith, it would be powerful enough to say to this large tree, 'My faith will pull you up by the roots and throw you into the sea,' and it will respond to your faith and obey you."
LUKE 17:6 TPT

"Believe in the Lord Jesus and you will be saved—you and all your family."
ACTS 16:31 TPT

Circumcision was a sign that Abraham already had faith and that God had already accepted him and declared him to be righteous—even before he was circumcised. So Abraham is the spiritual father of those who have faith but have not been circumcised. They are counted as righteous because of their faith.

ROMANS 4:11 NLT

The promise depends on faith so that it can be experienced as a grace-gift, and now it extends to all the descendants of Abraham. This promise is not only meant for those who obey the law, but also to those who enter into the faith of Abraham, the father of us all.

ROMANS 4:16 TPT

Because of our faith, Christ has brought us into this place of undeserved privilege where we now stand, and we confidently and joyfully look forward to sharing God's glory.

ROMANS 5:2 NLT

Faith, then, is birthed in a heart that responds to God's anointed utterance of the Anointed One.

ROMANS 10:17 TPT

We who are Jews by birth and not sinful Gentiles know that a person is not justified by the works of the law, but by faith in Jesus Christ. So we, too, have put our faith in Christ Jesus that we may be justified by faith in Christ and not by the works of the law, because by the works of the law no one will be justified.

GALATIANS 2:15-16 NIV

Understand, then, that those who have faith are children of Abraham.

GALATIANS 3:7 NIV

It was all laid out beforehand in Scripture that God would set things right with non-Jews by faith. Scripture anticipated this in the promise to Abraham: "All nations will be blessed in you." So those now who live by faith are blessed along with Abraham, who lived by faith—this is no new doctrine!

GALATIANS 3:8-9 MSG

For in Christ, neither our most conscientious religion nor disregard of religion amounts to anything. What matters is something far more interior: faith expressed in love.
GALATIANS 5:6 MSG

For it is by grace you have been saved, through faith—and this is not from yourselves, it is the gift of God.
EPHESIANS 2:8 NIV

There is one Lord, one faith, one baptism,
EPHESIANS 4:5 NLT

Now faith brings our hopes into reality and becomes the foundation needed to acquire the things we long for. It is all the evidence required to prove what is still unseen.
HEBREWS 11:1 TPT

And without faith it is impossible to please God, because anyone who comes to him must believe that he exists and that he rewards those who earnestly seek him.
HEBREWS 11:6 NIV

These were the true heroes, commended for their faith, yet they lived in hope without receiving the fullness of what was promised them. But now God has invited us to live in something better than what they had—faith's fullness! This is so that they could be brought to finished perfection alongside of us.
HEBREWS 11:39-40 TPT

So you see, faith by itself isn't enough. Unless it produces good deeds, it is dead and useless.
JAMES 2:17 NLT

So now it's clear that a person is seen as righteous in God's eyes not merely by faith alone, but by his works.
JAMES 2:24 TPT

And through your faith, God is protecting you by his power until you receive this salvation, which is ready to be revealed on the last day for all to see.
1 PETER 1:5 NLT

Faithfulness

"The land will be empty of them and enjoy its Sabbaths while they're gone. They'll pay for their sins because they refused my laws and treated my decrees with contempt. But in spite of their behavior, while they are among their enemies I won't reject or abhor or destroy them completely. I won't break my covenant with them: I am GOD, their God."
LEVITICUS 26:43–44 MSG

Know that Yahweh your God is God, the faithful God who keeps His gracious covenant loyalty for a thousand generations with those who love Him and keep His commands.
DEUTERONOMY 7:9 HCSB

He is the Rock, his works are perfect,
and all his ways are just.
A faithful God who does no wrong,
upright and just is he.
DEUTERONOMY 32:4 NIV

And now I am about to go the way of all the earth, and you know in your hearts and souls, all of you, that not one word has failed of all the good things that the LORD your God promised concerning you. All have come to pass for you; not one of them has failed.
JOSHUA 23:14 ESV

To the faithful you show yourself faithful;
to those with integrity you show integrity.
2 SAMUEL 22:26 NLT

Those who know your name trust in you,
for you, O LORD, do not abandon those who search for you.
PSALM 9:10 NLT

With the faithful
You prove Yourself faithful;
with the blameless man
You prove Yourself blameless;
> PSALM 18:25 HCSB

The LORD leads with unfailing love and faithfulness
all who keep his covenant and obey his demands.
> PSALM 25:10 NLT

I entrust my spirit into your hand.
Rescue me, LORD, for you are a faithful God.
> PSALM 31:5 NLT

Your faithfulness reaches beyond the clouds.
> PSALM 36:6 NLT

He will send from heaven and save me;
he will put to shame him who tramples on me.
God will send out this steadfast love and his faithfulness!
> PSALM 57:3 ESV

My faithful God will come to meet me;
God will let me look down on my adversaries.
> PSALM 59:10 HCSB

Your mercy and your truth have married each other.
Your righteousness and peace have kissed.
Flowers of your faithfulness are blooming on the earth.
Righteousness shines down from the sky.
> PSALM 85:10-11 TPT

Your unfailing love will last forever.
Your faithfulness is as enduring as the heavens.
> PSALM 89:2 NLT

You are faithful to all those who follow your ways and keep your Word.
> PSALM 103:18 TPT

Praise the LORD!
Give thanks to the LORD, for he is good!
His faithful love endures forever.
> PSALM 106:1 NLT

For His faithful love to us is great;
the LORD's faithfulness endures forever.
> PSALM 117:2 HCSB

Forever, O LORD, your word
is firmly fixed in the heavens.
Your faithfulness endures to all generations;
you have established the earth, and it stands fast.
> PSALM 119:89-90 ESV

"Remember these things, Jacob,
for you, Israel, are my servant.
I have made you, you are my servant;
Israel, I will not forget you."
> ISAIAH 44:21 NIV

"Return, faithless Israel," declares the LORD,
"I will frown on you no longer,
for I am faithful," declares the LORD,
"I will not be angry forever."
> JEREMIAH 3:12 NIV

"The sounds of joy and laughter. The joyful voices of bridegrooms and brides will be heard again, along with the joyous songs of people bringing thanksgiving offerings to the LORD. They will sing,
'Give thanks to the LORD of Heaven's Armies,
for the LORD is good.
His faithful love endures forever!'
For I will restore the prosperity of this land to what it was in the past,"
says the LORD.
> JEREMIAH 33:11 NLT

It turns out that Israel and Judah
are not widowed after all.
As their God, GOD of-the-Angel-Armies, I am still alive and well,
committed to them even though
They filled their land with sin
against Israel's most Holy God.
> JEREMIAH 51:5 MSG

Yet I still dare to hope
when I remember this:
The faithful love of the LORD never ends!
His mercies never cease.
Great is his faithfulness;
his mercies begin afresh each morning.
> LAMENTATIONS 3:21-23 NLT

Be glad, people of Zion,
rejoice in the LORD your God,
for he has given you the autumn rains
because he is faithful.
He sends you abundant showers,
both autumn and spring rains, as before.
> JOEL 2:23 NIV

He will also strengthen you to the end, so that you will be blameless in the day of our Lord Jesus Christ. God is faithful; you were called by Him into fellowship with His Son, Jesus Christ our Lord.
> 1 CORINTHIANS 1:8-9 HCSB

Now may the God of peace Himself sanctify you completely; and may your whole spirit, soul, and body be preserved blameless at the coming of our Lord Jesus Christ. He who calls you is faithful, who also will do it.
> 1 THESSALONIANS 5:23-24 NKJV

But the Lord is faithful; He will strengthen and guard you from the evil one.
> 2 THESSALONIANS 3:3 HCSB

But even if we are faithless, he will still be full of faith, for he never wavers in his faithfulness to us!
2 TIMOTHY 2:13 TPT

Let us hold on to the confession of our hope without wavering, for He who promised is faithful.
HEBREWS 10:23 HCSB

Family

The Man said,
"Finally! Bone of my bone,
flesh of my flesh!
Name her Woman
for she was made from Man."
Therefore a man leaves his father and mother and embraces his wife. They become one flesh.
The two of them, the Man and his Wife, were naked, but they felt no shame.

GENESIS 2:23-25 MSG

Then the LORD said to him, "No, your servant will not be your heir, for you will have a son of your own who will be your heir." Then the LORD took Abram outside and said to him, "Look up into the sky and count the stars if you can. That's how many descendants you will have!"

GENESIS 15:4-5 NLT

The angel of the LORD also said to her, "I will surely multiply your offspring so that they cannot be numbered for multitude." And the angel of the LORD said to her,
"Behold, you are pregnant
and shall bear a son.
You shall call his name Ishmael,
because the LORD has listened to your affliction.
He shall be a wild donkey of a man,
his hand against everyone
and everyone's hand against him,
and he shall dwell over against all his kinsmen."

GENESIS 16:10-12 ESV

"This is my covenant with you: I will make you the father of a multitude of nations! What's more, I am changing your name. It will no longer be Abram. Instead, you will be called Abraham, for you will be the father of many nations. I will make you extremely fruitful. Your descendants will become many nations, and kings will be among them!"

GENESIS 17:4-6 NLT

God said to Abraham, "As for your wife Sarai, do not call her Sarai, for Sarah will be her name. I will bless her; indeed, I will give you a son by her. I will bless her, and she will produce nations; kings of peoples will come from her."
GENESIS 17:15-16 HCSB

And the LORD said to her:
"Two nations are in your womb,
Two peoples shall be separated from your body;
One people shall be stronger than the other,
And the older shall serve the younger."
GENESIS 25:23 NKJV

"Say to the Israelites, 'If a man dies and leaves no son, give his inheritance to his daughter. If he has no daughter, give his inheritance to his brothers. If he has no brothers, give his inheritance to his father's brothers. If his father had no brothers, give his inheritance to the nearest relative in his clan, that he may possess it. This is to have the force of law for the Israelites, as the LORD commanded Moses."
NUMBERS 27:8-11 NIV

Cursed be anyone who dishonors his father or his mother.
DEUTERONOMY 27:16 ESV

Cursed is anyone who sleeps with his father's wife, for he dishonors his father's bed.
DEUTERONOMY 27:20 NIV

Cursed be anyone who lies with his sister, whether the daughter of his father or the daughter of his mother.
DEUTERONOMY 27:22 ESV

GOD'S curse on anyone who has sex with his mother-in-law.
DEUTERONOMY 27:23 MSG

There was a certain man of Zorah, of the tribe of the Danites, whose name was Manoah. And his wife was barren and had no children. And the angel of the LORD appeared to the woman and said to her, "Behold, you are barren and have not borne children, but you shall conceive and bear a son."
JUDGES 13:2-3 ESV

"When your life is complete and you're buried with your ancestors, then I'll raise up your child, your own flesh and blood, to succeed you, and I'll firmly establish his rule. He will build a house to honor me, and I will guarantee his kingdom's rule permanently."

2 SAMUEL 7:12-13 MSG

"Your family and your kingdom are permanently secured. I'm keeping my eye on them! And your royal throne will always be there, rock solid."

2 SAMUEL 7:16 MSG

So now, great GOD, this word that you have spoken to me and my family, guarantee it permanently! Do exactly what you've promised! Then your reputation will flourish always as people exclaim, "The GOD-of-the-Angel-Armies is God over Israel!" And the house of your servant David will remain sure and solid in your watchful presence.

2 SAMUEL 7:25-26 MSG

You will have many children;
your descendants will be as plentiful as grass!

JOB 5:25 NLT

He gives childless couples a family,
gives them joy as the parents of children.

PSALM 113:9 MSG

Children are a heritage from the LORD,
offspring a reward from him.
Like arrows in the hands of a warrior
are children born in one's youth.
Blessed is the man
whose quiver is full of them.

PSALM 127:3-5 NIV

Your wife will be like a fruitful grapevine,
flourishing within your home.
Your children will be like vigorous young olive trees
as they sit around your table.
That is the LORD's blessing
for those who fear him.
> PSALM 128:3-4 NLT

How wonderful, how beautiful,
when brothers and sisters get along!
> PSALM 133:1 MSG

"For just as the new heavens and the new earth,
which I will make,
will endure before Me"—
this is the LORD's declaration—
"so your offspring and your name will endure."
> ISAIAH 66:22 HCSB

Fear

The LORD said to Moses, "Do not be afraid of him, for I have delivered him into your hands, along with his whole army and his land. Do to him what you did to Sihon king of the Amorites, who reigned in Heshbon."
NUMBERS 21:34 NIV

"Then I said to you, 'Do not be terrified, or afraid of them.'"
DEUTERONOMY 1:29 NKJV

Then we turned and went up the way to Bashan. And Og the king of Bashan came out against us, he and all his people, to battle at Edrei. But the LORD said to me, "Do not fear him, for I have given him and all his people and his land into your hand. And you shall do to him as you did to Sihon the king of the Amorites, who lived at Heshbon."
DEUTERONOMY 3:1-2 ESV

"Don't be afraid of them, for the LORD your God fights for you."
DEUTERONOMY 3:22 HCSB

You may say to yourselves, "These nations are stronger than we are. How can we drive them out?" But do not be afraid of them; remember well what the LORD your God did to Pharaoh and to all Egypt.
DEUTERONOMY 7:17-18 NIV

"Don't be terrified of them, for the LORD your God, a great and awesome God, is among you."
DEUTERONOMY 7:21 HCSB

"When you go out to battle against your enemies, and see horses and chariots and people more numerous than you, do not be afraid of them; for the LORD your God is with you, who brought you up from the land of Egypt."
DEUTERONOMY 20:1 NKJV

"Have I not commanded you? Be strong and of good courage; do not be afraid, nor be dismayed, for the LORD your God is with you wherever you go."
JOSHUA 1:9 NKJV

And the LORD said to Joshua, "Do not fear and do not be dismayed. Take all the fighting men with you, and arise, go up to Ai. See, I have given into your hand the king of Ai, and his people, his city, and his land."
JOSHUA 8:1 ESV

And the LORD said to Joshua, "Do not be afraid of them, for tomorrow at this time I will give over all of them, slain, to Israel. You shall hamstring their horses and burn their chariots with fire."
JOSHUA 11:6 ESV

"Don't be afraid," the prophet answered. "Those who are with us are more than those who are with them."
2 KINGS 6:16 NIV

"Be strong and courageous. Do not be afraid or dismayed before the king of Assyria and all the horde that is with him, for there are more with us than with him. With him is an arm of flesh, but with us is the LORD our God, to help us and to fight our battles." And the people took confidence from the words of Hezekiah king of Judah.
2 CHRONICLES 32:7-8 ESV

And I looked, and arose and said to the nobles, to the leaders, and to the rest of the people, "Do not be afraid of them. Remember the Lord, great and awesome, and fight for your brethren, your sons, your daughters, your wives, and your houses."
NEHEMIAH 4:14 NKJV

You'll shrug off disaster and famine,
and stroll fearlessly among wild animals.
JOB 5:22 MSG

You will lie down, with no one to make you afraid,
and many will court your favor.
But the eyes of the wicked will fail,
and escape will elude them;
their hope will become a dying gasp.
JOB 11:19-20 NIV

I lie down and sleep;
I wake again, because the LORD sustains me.
I will not fear though tens of thousands
assail me on every side.
> PSALM 3:5-6 NIV

What harm could man do to me?
With God on my side I will not be afraid of what comes.
My heart overflows with praise to God and for his promises.
I will always trust in him.
> PSALM 56:11 TPT

You will not fear the terror of the night,
the arrow that flies by day.
> PSALM 91:5 HCSB

[The righteous] will have no fear of bad news;
their hearts are steadfast, trusting in the LORD.
> PSALM 112:7 NIV

The LORD is with me; I will not be afraid.
What can mere mortals do to me?
> PSALM 118:6 NIV

You need not be afraid of sudden disaster
or the destruction that comes upon the wicked,
> PROVERBS 3:25 NLT

Say to the cowardly:
"Be strong; do not fear!
Here is your God; vengeance is coming.
God's retribution is coming; He will save you."
> ISAIAH 35:4 HCSB

"Do not fear, for I am with you;
do not be afraid, for I am your God."
> ISAIAH 41:10A HCSB

"Fear not, you worm Jacob,
you men of Israel!
I am the one who helps you, declares the LORD;
your Redeemer is the Holy One of Israel."
   ISAIAH 41:14 ESV

"Fear not, for I am with you;
I will bring your descendants from the east,
And gather you from the west."
   ISAIAH 43:5 NKJV

Don't be afraid, dear servant Jacob,
Jeshurun, the one I chose.
For I will pour water on the thirsty ground
and send streams coursing through the parched earth.
I will pour my Spirit into your descendants
and my blessing on your children.
   ISAIAH 44:2B-3 MSG

"Do not be afraid of them, for I am with you and will rescue you," declares the LORD.
   JEREMIAH 1:8 NIV

"Get yourself ready! Stand up and say to them whatever I command you. Do not be terrified by them, or I will terrify you before them."
   JEREMIAH 1:17 NIV

"Don't be afraid of the king of Babylon whom you now fear; don't be afraid of him"—this is the LORD's declaration—"because I am with you to save you and deliver you from him. I will grant you compassion, and he will have compassion on you and allow you to return to your own soil."
   JEREMIAH 42:11-12 HCSB

"Do not be afraid, land of Judah;
be glad and rejoice.
Surely the LORD has done great things!"
   JOEL 2:22 NIV

For the LORD your God is living among you.
He is a mighty savior.
He will take delight in you with gladness.
With his love, he will calm all your fears.
He will rejoice over you with joyful songs.
ZEPHANIAH 3:17 NLT

"Don't be afraid of those who want to kill your body; they cannot touch your soul. Fear only God, who can destroy both soul and body in hell."
MATTHEW 10:28 NLT

"Don't be afraid, Mary," the angel told her, "for you have found favor with God!"
LUKE 1:30 NLT

"So don't ever be afraid, dearest friends! Your loving Father joyously gives you his kingdom realm with all its promises!"
LUKE 12:32 TPT

One night, the Lord spoke to Paul in a supernatural vision and said, "Don't ever be afraid. Speak the words that I give you and don't be intimidated, because I AM with you. No one will be able to hurt you, for there are many in this city whom I call my own."
ACTS 18:9-10 TPT

There is no fear in love. But perfect love drives out fear, because fear has to do with punishment. The one who fears is not made perfect in love.
1 JOHN 4:18 NIV

Forgiveness

GOD passed in front of him and called out, "GOD, GOD, a God of mercy and grace, endlessly patient—so much love, so deeply true—loyal in love for a thousand generations, forgiving iniquity, rebellion, and sin. Still, he doesn't ignore sin. He holds sons and grandsons responsible for a father's sins to the third and even fourth generation."
EXODUS 34:6-7 MSG

"They are to bring to the priest as a guilt offering a ram from the flock, one without defect and of the proper value. In this way the priest will make atonement for them for the wrong they have committed unintentionally, and they will be forgiven. It is a guilt offering; they have been guilty of wrongdoing against the LORD."
LEVITICUS 5:18-19 NIV

The LORD replied, "I have forgiven them, as you asked."
NUMBERS 14:20 NIV

"But if it's just one person who sins by mistake, not realizing what he's doing, he is to bring a yearling she-goat as an Absolution-Offering. The priest then is to atone for the person who accidentally sinned, to make atonement before GOD so that it won't be held against him."
NUMBERS 15:27-28 MSG

"The LORD will not abandon His people, because of His great name and because He has determined to make you His own people."
1 SAMUEL 12:22 HCSB

So David said to Nathan, "I have sinned against the LORD." And Nathan said to David, "The LORD also has put away your sin; you shall not die."
2 SAMUEL 12:13 NKJV

"If my people, who are called by my name, will humble themselves and pray and seek my face and turn from their wicked ways, then I will hear from heaven, and I will forgive their sin and will heal their land."
2 CHRONICLES 7:14 NIV

If you are unfaithful, I will scatter you among the nations, but if you return to me and obey my commands, then even if your exiled people are at the farthest horizon, I will gather them from there and bring them to the place I have chosen as a dwelling for my Name.

NEHEMIAH 1:8-9 NIV

You are a forgiving God, gracious and compassionate, slow to anger and rich in faithful love, and You did not abandon them.

NEHEMIAH 9:17 HCSB

You, Lord, are forgiving and good,
abounding in love to all who call to you.

PSALM 86:5 NIV

He forgives your sins—every one.

PSALM 103:3A MSG

He will not always accuse us
or be angry forever.

PSALM 103:9 HCSB

As far as the east is from the west,
So far has He removed our transgressions from us.

PSALM 103:12 NKJV

"Come now, let us settle the matter,"
says the LORD.
"Though your sins are like scarlet,
they shall be as white as snow;
though they are red as crimson,
they shall be like wool."

ISAIAH 1:18 NIV

The people of Israel will no longer say,
"We are sick and helpless,"
for the LORD will forgive their sins.

ISAIAH 33:24 NLT

"I have swept away your offenses like a cloud,
your sins like the morning mist.
Return to me,
for I have redeemed you."
   ISAIAH 44:22 NIV

"The LORD will call you back
as if you were a wife deserted and distressed in spirit—
a wife who married young,
only to be rejected," says your God.
   ISAIAH 54:6 NIV

"Let the wicked one abandon his way
and the sinful one his thoughts;
let him return to the LORD,
so He may have compassion on him,
and to our God, for He will freely forgive."
   ISAIAH 55:7 HCSB

"For I will not accuse you forever,
and I will not always be angry;
for then the spirit would grow weak before Me,
even the breath of man, which I have made."
   ISAIAH 57:16 HCSB

"All who invoke a blessing or take an oath
will do so by the God of truth.
For I will put aside my anger
and forget the evil of earlier days."
   ISAIAH 65:16 NLT

"For I will forgive their wrongdoing and never again remember their sin."
   JEREMIAH 31:34 NKJV

"I am about to gather them from all the lands where I have banished them in My anger, rage and great wrath, and I will return them to this place and make them live in safety. They will be My people, and I will be their God. I will give them one heart and one way so that for their good and for the good of their descendants after them, they will fear Me always."
JEREMIAH 32:37-39 HCSB

"I will restore the fortunes of Judah and of Israel and will rebuild them as in former times."
JEREMIAH 33:7 HCSB

"If you will indeed stay in this land, then I will rebuild and not demolish you, and I will plant and not uproot you, because I relent concerning the disaster that I have brought on you."
JEREMIAH 42:10 HCSB

"In those days," says the LORD,
"no sin will be found in Israel or in Judah,
for I will forgive the remnant I preserve."
JEREMIAH 50:20 NLT

Now this is what the Sovereign LORD says: "I will give you what you deserve, for you have taken your solemn vows lightly by breaking your covenant. Yet I will remember the covenant I made with you when you were young, and I will establish an everlasting covenant with you."
EZEKIEL 16:59-60 NLT

The Lord our God is merciful and forgiving, even though we have rebelled against him.
DANIEL 9:9 NIV

Because I have sinned against Him,
I must endure the LORD's rage
until He argues my case
and establishes justice for me.
He will bring me into the light;
I will see His salvation.
MICAH 7:9 HCSB

The LORD is slow to anger but great in power;
the LORD will never leave the guilty unpunished.
His path is in the whirlwind and storm,
and clouds are the dust beneath His feet.
NAHUM 1:3 HCSB

The LORD has taken away your punishment,
he has turned back your enemy.
The LORD, the King of Israel, is with you;
never again will you fear any harm.
ZEPHANIAH 3:15 NIV

"If you forgive those who sin against you, your heavenly Father will forgive you. But if you refuse to forgive others, your Father will not forgive your sins."
MATTHEW 6:14-15 NLT

"Therefore, everyone who will acknowledge Me before men, I will also acknowledge him before My Father in heaven. But whoever denies Me before men, I will also deny him before My Father in heaven."
MATTHEW 10:32-33 HCSB

"Therefore I say to you, every sin and blasphemy will be forgiven men, but the blasphemy against the Spirit will not be forgiven men. Anyone who speaks a word against the Son of Man, it will be forgiven him; but whoever speaks against the Holy Spirit, it will not be forgiven him, either in this age or in the age to come."
MATTHEW 12:31-32 NIV

"So also my heavenly Father will do to every one of you, if you do not forgive your brother from your heart."
MATTHEW 18:35 ESV

"Which is simpler: to say to the paraplegic, 'I forgive your sins,' or say, 'Get up, take your stretcher, and start walking'? Well, just so it's clear that I'm the Son of Man and authorized to do either, or both..." (he looked now at the paraplegic), "Get up. Pick up your stretcher and go home."
MARK 2:9-11 MSG

"I assure you: People will be forgiven for all sins and whatever blasphemies they may blaspheme. But whoever blasphemes against the Holy Spirit never has forgiveness, but is guilty of an eternal sin"

MARK 3:28-29 HCSB

"But when you are praying, first forgive anyone you are holding a grudge against, so that your Father in heaven will forgive your sins, too."

MARK 11:25 NLT

"And child, you will be called
a prophet of the Most High,
for you will go before the Lord
to prepare His ways,
to give His people knowledge of salvation
through the forgiveness of their sins."

LUKE 1:76-77 HCSB

Jesus, knowing their thoughts, said to them, "Why do you argue in your hearts over what I do and think that it is blasphemy for me to say his sins are forgiven? Let me ask you, which is easier to prove: when I say, 'Your sins are forgiven,' or when I say, 'Stand up, carry your stretcher, and walk'?" Jesus turned to the paraplegic man and said, "To prove to you all that I, the Son of Man, have the lawful authority on earth to forgive sins, I say to you now, stand up! Carry your stretcher and go on home, for you are healed."

LUKE 5:22-24 TPT

"Judge not, and you shall not be judged. Condemn not, and you shall not be condemned. Forgive, and you will be forgiven."

LUKE 6:37 NKJV

"If anyone speaks evil of me, the Son of Man, he can be forgiven. But if anyone scornfully speaks against the Holy Spirit, it will never be forgiven."

LUKE 12:10 TPT

The very next day John saw Jesus coming to him to be baptized, and John cried out, "Look! There he is—God's Lamb! He will take away the sins of the world!"

JOHN 1:29 TPT

"I send you to preach the forgiveness of sins—and people's sins will be forgiven. But if you don't proclaim the forgiveness of their sins, they will remain guilty."
JOHN 20:23 TPT

"Now it's time to change your ways! Turn to face God so he can wipe away your sins, pour out showers of blessing to refresh you, and send you the Messiah he prepared for you, namely, Jesus."
ACTS 3:19-20 MSG

"Brothers, listen! We are here to proclaim that through this man Jesus there is forgiveness for your sins."
ACTS 13:38 NLT

Here's what David says:
"What happy fulfillment is ahead for those
whose rebellion has been forgiven
and whose sins are covered by blood.
What happy progress comes to them
when they hear the Lord speak over them,
'I will never hold your sins against you!'"
ROMANS 4:7-8 TPT

Since we are now joined to Christ, we have been given the treasures of salvation by his blood—the total cancellation of our sins—all because of the cascading riches of his grace.
EPHESIANS 1:7 TPT

We have redemption, the forgiveness of sins, in Him.
COLOSSIANS 1:14 HCSB

You were dead because of your sins and because your sinful nature was not yet cut away. Then God made you alive with Christ, for he forgave all our sins. He canceled the record of the charges against us and took it away by nailing it to the cross.
COLOSSIANS 2:13-14 NLT

So if our sins have been forgiven and forgotten, why would we ever need to offer another sacrifice for sin?

HEBREWS 10:18 TPT

He personally carried our sins
in his body on the cross
so that we can be dead to sin
and live for what is right.
By his wounds
you are healed.

1 PETER 2:24 NLT

I am writing to you, dear children,
because your sins have been forgiven on account of his name.

1 JOHN 2:12 NIV

Freedom

But the Lord has paid for the freedom of his servants,
and he will freely pardon those who love him.
He will declare them free and innocent
when they turn to hide themselves in him.

PSALM 34:22 TPT

"From now on I'm taking the yoke from your neck
and splitting it up for kindling.
I'm cutting you free
from the ropes of your bondage."

NAHUM 1:13 MSG

"The Spirit of the Lord is on Me,
because He has anointed Me
to preach good news to the poor.
He has sent Me
to proclaim freedom to the captives
and recovery of sight to the blind,
to set free the oppressed,
to proclaim the year of the Lord's favor."

LUKE 4:18-19 HCSB

"Everyone who believes in him is set free from sin and guilt—something the law of Moses had no power to do."

ACTS 13:39 TPT

Death once held us in its grip, and by the blunder of one man, death reigned over humanity. But now we are held in the grip of grace and reign as kings in life, enjoying our regal freedom through the gift of perfect righteousness in the one and only Jesus, the Messiah!

ROMANS 5:17 TPT

For when we died with Christ we were set free from the power of sin.
ROMANS 6:7 NLT

And God is pleased with you, for in the past you were servants of sin, but now your obedience is heart deep, and your life is being molded by truth through the teaching you are devoted to. And now you celebrate your freedom from your former master—sin. You've left its bondage, and now God's perfect righteousness holds power over you as his loving servants.
ROMANS 6:17-18 TPT

God has united you with Christ Jesus. For our benefit God made him to be wisdom itself. Christ made us right with God; he made us pure and holy, and he freed us from sin.
1 CORINTHIANS 1:30 NLT

Now the Lord is the Spirit, and where the Spirit of the Lord is, there is freedom.
2 CORINTHIANS 3:17 HCSB

Yet, Christ, our Anointed Substitute, paid the full price to set us free from the curse of the law. He absorbed it completely as he became a "curse" in our place.
GALATIANS 3:13 TPT

But the Scriptures declare that we are all prisoners of sin, so we receive God's promise of freedom only by believing in Jesus Christ.
GALATIANS 3:22 NLT

You have died with Christ, and he has set you free from the spiritual powers of this world.
COLOSSIANS 2:20 NLT

To him who loves us and has freed us from our sins by his blood and made us a kingdom, priests to his God and Father, to him be glory and dominion forever and ever. Amen.
REVELATION 1:5-6 ESV

Friendship

"I have never called you 'servants,' because a master doesn't confide in his servants, and servants don't always understand what the master is doing. But I call you my most intimate friends, for I reveal to you everything that I've heard from my Father."

JOHN 15:15 TPT

Since our friendship with God was restored by the death of his Son while we were still his enemies, we will certainly be saved through the life of his Son.

ROMANS 5:10 NLT

"Here I am! I stand at the door and knock. If anyone hears my voice and opens the door, I will come in and eat with that person, and they with me."

REVELATION 3:20 NIV

Fruit

"You didn't choose me, but I've chosen and commissioned you to go into the world to bear fruit. And your fruit will last, because whatever you ask of my Father, for my sake, he will give it to you!"

JOHN 15:16 TPT

Those who live only to satisfy their own sinful nature will harvest decay and death from that sinful nature. But those who live to please the Spirit will harvest everlasting life from the Spirit.

GALATIANS 6:8 TPT

Fulfillment

"Remember the LORD your God. He is the one who gives you power to be successful, in order to fulfill the covenant he confirmed to your ancestors with an oath."

DEUTERONOMY 8:18 NLT

Not a single one of all the good promises the LORD had given to the family of Israel was left unfulfilled; everything he had spoken came true.

JOSHUA 21:45 NLT

"LORD God of Israel,
there is no God like You
in heaven or on earth,
keeping His gracious covenant
with Your servants who walk before You
with their whole heart.
You have kept what You promised
to Your servant, my father David.
You spoke directly to him,
and You fulfilled Your promise by Your power,
as it is today."

2 CHRONICLES 6:14–15 HCSB

You are the Lord that reigns over your never-ending kingdom,
through all the ages of time and eternity!
You are faithful to fulfill every promise you've made.
You manifest yourself as Kindness in all you do!

PSALM 145:13 TPT

"The days are coming," declares the LORD, "when I will fulfill the good promise I made to the people of Israel and Judah."

JEREMIAH 33:14 NIV

Future

Watch the blameless and observe the upright,
for the man of peace will have a future.
But transgressors will all be eliminated;
the future of the wicked will be destroyed.

PSALM 37:37-38 HCSB

"Only I can tell you the future
before it even happens.
Everything I plan will come to pass,
for I do whatever I wish."

ISAIAH 46:10 NLT

Many who have been long dead and buried will wake up, some to eternal life, others to eternal shame.

DANIEL 12:2 MSG

I don't mean to say that I have already achieved these things or that I have already reached perfection. But I press on to possess that perfection for which Christ Jesus first possessed me. No, dear brothers and sisters, I have not achieved it, but I focus on this one thing: Forgetting the past and looking forward to what lies ahead, I press on to reach the end of the race and receive the heavenly prize for which God, through Christ Jesus, is calling us.

PHILIPPIANS 3:12-14 NLT

Now, brothers and sisters, about times and dates we do not need to write to you, for you know very well that the day of the Lord will come like a thief in the night. While people are saying, "Peace and safety," destruction will come on them suddenly, as labor pains on a pregnant woman, and they will not escape.

1 THESSALONIANS 5:1-3 NIV

But the day of the Lord will come as a thief in the night, in which the heavens will pass away with a great noise, and the elements will melt with fervent heat; both the earth and the works that are in it will be burned up.

2 PETER 3:10 NKJV

Behold, he is coming with the clouds, and every eye will see him, even those who pierced him, and all tribes of the earth will wail on account of him. Even so. Amen.
REVELATION 1:7 ESV

"I'm on my way; I'll be there soon. Keep a tight grip on what you have so no one distracts you and steals your crown."
REVELATION 3:11 MSG

Each of these living beings had six wings, and their wings were covered all over with eyes, inside and out. Day after day and night after night they keep on saying,
"Holy, holy, holy is the Lord God, the Almighty—
the one who always was, who is, and who is still to come."
REVELATION 4:8 NLT

When he opened the fifth seal, I saw under the altar the souls of those who had been slain because of the word of God and the testimony they had maintained. They called out in a loud voice, "How long, Sovereign Lord, holy and true, until you judge the inhabitants of the earth and avenge our blood?" Then each of them was given a white robe, and they were told to wait a little longer, until the full number of their fellow servants, their brothers and sisters, were killed just as they had been.
REVELATION 6:9-11 NIV

"We give thanks to you, Lord God Almighty,
the One who is and who was,
because you have taken your great power
and have begun to reign."
REVELATION 11:17 NIV

"It has come at last—
salvation and power
and the Kingdom of our God,
and the authority of his Christ.
For the accuser of our brothers and sisters
has been thrown down to earth—
the one who accuses them
before our God day and night.
And they have defeated him by the blood of the Lamb
and by their testimony.
And they did not love their lives so much
that they were afraid to die."
REVELATION 12:10-11 NLT

After these things I heard a loud voice of a great multitude in heaven, saying, "Alleluia! Salvation and glory and honor and power belong to the Lord our God! For true and righteous are His judgments, because He has judged the great harlot who corrupted the earth with her fornication; and He has avenged on her the blood of His servants shed by her."
REVELATION 19:1-2 NKJV

"Alleluia! For the Lord God Omnipotent reigns! Let us be glad and rejoice and give Him glory, for the marriage of the Lamb has come, and His wife has made herself ready." And to her it was granted to be arrayed in fine linen, clean and bright, for the fine linen is the righteous acts of the saints.
REVELATION 19:6-8 NKJV

I saw the Beast and, assembled with him, earth's kings and their armies, ready to make war against the One on the horse and his army. The Beast was taken, and with him, his puppet, the False Prophet, who used signs to dazzle and deceive those who had taken the mark of the Beast and worshiped his image. They were thrown alive, those two, into Lake Fire and Brimstone. The rest were killed by the sword of the One on the horse, the sword that comes from his mouth. All the birds held a feast on their flesh.
REVELATION 19:19-21 MSG

And I saw an angel coming down out of heaven, having the key to the Abyss and holding in his hand a great chain. He seized the dragon, that ancient serpent, who is the devil, or Satan, and bound him for a thousand years. He threw him into the Abyss, and locked and sealed it over him, to keep him from deceiving the nations anymore until the thousand years were ended. After that, he must be set free for a short time.
REVELATION 20:1-3 NIV

Then I saw thrones, and the people sitting on them had been given the authority to judge. And I saw the souls of those who had been beheaded for their testimony about Jesus and for proclaiming the word of God. They had not worshiped the beast or his statue, nor accepted his mark on their forehead or their hands. They all came to life again, and they reigned with Christ for a thousand years.
REVELATION 20:4 NLT

Blessed and holy are those who share in the first resurrection. For them the second death holds no power, but they will be priests of God and of Christ and will reign with him a thousand years.
REVELATION 20:6 NLT

And I saw the dead, great and small, standing before the throne, and books were opened. Another book was opened, which is the book of life. The dead were judged according to what they had done as recorded in the books. The sea gave up the dead that were in it, and death and Hades gave up the dead that were in them, and each person was judged according to what they had done. Anyone whose name was not found written in the book of life was thrown into the lake of fire.
REVELATION 20:12-13, 15 NIV

I did not see a temple in the city, because the Lord God Almighty and the Lamb are its temple. The city does not need the sun or the moon to shine on it, for the glory of God gives it light, and the Lamb is its lamp. The nations will walk by its light, and the kings of the earth will bring their splendor into it. On no day will its gates ever be shut, for there will be no night there. The glory and honor of the nations will be brought into it.
REVELATION 21:22-26 NIV

Then the angel showed me a river with the water of life, clear as crystal, flowing from the throne of God and of the Lamb. It flowed down the center of the main street. On each side of the river grew a tree of life, bearing twelve crops of fruit, with a fresh crop each month. The leaves were used for medicine to heal the nations.
REVELATION 22:1-2 NLT

Generosity

Give generously to them and do so without a grudging heart; then because of this the LORD your God will bless you in all your work and in everything you put your hand to. There will always be poor people in the land. Therefore I command you to be openhanded toward your fellow Israelites who are poor and needy in your land.

DEUTERONOMY 15:10-11 NIV

For the Lord God is brighter
than the brilliance of a sunrise!
Wrapping himself around me like a shield,
he is so generous with his gifts of grace and glory.

PSALM 84:11 TPT

Whoever is generous to the poor lends to the LORD,
and he will repay him for his deed.

PROVERBS 19:17 ESV

When you are generous to the poor,
you are enriched with blessings in return.

PROVERBS 22:9 TPT

"Listen carefully to what I am saying—and be wary of the shrewd advice that tells you how to get ahead in the world on your own. Giving, not getting, is the way. Generosity begets generosity. Stinginess impoverishes."

MARK 4:24-25 MSG

"Give generously and generous gifts will be given back to you, shaken down to make room for more. Abundant gifts will pour out upon you with such an overflowing measure that it will run over the top! Your measurement of generosity becomes the measurement of your return."

LUKE 6:38 TPT

"If you free your heart of greed, showing compassion and true generosity to the poor, you have more than clean hands; you will be clean within."

LUKE 11:41 TPT

He looked up and saw the rich dropping their offerings into the temple treasury. He also saw a poor widow dropping in two tiny coins. "I tell you the truth," He said. "This poor widow has put in more than all of them. For all these people have put in gifts out of their surplus, but she out of her poverty has put in all she had to live on."
LUKE 21:1-4 HCSB

In everything I did, I showed you that by this kind of hard work we must help the weak, remembering the words the Lord Jesus himself said: "It is more blessed to give than to receive."
ACTS 20:35 NIV

Remember this: The person who sows sparingly will also reap sparingly, and the person who sows generously will also reap generously.
2 CORINTHIANS 9:6 HCSB

Anyone who neglects to care for family members in need repudiates the faith. That's worse than refusing to believe in the first place.
1 TIMOTHY 5:8 MSG

We will show mercy to the poor and not miss an opportunity to do acts of kindness for others, for these are the true sacrifices that delight God's heart.
HEBREWS 13:16 TPT

Glory

So Moses said to Aaron, "This is what the LORD meant when He said:
I will show My holiness,
to those who are near Me,
and I will reveal My glory,
before all the people."
>   LEVITICUS 10:3 HCSB

Listen! It's the voice of someone shouting,
"Clear the way through the wilderness
for the LORD!
Make a straight highway through the wasteland
for our God!
Fill in the valleys,
and level the mountains and hills.
Straighten the curves,
and smooth out the rough places.
Then the glory of the LORD will be revealed,
and all people will see it together.
The LORD has spoken!"
>   ISAIAH 40:3-5 NLT

"You also will command nations you do not know,
and peoples unknown to you will come running to obey,
because I, the LORD your God,
the Holy One of Israel, have made you glorious."
>   ISAIAH 55:5 NLT

God

"I will consecrate the tent of meeting and the altar. Aaron also and his sons I will consecrate to serve me as priests. I will dwell among the people of Israel and will be their God."
EXODUS 29:44-45 ESV

"I am your GOD who rescued you from the land of Egypt to be your personal God. Yes, I am GOD, your God."
NUMBERS 15:41 MSG

So stay alert. Don't for a minute forget the covenant which GOD, your God, made with you. And don't take up with any carved images, no forms of any kind—GOD, your God, issued clear commands on that. GOD, your God, is not to be trifled with—he's a consuming fire, a jealous God.
DEUTERONOMY 4:23-24 MSG

But even there, if you seek GOD, your God, you'll be able to find him if you're serious, looking for him with your whole heart and soul.
DEUTERONOMY 4:29 MSG

You were shown these things so that you would know that the LORD is God; there is no other besides Him. He let you hear His voice from heaven to instruct you. He showed you His great fire on earth, and you heard His words from the fire.
DEUTERONOMY 4:35-36 HCSB

"No using the name of GOD, your God, in curses or silly banter; GOD won't put up with the irreverent use of his name."
DEUTERONOMY 5:11 MSG

Deeply respect GOD, your God. Serve and worship him exclusively. Back up your promises with his name only. Don't fool around with other gods, the gods of your neighbors, because GOD, your God, who is alive among you is a jealous God. Don't provoke him, igniting his hot anger that would burn you right off the face of the Earth.
DEUTERONOMY 6:13-15 MSG

Cursed is the one who makes a carved or molded image, an abomination to the LORD, the work of the hands of the craftsman, and sets it up in secret.
DEUTERONOMY 27:15 NKJV

No wonder our hearts have melted in fear! No one has the courage to fight after hearing such things. For the LORD your God is the supreme God of the heavens above and the earth below.
JOSHUA 2:11 NLT

"There is no one holy like the LORD;
there is no one besides you;
there is no Rock like our God."
1 SAMUEL 2:2 NIV

And he who is the Glory of Israel will not lie, nor will he change his mind, for he is not human that he should change his mind!
1 SAMUEL 15:29 NLT

"You are great, O Lord GOD. For there is none like You, nor is there any God besides You, according to all that we have heard with our ears."
2 SAMUEL 7:22 NKJV

He then went back to the Holy Man, he and his entourage, stood before him, and said, "I now know beyond a shadow of a doubt that there is no God anywhere on earth other than the God of Israel. In gratitude let me give you a gift."
2 KINGS 5:15 MSG

There is none like you, O LORD, and there is no God besides you, according to all that we have heard with our ears.
1 CHRONICLES 17:20 ESV

Then people will say, "The LORD Almighty, the God over Israel, is Israel's God!" And the house of your servant David will be established before you.
1 CHRONICLES 17:24 NIV

"And Solomon, my son, learn to know the God of your ancestors intimately. Worship and serve him with your whole heart and a willing mind. For the LORD sees every heart and knows every plan and thought. If you seek him, you will find him. But if you forsake him, he will reject you forever."
1 CHRONICLES 28:9 NLT

Indeed, I know that this is true.
But how can mere mortals prove their innocence before God?
Though they wished to dispute with him,
they could not answer him one time out of a thousand.
His wisdom is profound, his power is vast.
Who has resisted him and come out unscathed?
JOB 9:2-4 NIV

But I know my living Redeemer,
and He will stand on the dust at last.
Even after my skin has been destroyed,
yet I will see God in my flesh.
I will see Him myself;
my eyes will look at Him, and not as a stranger.
My heart longs within me.
JOB 19:25-27 HCSB

Indeed, it is true that God does not act wickedly
and the Almighty does not pervert justice.
JOB 34:12 HCSB

God is mighty, but he does not despise anyone!
He is mighty in both power and understanding.
JOB 36:5 NLT

The Almighty is beyond our reach and exalted in power;
in his justice and great righteousness, he does not oppress.
JOB 37:23 NIV

The LORD is in His holy temple;
the LORD's throne is in heaven.
His eyes watch; He examines everyone.
> PSALM 11:4 HCSB

As for God, his way is perfect:
The LORD'S word is flawless;
> PSALM 18:30 NIV

For the word of the LORD holds true,
 and we can trust everything he does.
> PSALM 33:4 NLT

He's Lord over earth,
so sing your best songs to God.
God is Lord of godless nations—
sovereign, he's King of the mountain.
Princes from all over are gathered,
people of Abraham's God.
The powers of earth are God's—
he soars over all.
> PSALM 47:7-9 MSG

God, there's just no one like you—
there's no other god as famous as you.
You outshine all others,
and your miracles make it easy to know you.
You are the one and only God!
> PSALM 86:8, 10 TPT

The eyes of the Lord are everywhere
and he takes note of everything that happens.
He watches over his lovers,
and he also sees the wickedness of the wicked.
> PROVERBS 15:3 TPT

I know that all God does will last forever; there is no adding to it or taking from it. God works so that people will be in awe of Him.
> ECCLESIASTES 3:14 HCSB

My beloved is mine, and I am his;
he grazes among the lilies.
> SONG OF SONGS 2:16 ESV

I am my beloved's and my beloved is mine;
he grazes among the lilies.
> SONG OF SONGS 6:3 ESV

I am my beloved's,
and his desire is for me.
> SONG OF SONGS 7:10 ESV

For your Maker is your bridegroom,
his name, GOD of-the-Angel-Armies!
Your Redeemer is The Holy of Israel,
known as God of the whole earth.
> ISAIAH 54:5 MSG

"You are my sheep, the sheep of my pasture, and I am your God," declares the Sovereign LORD.
> EZEKIEL 34:31 NIV

"Now I, Nebuchadnezzar, praise and exalt and glorify the King of heaven, because everything he does is right and all his ways are just. And those who walk in prided he is able to humble."
> DANIEL 4:37 NIV

Oh, that we might know the LORD!
Let us press on to know him.
He will respond to us as surely as the arrival of dawn
or the coming of rains in early spring.
> HOSEA 6:3 NLT

For the LORD is the one who shaped the mountains,
stirs up the winds, and reveals his thoughts to mankind.
He turns the light of dawn into darkness
and treads on the heights of the earth.
The LORD God of Heaven's Armies is his name!
   AMOS 4:13 NLT

"For the earth will be filled
with the knowledge of the LORD's glory,
as the waters cover the sea."
   HABAKKUK 2:14 HCSB

"I am the LORD, and I do not change."
   MALACHI 3:6 NLT

"The true God is the Creator of all things. He is the owner and Lord of the heavenly realm and the earthly realm, and he doesn't live in man-made temples. He supplies life and breath and all things to every living being. He doesn't lack a thing that we mortals could supply for him, for he has all things and everything he needs."
   ACTS 17:24-25 TPT

They say—again, quite rightly—that there is only one God the Father, that everything comes from him, and that he wants us to live for him. Also, they say that there is only one Master—Jesus the Messiah—and that everything is for his sake, including us. Yes. It's true.
   1 CORINTHIANS 8:6 MSG

He wants not only us but everyone saved, you know, everyone to get to know the truth we've learned.
   1 TIMOTHY 2:4 MSG

Move your heart closer and closer to God, and he will come even closer to you.
   JAMES 4:8 TPT

We know how much God loves us, and we have put our trust in his love. God is love, and all who live in love live in God, and God lives in them.
   1 JOHN 4:16 NLT

Goodness

"And now, O Lord GOD, You are God, and Your words are true, and You have promised this goodness to Your servant. Now therefore, let it please You to bless the house of Your servant, that it may continue before You forever; for You, O Lord GOD, have spoken it, and with Your blessing let the house of Your servant be blessed forever."
>   2 SAMUEL 7:28-29 NKJV

And they sang responsively, praising and giving thanks to the LORD, "For he is good, for his steadfast love endures forever toward Israel."
>   EZRA 3:11 ESV

Only goodness and faithful love will pursue me
all the days of my life,
and I will dwell in the house of the LORD
as long as I live.
>   PSALM 23:6 HCSB

How abundant are the good things
that you have stored up for those who fear you,
that you bestow in the sight of all,
on those who take refuge in you.
>   PSALM 31:19 NIV

No doubt about it! God is good—
good to good people, good to the good-hearted.
>   PSALM 73:1 MSG

Yes, the LORD will give what is good;
And our land will yield its increase.
>   PSALM 85:12 NKJV

Good comes to those who lend money generously
and conduct their business fairly.
>   PSALM 112:5 NLT

Return to your rest, my soul,
for the LORD has been good to you.
>   PSALM 116:7 NKJV

"And when your land is once more filled with people," says the LORD, "you will no longer wish for 'the good old days' when you possessed the Ark of the LORD's Covenant. You will not miss those days or even remember them, and there will be no need to rebuild the Ark."
>   JEREMIAH 3:16 NLT

"This city will bear on My behalf a name of joy, praise, and glory before all the nations of the earth, who will hear of all the good I will do for them. They will tremble with awe because of all the good and all the peace I will bring about for them."
>   JEREMIAH 33:9 HCSB

Gospel

For the message of the cross is foolishness to those who are perishing, but it is God's power to us who are being saved.
　　1 CORINTHIANS 1:18 HCSB

For whenever you eat this bread and drink this cup, you proclaim the Lord's death until he comes.
　　1 CORINTHIANS 11:26 NIV

Now, brothers and sisters, I want to remind you of the gospel I preached to you, which you received and on which you have taken your stand. By this gospel you are saved, if you hold firmly to the word I preached to you. Otherwise, you have believed in vain.
　　1 CORINTHIANS 15:1-2 NIV

That is, in Christ, God was reconciling the world to Himself, not counting their trespasses against them, and He has committed the message of reconciliation to us.
　　2 CORINTHIANS 5:19 HCSB

Grace

He has not dealt with us as our sins deserve
or repaid us according to our offenses.
>   PSALM 103:10 HCSB

The LORD is gracious and compassionate.
>   PSALM 111:4B HCSB

Sunrise breaks through the darkness for good people—
God's grace and mercy and justice!
>   PSALM 112:4 MSG

Gracious is the LORD, and righteous;
Yes, our God is merciful.
>   PSALM 116:5 NKJV

The LORD is righteous in all His ways,
Gracious in all His works.
>   PSALM 145:17 NKJV

"Therefore the LORD will wait, that He may be gracious to you;
And therefore He will be exalted, that He may have mercy on you.
For the LORD is a God of justice;
Blessed are all those who wait for Him."
>   ISAIAH 30:18 NKJV

But if you stop your sinning and begin to obey the LORD your God, he will change his mind about this disaster that he has announced against you.
>   JEREMIAH 26:13 NLT

You will know that I am the LORD, when I deal with you for my name's sake and not according to your evil ways and your corrupt practices, you people of Israel, declares the Sovereign LORD.
>   EZEKIEL 20:44 NIV

I will not vent the full fury of My anger;
I will not turn back to destroy Ephraim.
For I am God and not man,
the Holy One among you;
I will not come in rage.
>   HOSEA 11:9 HCSB

Now, there is no comparison between Adam's transgression and the gracious gift that we experience. For the magnitude of the gift far outweighs the crime. It's true that many died because of one man's transgression, but how much greater will God's grace and his gracious gift of acceptance overflow to many because of what one Man, Jesus, the Messiah, did for us!
>   ROMANS 5:15 TPT

Now then, the law was introduced into God's plan to bring the reality of human sinfulness out of hiding. And yet, wherever sin increased, there was more than enough of God's grace to triumph all the more! And just as sin reigned through death, so also this sin-conquering grace will reign as king through righteousness, imparting eternal life through Jesus, our Lord and Messiah!
>   ROMANS 5:20-21 TPT

Sin is no longer your master, for you no longer live under the requirements of the law. Instead, you live under the freedom of God's grace.
>   ROMANS 6:14 NLT

For you know the grace of our Lord Jesus Christ, that though he was rich, yet for your sake he became poor, so that you by his poverty might become rich.
>   2 CORINTHIANS 8:9 ESV

"My grace is sufficient for you, for power is perfected in weakness."
>   2 CORINTHIANS 12:9 HCSB

This superabundant grace is already powerfully working in us and flooding into every part of our being, releasing within us all forms of wisdom and practical understanding.
>   EPHESIANS 1:8 TPT

Together with Christ Jesus He also raised us up and seated us in the heavens, so that in the coming ages He might display the immeasurable riches of His grace through His kindness to us in Christ Jesus.

EPHESIANS 2:6-7 HCSB

For the grace of God has appeared that offers salvation to all people.

TITUS 2:11 NIV

He generously poured out the Spirit upon us through Jesus Christ our Savior. Because of his grace he declared us righteous and gave us confidence that we will inherit eternal life.

TITUS 3:6-7 NLT

But we see Jesus, who as a man, lived for a short time lower than the angels and has now been crowned with glorious honor because of what he suffered in his death. For it was by God's grace that he experienced death's bitterness on behalf of everyone!

HEBREWS 2:9 TPT

Guidance

For you are my lamp, O LORD,
and my God lightens my darkness.
> 2 SAMUEL 22:29 ESV

As for God, his way is perfect:
The LORD'S word is flawless.
> 2 SAMUEL 22:31 NIV

"He teaches my hands to make war,
So that my arms can bend a bow of bronze."
> 2 SAMUEL 22:35 NKJV

I will bless the LORD who guides me;
even at night my heart instructs me.
> PSALM 16:7 NLT

You reveal the path of life to me;
in Your presence is abundant joy;
in Your right hand are eternal pleasures.
> PSALM 16:11 HCSB

God, all at once, you turned on a floodlight for me!
You are the revelation light in my darkness,
and in your brightness I can see the path ahead.
> PSALM 18:28 TPT

He trains my hands for war,
so that my arms can bend a bow of bronze.
> PSALM 18:34 ESV

The life-maps of GOD are right,
showing the way to joy.
The directions of GOD are plain
and easy on the eyes.
>   PSALM 19:8 MSG

The rarest treasures of life are found in his truth.
That's why I prize God's Word like others prize the finest gold.
Nothing brings the soul such sweetness
as seeking his living words.
>   PSALM 19:10 TPT

There's more: God's Word warns us of danger
and directs us to hidden treasure.
Otherwise how will we find our way?
Or know when we play the fool?
>   PSALM 19:11-12 MSG

True to your word,
you let me catch my breath
and send me in the right direction.
>   PSALM 23:3 MSG

Good and upright is the LORD;
therefore he instructs sinners in his ways.
He guides the humble in what is right
and teaches them his way.
>   PSALM 25:8-9 NIV

Who, then, are those who fear the LORD?
He will instruct them in the ways they should choose.
>   PSALM 25:12 NIV

The Lord is my Revelation Light
to guide me along the way.
>   PSALM 27:1 TPT

I hear the Lord saying, "I will stay close to you,
instructing and guiding you
along the pathway for your life.
I will advise you along the way,
and lead you forth with my eyes as your guide.
So don't make it difficult, don't be stubborn
when I take you where you've not been before.
Don't make me tug you and pull you along.
Just come with me!"
  PSALM 32:8 TPT

For that is what God is like.
He is our God forever and ever,
and he will guide us until we die.
  PSALM 48:14 NLT

You guide me with your counsel,
and afterward you will take me into glory.
  PSALM 73:24 NIV

Blessed is the one you discipline, LORD,
the one you teach from your law;
  PSALM 94:12 NIV

The LORD will watch over your coming and going both now and forevermore.
  PSALM 121:8 NIV

May the LORD, my rock, be praised,
who trains my hands for battle
and my fingers for warfare.
  PSALM 144:1-2 HCSB

For the LORD gives wisdom;
From His mouth come knowledge and understanding;
  PROVERBS 2:6 NKJV

Trust in the Lord completely,
and do not rely on your own opinions.
With all your heart rely on him to guide you
and he will lead you in every decision you make.
PROVERBS 3:5 TPT

I am teaching you the way of wisdom;
I am guiding you on straight paths.
When you walk, your steps will not be hindered;
when you run, you will not stumble.
PROVERBS 4:11-12 HCSB

Whether you turn to the right or to the left, your ears will hear a voice behind you, saying, "This is the way; walk in it."
ISAIAH 30:21 NIV

"I will lead the blind by a way they did not know;
I will guide them on paths they have not known.
I will turn darkness to light in front of them
and rough places into level ground.
This is what I will do for them,
and I will not forsake them."
ISAIAH 42:16 HCSB

"I'll go ahead of you,
clearing and paving the road.
I'll break down bronze city gates,
smash padlocks, kick down barred entrances.
I'll lead you to buried treasures,
secret caches of valuables—
Confirmations that it is, in fact, I, GOD,
the God of Israel, who calls you by your name."
ISAIAH 45:2 MSG

"I am the LORD your God,
who teaches you for your benefit,
who leads you in the way you should go."
ISAIAH 48:17 HCSB

"Come to me with your ears wide open.
Listen, and you will find life.
I will make an everlasting covenant with you.
I will give you all the unfailing love I promised to David."
    ISAIAH 55:3 NLT

"Feed the hungry,
and help those in trouble.
Then your light will shine out from the darkness,
and the darkness around you will be as bright as noon.
The LORD will guide you continually,
giving you water when you are dry
and restoring your strength.
You will be like a well-watered garden,
like an ever-flowing spring."
    ISAIAH 58:10-11 NLT

"But this is the new covenant I will make with the people of Israel on that day," says the LORD. "I will put my instructions deep within them, and I will write them on their hearts. I will be their God, and they will be my people. And they will not need to teach their neighbors, nor will they need to teach their relatives, saying, 'You should know the LORD.' For everyone, from the least to the greatest, will know me already," says the LORD.
    JEREMIAH 31:33-34 NLT

If you want to live well,
make sure you understand all of this.
If you know what's good for you,
you'll learn this inside and out.
GOD'S paths get you where you want to go.
Right-living people walk them easily;
wrong-living people are always tripping and stumbling.
    HOSEA 14:9 MSG

People from many nations will come and say,
"Come, let us go up to the mountain of the LORD,
to the house of Jacob's God.
There he will teach us his ways,
and we will walk in his paths."
For the LORD's teaching will go out from Zion;
his word will go out from Jerusalem.

MICAH 4:2 NLT

"Walk with me and work with me—watch how I do it. Learn the unforced rhythms of grace. I won't lay anything heavy or ill-fitting on you. Keep company with me and you'll learn to live freely and lightly."

MATTHEW 11:29-30 MSG

Then Jesus said, "I am light to the world and those who embrace me will experience life-giving light, and they will never walk in darkness."

JOHN 8:12 TPT

"There is so much more I would like to say to you, but it's more than you can grasp at this moment. But when the truth-giving Spirit comes, he will unveil the reality of every truth within you. He won't speak his own message, but only what he hears from the Father, and he will reveal prophetically to you what is to come."

JOHN 16:12-13 TPT

He is the perfect Father who leads us all, works through us all, and lives in us all!

EPHESIANS 4:6 TPT

Healing

Then the LORD told him, "Make a replica of a poisonous snake and attach it to a pole. All who are bitten will live if they simply look at it!" So Moses made a snake out of bronze and attached it to a pole. Then anyone who was bitten by a snake could look at the bronze snake and be healed!
NUMBERS 21:8-9 NLT

"And the LORD will take away from you all sickness, and will afflict you with none of the terrible diseases of Egypt which you have known, but will lay them on all those who hate you."
DEUTERONOMY 7:15 NKJV

"Go back and tell Hezekiah, the ruler of my people, 'This is what the LORD, the God of your father David, says: I have heard your prayer and seen your tears; I will heal you. On the third day from now you will go up to the temple of the LORD. I will add fifteen years to your life. And I will deliver you and this city from the hand of the king of Assyria. I will defend this city for my sake and for the sake of my servant David.'"
2 KINGS 20:5-6 NIV

When [the poor and helpless] are sick, God will restore them,
lying upon their bed of suffering.
He will raise them up again
and restore them back to health.
PSALM 41:3 TPT

He heals your diseases—every one.
PSALM 103:3 MSG

Blind eyes will be opened,
deaf ears unstopped,
Lame men and women will leap like deer,
the voiceless break into song.
ISAIAH 35:5-6 HCSB

Heal me, LORD, and I will be healed;
save me and I will be saved,
for you are the one I praise.
 JEREMIAH 17:14 NIV

"But I will restore you to health
and heal your wounds,"
declares the LORD,
"because you are called an outcast,
Zion for whom no one cares."
 JEREMIAH 30:17 NIV

"Yet I will certainly bring health and healing to it and will indeed heal them. I will let them experience the abundance of peace and truth."
 JEREMIAH 33:6 HCSB

"But for you who fear my name, the Sun of Righteousness will rise with healing in his wings. And you will go free, leaping with joy like calves let out to pasture."
 MALACHI 4:2 NLT

A man with leprosy came and knelt in front of Jesus, begging to be healed. "If you are willing, you can heal me and make me clean," he said. Moved with compassion, Jesus reached out and touched him. "I am willing," he said. "Be healed!"
 MARK 1:40-41 NLT

One day, while Jesus was ministering in a certain city, he came upon a man covered with leprous sores. When the man recognized Jesus, he fell on his face at Jesus' feet and begged to be healed, saying, "If you are only willing, you could completely heal me." Jesus reached out and touched him and said, "Of course I am willing to heal you, and now you will be healed." Instantly the leprous sores were healed and his skin became smooth.
 LUKE 5:12-14 TPT

Jesus responded, "Beloved daughter, your faith in me has released your healing. You may go with my peace."
 LUKE 8:48 TPT

Are any of you sick? You should call for the elders of the church to come and pray over you, anointing you with oil in the name of the Lord. Such a prayer offered in faith will heal the sick, and the Lord will make you well. And if you have committed any sins, you will be forgiven.

JAMES 5:14-15 NLT

Heaven

"So, now, go and sell what you have and give to those in need, making deposits in your account in heaven, an account that will never be taken from you. Your gifts will become a secure and unfailing treasure, deposited in heaven forever. Where you deposit your treasure, that is where your thoughts will turn to—and your heart will long to be there also."
LUKE 12:33-34 TPT

"Don't let your hearts be troubled. Trust in God, and trust also in me. There is more than enough room in my Father's home. If this were not so, would I have told you that I am going to prepare a place for you?"
JOHN 14:1-2 NLT

For we know that if the earthly tent we live in is destroyed, we have a building from God, an eternal house in heaven, not built by human hands.
2 CORINTHIANS 5:1 NIV

For our citizenship is in heaven, from which we also eagerly wait for the Savior, the Lord Jesus Christ, who will transform our lowly body that it may be conformed to His glorious body, according to the working by which He is able even to subdue all things to Himself.
PHILIPPIANS 3:20-21 NKJV

When the Messiah, who is your life, is revealed, then you also will be revealed with Him in glory.
COLOSSIANS 3:4 HCSB

But now they desire a better, that is, a heavenly country. Therefore God is not ashamed to be called their God, for He has prepared a city for them.
HEBREWS 11:16 NKJV

Help

And God heard the voice of the boy, and the angel of God called to Hagar from heaven and said to her, "What troubles you, Hagar? Fear not, for God has heard the voice of the boy where he is. Up! Lift up the boy, and hold him fast with your hand, for I will make him into a great nation."
GENESIS 21:17-18 ESV

"The LORD will fight for you, and you have only to be silent."
EXODUS 14:14 ESV

LORD, who is like You among the gods?
Who is like You, glorious in holiness,
revered with praises, performing wonders?
EXODUS 15:11 HCSB

And the LORD said to Moses, "I will do the very thing you have asked, because I am pleased with you and I know you by name."
EXODUS 33:17 NIV

"The LORD your God who goes before you will fight for you, just as you saw Him do for you in Egypt. And you saw in the wilderness how the LORD your God carried you as a man carries his son all along the way you traveled until you reached this place."
DEUTERONOMY 1:30-31 HCSB

"Rise up, set out on your journey and go over the Valley of the Arnon. Behold, I have given into your hand Sihon the Amorite, king of Heshbon, and his land. Begin to take possession, and contend with him in battle. This day I will begin to put the dread and fear of you on the peoples who are under the whole heaven, who shall hear the report of you and shall tremble and be in anguish because of you."
DEUTERONOMY 2:24-25 ESV

And the LORD said to me, "See, I have begun to give Sihon and his land over to you. Begin to possess it, that you may inherit his land."
DEUTERONOMY 2:31 NKJV

"I commanded Joshua at that time: Your own eyes have seen everything the LORD your God has done to these two kings. The LORD will do the same to all the kingdoms you are about to enter."

DEUTERONOMY 3:21 HCSB

"When GOD, your God, brings you into the country that you are about to enter and take over, he will clear out the superpowers that were there before you: the Hittite, the Girgashite, the Amorite, the Canaanite, the Perizzite, the Hivite, and the Jebusite. Those seven nations are all bigger and stronger than you are."

DEUTERONOMY 7:1 MSG

"Know therefore today that he who goes over before you as a consuming fire is the LORD your God. He will destroy them and subdue them before you. So you shall drive them out and make them perish quickly, as the LORD has promised you."

DEUTERONOMY 9:3 ESV

"If you diligently keep all this commandment that I command you to obey—love GOD, your God, do what he tells you, stick close to him—GOD on his part will drive out all these nations that stand in your way. Yes, he'll drive out nations much bigger and stronger than you. Every square inch on which you place your foot will be yours."

DEUTERONOMY 11:22-24A MSG

"GOD, your God, is right there with you, fighting with you against your enemies, fighting to win."

DEUTERONOMY 20:4 MSG

"The LORD your God is the One who will cross ahead of you. He will destroy these nations before you, and you will drive them out."

DEUTERONOMY 31:3A HCSB

"There is no one like the God of Israel.
He rides across the heavens to help you,
across the skies in majestic splendor."

DEUTERONOMY 33:26 NLT

"Attention! Listen to what GOD, your God, has to say. This is how you'll know that God is alive among you—he will completely dispossess before you the Canaanites, Hittites, Hivites, Perizzites, Girgashites, Amorites, and Jebusites."
JOSHUA 3:9-10 MSG

"When the feet of the priests who carry the ark of the LORD, the Lord of all the earth, come to rest in the Jordan's waters, its waters will be cut off. The water flowing downstream will stand up in a mass."
JOSHUA 3:13 HCSB

And the LORD said to Joshua, "See, I have given Jericho into your hand, with its king and mighty men of valor."
JOSHUA 6:2 ESV

The seventh time around, when the priests sounded the trumpet blast, Joshua commanded the army, "Shout! For the LORD has given you the city!"
JOSHUA 6:16 NIV

Then the LORD said to Joshua, "Stretch out the spear that is in your hand toward Ai, for I will give it into your hand." And Joshua stretched out the spear that was in his hand toward the city.
JOSHUA 8:18 NKJV

So Joshua marched up from Gilgal with his entire army, including all the best fighting men. The LORD said to Joshua, "Do not be afraid of them; I have given them into your hand. Not one of them will be able to withstand you."
JOSHUA 10:7-8 NIV

When Joshua had grown old, the LORD said to him, "You are now very old, and there are still very large areas of land to be taken over. As for all the inhabitants of the mountain regions from Lebanon to Misrephoth Maim, that is, all the Sidonians, I myself will drive them out before the Israelites. Be sure to allocate this land to Israel for an inheritance, as I have instructed you."
JOSHUA 13:1, 6 NIV

"You yourselves have seen everything the LORD your God has done to all these nations for your sake; it was the LORD your God who fought for you."
JOSHUA 23:3 NIV

"The LORD has driven out before you great and powerful nations; to this day no one has been able to withstand you. One of you routs a thousand, because the LORD your God fights for you, just as he promised. So be very careful to love the LORD your God."
JOSHUA 23:9-11 NIV

"The Spirit of the LORD will control you, you will prophesy with them, and you will be transformed into a different person. When these signs have happened to you, do whatever your circumstances require, because God is with you."
1 SAMUEL 10:6-7 HCSB

"Let's go across to the outpost of those pagans," Jonathan said to his armor bearer. "Perhaps the LORD will help us, for nothing can hinder the LORD. He can win a battle whether he has many warriors or only a few!"
1 SAMUEL 14:6 NLT

David said to the Philistine: "You come against me with a dagger, spear, and sword, but I come against you in the name of Yahweh of Hosts, the God of Israel's armies—you have defied Him. Today, the LORD will hand you over to me. Today, I'll strike you down, cut your head off, and give the corpses of the Philistine camp to the birds of the sky and the creatures of the earth. Then all the world will know that Israel has a God, and this whole assembly will know that it is not by sword or by spear that the LORD saves, for the battle is the LORD's. He will hand you over to us."
1 SAMUEL 17:45-47 HCSB

David continued to succeed in everything he did, for the LORD was with him.
1 SAMUEL 18:14 NLT

So David inquired of the LORD, saying, "Shall I go up against the Philistines? Will You deliver them into my hand?" And the LORD said to David, "Go up, for I will doubtless deliver the Philistines into your hand."
2 SAMUEL 5:19 NKJV

David inquired of the LORD, and He said, "You shall not go up; circle around behind them, and come upon them in front of the mulberry trees. And it shall be, when you hear the sound of marching in the tops of the mulberry trees, then you shall advance quickly. For then the LORD will go out before you to strike the camp of the Philistines."
2 SAMUEL 5:23-24 NKJV

So David again inquired of God, and God answered him, "Do not pursue them directly. Circle around them and attack them opposite the balsam trees. When you hear the sound of marching in the tops of the balsam trees, then march out to battle, for God will have marched out ahead of you to attack the camp of the Philistines."
1 CHRONICLES 14:14-16 HCSB

"I have been with you wherever you have gone, and I have destroyed all your enemies before you. I will make a name for you like that of the greatest in the land."
1 CHRONICLES 17:8 HCSB

"And now, O LORD, I am your servant; do as you have promised concerning me and my family. May it be a promise that will last forever."
1 CHRONICLES 17:23 NLT

"God is with us; he is our leader. His priests with their trumpets will sound the battle cry against you."
2 CHRONICLES 13:12A NIV

"LORD, there is no one besides You to help the mighty and those without strength. Help us, LORD our God, for we depend on You, and in Your name we have come against this large army. Yahweh, You are our God. Do not let a mere mortal hinder You."
2 CHRONICLES 14:11 HCSB

For a long time Israel was without the true God, without a priest to teach them, and without the Law to instruct them. But whenever they were in trouble and turned to the LORD, the God of Israel, and sought him out, they found him.
2 CHRONICLES 15:3-4 NLT

"GOD is always on the alert, constantly on the lookout for people who are totally committed to him. You were foolish to go for human help when you could have had God's help. Now you're in trouble—one round of war after another."
2 CHRONICLES 16:9 MSG

"The work is great and widely spread, and we are separated on the wall, far from one another. In the place where you hear the sound of the trumpet, rally to us there. Our God will fight for us."
NEHEMIAH 4:19-20 ESV

But if I were you, I would appeal to God;
I would lay my cause before him.
He performs wonders that cannot be fathomed,
miracles that cannot be counted.
> JOB 5:8-9 NIV

But look, God will not reject a person of integrity,
nor will he lend a hand to the wicked.
> JOB 8:20 NLT

"Even now my witness is in heaven,
and my advocate is in the heights!"
> JOB 16:19 HCSB

The poor and helpless ones trust in you, Lord,
for you are famous for being the Helper of the fatherless.
I know you won't let them down.
> PSALM 10:14 TPT

The eyes of the LORD are on the righteous,
and His ears are open to their cry for help.
> PSALM 34:15 HCSB

Join me, everyone! Trust only in God every moment!
Tell him all your troubles and
Pour out your heart-longings to him.
Believe me when I tell you—he will help you!
> PSALM 62:8 TPT

I am afflicted and needy;
hurry to me, God.
You are my help and my deliverer;
LORD, do not delay.
> PSALM 70:5 HCSB

He will rescue the poor when they cry to him;
he will help the oppressed, who have no one to defend them.
> PSALM 72:12 NLT

Even though others succumb all around,
drop like flies right and left,
no harm will even graze you.
>   PSALM 91:7 MSG

If you stumble, [God's angels] will catch you;
their job is to keep you from falling.
>   PSALM 91:12 MSG

With God's help we will do mighty things,
for he will trample down our foes.
>   PSALM 108:13 NLT

O Israel, trust the LORD!
He is your helper and your shield.
>   PSALM 115:9 NLT

The LORD is with me; he is my helper.
I look in triumph on my enemies.
>   PSALM 118:7 NIV

I lift my eyes toward the mountains.
Where will my help come from?
My help comes from the LORD,
the Maker of heaven and earth.
>   PSALM 121:1-2 HCSB

Our help is in the name of the LORD,
the Maker of heaven and earth.
>   PSALM 124:8 NIV

Through your mighty power
I can walk through any devastation,
and you will keep me alive, reviving me.
Your power set me free from the hatred of my enemies.
>   PSALM 138:7 TPT

If I take the wings of the morning,
And dwell in the uttermost parts of the sea,
Even there Your hand shall lead me,
And Your right hand shall hold me.
> PSALM 139:9-10 NKJV

The LORD helps all who fall;
He raises up all who are oppressed.
> PSALM 145:14 HCSB

He fulfills the desires of those who fear Him;
He hears their cry for help and saves them.
> PSALM 145:19 HCSB

The LORD helps the afflicted
but brings the wicked to the ground.
> PSALM 147:6 HCSB

In all your ways acknowledge him,
and he will make straight your paths.
> PROVERBS 3:6 ESV

"I will strengthen you; I will help you;
I will hold on to you with My righteous right hand."
> ISAIAH 41:10B HCSB

"Though you search for your enemies,
you will not find them.
Those who wage war against you
will be as nothing at all.
For I am the LORD your God
who takes hold of your right hand
and says to you, Do not fear;
I will help you."
> ISAIAH 41:12-13 NIV

"I'm ready to help you right now.
Deliverance is not a long-range plan.
Salvation isn't on hold.
I'm putting salvation to work in Zion now,
and glory in Israel."
>   ISAIAH 46:13 MSG

"I will answer you in a time of favor,
and I will help you in the day of salvation.
I will keep you, and I will appoint you
to be a covenant for the people,
to restore the land,
to make them possess the desolate inheritances."
>   ISAIAH 49:8 HCSB

Because the Sovereign LORD helps me,
I will not be disgraced.
Therefore have I set my face like flint,
and I know I will not be put to shame.
>   ISAIAH 50:7 NIV

It is the Sovereign LORD who helps me.
Who will condemn me?
They will all wear out like a garment;
the moths will eat them up.
>   ISAIAH 50:9 NIV

"His children will be as in past days;
his congregation will be established in My presence.
I will punish all his oppressors."
>   JEREMIAH 30:20 HCSB

"Do not fear, O Jacob My servant," says the LORD,
"For I am with you;
For I will make a complete end of all the nations
To which I have driven you,
But I will not make a complete end of you.
I will rightly correct you,
For I will not leave you wholly unpunished."

JEREMIAH 46:48 NKJV

"I will drive away these armies from the north.
I will send them into the parched wastelands.
Those in the front will be driven into the Dead Sea,
and those at the rear into the Mediterranean.
The stench of their rotting bodies will rise over the land.
Surely the LORD has done great things!"

JOEL 2:20 NLT

"Look among the nations, and see;
wonder and be astounded.
For I am doing a work in your days
that you would not believe if told."

HABAKKUK 1:5 ESV

I have heard all about you, LORD.
I am filled with awe by your amazing works.
In this time of our deep need,
help us again as you did in years gone by.
And in your anger,
remember your mercy.

HABAKKUK 3:2 NLT

"Be strong, Joshua son of Jehozadak, high priest. Be strong, all you people of the land"—this is the LORD's declaration. "Work! For I am with you"—the declaration of the LORD of Hosts.

HAGGAI 2:4 HCSB

For thus said the LORD of hosts, after his glory sent me to the nations who plundered you, for he who touches you touches the apple of his eye: "Behold, I will shake my hand over them, and they shall become plunder for those who served them. Then you will know that the LORD of hosts has sent me."

ZECHARIAH 2:8-9 ESV

"Look! I am sending my messenger, and he will prepare the way before me. Then the Lord you are seeking will suddenly come to his Temple. The messenger of the covenant, whom you look for so eagerly, is surely coming," says the LORD of Heaven's Armies.

MALACHI 3:1 NLT

"Look, I am sending you the prophet Elijah before the great and dreadful day of the LORD arrives."

MALACHI 4:6 NLT

"Mighty power flows from him
to scatter all those who walk in pride.
Powerful princes he tears from their thrones
and he lifts up the lowly to take their place."

LUKE 1:51-52 TPT

"Will not God grant justice to His elect who cry out to Him day and night? Will He delay to help them? I tell you that He will swiftly grant them justice. Nevertheless, when the Son of Man comes, will He find that faith on earth?"

LUKE 18:7-8 HCSB

And the Holy Spirit helps us in our weakness. For example, we don't know what God wants us to pray for. But the Holy Spirit prays for us with groanings that cannot be expressed in words.

ROMANS 8:26 NLT

The God of peace will soon crush Satan under your feet. May the grace of our Lord Jesus be with you.

ROMANS 16:20 NLT

For God says,
"At just the right time, I heard you.
On the day of salvation, I helped you."

2 CORINTHIANS 6:2 NLT

And God will provide rest for you who are being persecuted and also for us when the Lord Jesus appears from heaven. He will come with his mighty angels, in flaming fire, bringing judgment on those who don't know God and on those who refuse to obey the Good News of our Lord Jesus.

2 THESSALONIANS 1:7-8 NLT

So now we come freely and boldly to where love is enthroned, to receive mercy's kiss and discover the grace we urgently need to strengthen us in our time of weakness.

HEBREWS 4:16 TPT

Now to him who is able to keep you from stumbling and to present you blameless before the presence of his glory with great joy, to the only God, our Savior, through Jesus Christ our Lord, be glory, majesty, dominion, and authority, before all time and now and forever. Amen.

JUDE 24-25 ESV

Holiness

"For I am Yahweh your God, so you must consecrate yourselves and be holy because I am holy. You must not defile yourselves by any swarming creature that crawls on the ground. For I am Yahweh, who brought you up from the land of Egypt to be your God, so you must be holy because I am holy."
LEVITICUS 11:44–45 HCSB

"So set yourselves apart to be holy, for I am the LORD your God. Keep all my decrees by putting them into practice, for I am the LORD who makes you holy."
LEVITICUS 20:7–8 NLT

"Live holy lives before me because I, GOD, am holy. I have distinguished you from the nations to be my very own."
LEVITICUS 20:26 MSG

There will be a highway
called the Holy Road.
No one rude or rebellious
is permitted on this road.
It's for GOD'S people exclusively—
impossible to get lost on this road.
Not even fools can get lost on it.
No lions on this road,
no dangerous wild animals—
Nothing and no one dangerous or threatening.
Only the redeemed will walk on it.
ISAIAH 35:8–9 MSG

"You therefore must be perfect, as your heavenly Father is perfect."
MATTHEW 5:48 ESV

For God's will was for us to be made holy by the sacrifice of the body of Jesus Christ, once for all time.
HEBREWS 10:10 NLT

Holy Spirit

"And I will never again turn my face from them, for I will pour out my Spirit upon the people of Israel. I, the Sovereign LORD, have spoken!"

EZEKIEL 39:29 NLT

"Whenever you are arrested and brought to trial, do not worry beforehand about what to say. Just say whatever is given you at the time, for it is not you speaking, but the Holy Spirit."

MARK 13:11 NIV

John answered them all, "I baptize you with water. But one who is more powerful than I will come, the straps of whose sandals I am not worthy to untie. He will baptize you with the Holy Spirit and fire. His winnowing fork is in his hand to clear his threshing floor and to gather the wheat into his barn, but he will burn up the chaff with unquenchable fire."

LUKE 3:16-17 NIV

Jesus replied, "I assure you, no one can enter the Kingdom of God without being born of water and the Spirit. Humans can reproduce only human life, but the Holy Spirit gives birth to spiritual life."

JOHN 3:5-6 NLT

"I will talk to the Father, and he'll provide you another Friend so that you will always have someone with you. This Friend is the Spirit of Truth. The godless world can't take him in because it doesn't have eyes to see him, doesn't know what to look for. But you know him already because he has been staying with you, and will even be in you!"

JOHN 14:15-17 MSG

"Do not leave Jerusalem until the Father sends you the gift he promised, as I told you before. John baptized with water, but in just a few days you will be baptized with the Holy Spirit."

ACTS 1:4-5 NLT

Peter replied, "Repent and return to God, and each one of you must be baptized in the name of Jesus, the Anointed One, to have your sins removed. Then you may take hold of the gift of the Holy Spirit. For God's promise of the Holy Spirit is for you and your families, for those yet to be born and for everyone whom the Lord our God calls to himself."

ACTS 2:38-39 TPT

And the Father who knows all hearts knows what the Spirit is saying, for the Spirit pleads for us believers in harmony with God's own will.

ROMANS 8:27 NLT

Do you not know that your bodies are temples of the Holy Spirit, who is in you, whom you have received from God? You are not your own;

1 CORINTHIANS 6:19 NIV

All these gifts have a common origin, but are handed out one by one by the one Spirit of God. He decides who gets what, and when.

1 CORINTHIANS 12:11 MSG

He has also sealed us and given us the Spirit as a down payment in our hearts.

2 CORINTHIANS 1:22 HCSB

Indeed, we groan while we are in this tent, burdened as we are, because we do not want to be unclothed but clothed, so that mortality may be swallowed up by life. And the One who prepared us for this very purpose is God, who gave us the Spirit as a down payment.

2 CORINTHIANS 5:4-5 HCSB

Through Christ Jesus, God has blessed the Gentiles with the same blessing he promised to Abraham, so that we who are believers might receive the promised Holy Spirit through faith.

GALATIANS 3:14 TPT

Because you are his sons, God sent the Spirit of his Son into our hearts, the Spirit who calls out, "Abba, Father."

GALATIANS 4:6 NIV

As you yield freely and fully to the dynamic life and power of the Holy Spirit, you will abandon the cravings of your self-life.
GALATIANS 5:16 TPT

Now all of us can come to the Father through the same Holy Spirit because of what Christ has done for us.
EPHESIANS 2:18 NLT

But you have an anointing from the Holy One, and you know all things.
1 JOHN 2:20 NKJV

But you have received the Holy Spirit, and he lives within you, so you don't need anyone to teach you what is true. For the Spirit teaches you everything you need to know, and what he teaches is true—it is not a lie. So just as he has taught you, remain in fellowship with Christ.
1 JOHN 2:27 NLT

This is how we know that we live in him and he in us: He has given us of his Spirit.
1 JOHN 4:13 NIV

Hope

And so at last the poor have hope,
and the snapping jaws of the wicked are shut.
> JOB 5:16 NLT

You'll forget your troubles;
they'll be like old, faded photographs.
Your world will be washed in sunshine,
every shadow dispersed by dayspring.
Full of hope, you'll relax, confident again;
you'll look around, sit back, and take it easy.
> JOB 11:16-18 MSG

But the needy will not be ignored forever;
the hopes of the poor will not always be crushed.
> PSALM 9:18 NLT

No one who trusts in you will ever be disgraced,
but disgrace comes to those who try to deceive others.
> PSALM 25:3 NLT

You are the hope of everyone on earth,
even those who sail on distant seas.
> PSALM 65:5B NLT

As for me, I will always have hope;
I will praise you more and more.
> PSALM 71:14 NIV

You are my refuge and my shield;
your word is my source of hope.
> PSALM 119:114 NLT

The LORD values those who fear Him,
those who put their hope in His faithful love.
> PSALM 147:11 HCSB

O GOD, you're the hope of Israel.
All who leave you end up as fools,
Deserters with nothing to show for their lives,
who walk off from GOD, fountain of living waters—
and wind up dead!
> JEREMIAH 17:13 MSG

I say: The LORD is my portion,
therefore I will put my hope in Him.
> LAMENTATIONS 3:24 HCSB

"Glory to God in the highest realms of heaven!
For there is peace and a good hope given to the sons of men."
> LUKE 2:14 TPT

And hope does not put us to shame, because God's love has been poured out into our hearts through the Holy Spirit, who has been given to us.
> ROMANS 5:5 NIV

He is given to us like an engagement ring is given to a bride, as the first installment of what's coming! He is our promised hope of a future inheritance for all who have been made alive in Christ. This hope-promise seals us until we have all of redemption's promises and experience complete freedom—all for the supreme glory and honor of God!
> EPHESIANS 1:14 TPT

For we have heard of your faith in Christ Jesus and your love for all of God's people, which come from your confident hope of what God has reserved for you in heaven. You have had this expectation ever since you first heard the truth of the Good News.
> COLOSSIANS 1:4–5 NLT

For the sake of this ministry, we toil tirelessly and are criticized continually, simply because our hope is in the Living God. He is the wonderful Life-Giver of all the children of men, and even more so to those who believe.
1 TIMOTHY 4:10 TPT

God can't break his word. And because his word cannot change, the promise is likewise unchangeable.
We who have run for our very lives to God have every reason to grab the promised hope with both hands and never let go. It's an unbreakable spiritual lifeline, reaching past all appearances right to the very presence of God.
HEBREWS 6:18-19 MSG

Humility

He humbles the proud
and brings down the arrogant city.
He brings it down to the dust.
>   ISAIAH 26:5 NLT

"For everyone who is proud and feels that he is superior to others will one day be humiliated before all, and everyone who humbles himself will one day be lifted up and honored before all."
>   LUKE 18:14 TPT

Be willing to be made low before the Lord and he will exalt you!
>   JAMES 4:10 TPT

You who are younger, be subject to the elders. Clothe yourselves, all of you, with humility toward one another, for "God opposes the proud but gives grace to the humble."
>   1 PETER 5:5 ESV

Humble yourselves, therefore, under God's mighty hand, that he may lift you up in due time.
>   1 PETER 5:6 NIV

Hunger

The well-fed are out begging in the streets for crusts,
while the hungry are getting second helpings.
The barren woman has a houseful of children,
while the mother of many is bereft.
> 1 SAMUEL 2:5 MSG

He fills the sky with clouds, sending showers to water the earth
so that the grass springs up on the mountain fields
and the earth produces food for man.
All the birds and beasts that cry with hunger to him
are fed from his hands.
> PSALM 147:8-9 TPT

"I will raise up for them a garden of renown, and they shall no longer be consumed with hunger in the land, nor bear the shame of the Gentiles anymore."
> EZEKIEL 34:29 NKJV

"God blesses you who are hungry now,
for you will be satisfied."
> LUKE 6:21 NLT

The One seated on the throne will shelter them:
They will no longer hunger;
they will no longer thirst;
the sun will no longer strike them,
nor will any heat.
For the Lamb who is at the center of the throne
will shepherd them;
He will guide them to springs of living waters,
and God will wipe away every tear from their eyes.
> REVELATION 7:15-17 HCSB

Identity

Then God said, "Let us make mankind in our image, in our likeness, so that they may rule over the fish in the sea and the birds in the sky, over the livestock and all the wild animals, and over all the creatures that move along the ground."
So God created mankind in his own image,
in the image of God he created them;
male and female he created them.
GENESIS 1:26–28 NIV

"Your name will no longer be Jacob," the man told him. "From now on you will be called Israel, because you have fought with God and with men and have won."
GENESIS 32:28 NLT

God appeared to Jacob again, when he came from Paddan-aram, and blessed him. And God said to him, "Your name is Jacob; no longer shall your name be called Jacob, but Israel shall be your name." So he called his name Israel. And God said to him, "I am God Almighty: be fruitful and multiply. A nation and a company of nations shall come from you, and kings shall come from your own body."
GENESIS 35:9–13 ESV

But the LORD said to Samuel, "Do not look on his appearance or on the height of his stature, because I have rejected him. For the LORD sees not as man sees: man looks on the outward appearance, but the LORD looks on the heart."
1 SAMUEL 16:7 ESV

"And I have been with you wherever you have gone, and have cut off all your enemies from before you, and have made you a great name, like the name of the great men who are on the earth."
2 SAMUEL 7:9 NKJV

"What is man, that You think so highly of him
and pay so much attention to him?
You inspect him every morning,
and put him to the test every moment."
JOB 7:17–18 HCSB

"The Spirit of God has made me;
the breath of the Almighty gives me life."
> JOB 33:4 NIV

You have made [mankind] a little lower than the angels
and crowned them with glory and honor.
You made them rulers over the works of your hands;
you put everything under their feet:
all flocks and herds,
and the animals of the wild,
the birds in the sky,
and the fish in the sea,
all that swim the paths of the seas.
> PSALM 8:5-8 NIV

Know that the LORD is God.
It is he who made us, and we are his;
we are his people, the sheep of his pasture.
> PSALM 100:3 NIV

With your very own hands you formed me;
now breathe your wisdom over me so I can understand you.
> PSALM 119:73 MSG

Lord, you know everything there is to know about me.
You've examined my innermost being with your loving gaze.
You perceive every movement of my heart and soul,
and understand my every thought before it even enters my mind.
You are so intimately aware of me, Lord,
you read my heart like an open book
and you know all the words I'm about to speak
before I even start a sentence!
You know every step I will take.
> PSALM 139:1-4 TPT

For you created my inmost being;
you knit me together in my mother's womb.
> PSALM 139:13 NIV

I thank you, High God—you're breathtaking!
Body and soul, I am marvelously made!
I worship in adoration—what a creation!
You know me inside and out,
you know every bone in my body;
You know exactly how I was made, bit by bit,
how I was sculpted from nothing into something.
> PSALM 139:14-15 MSG

You saw me before I was born.
Every day of my life was recorded in your book.
Every moment was laid out
before a single day had passed.
> PSALM 139:16 NLT

Every single moment you are thinking of me!
How precious and wonderful to consider,
that you cherish me constantly in your every thought!
O God, your desires toward me are more
than the grains of sand on every shore!
When I awake each morning, you're still thinking of me.
> PSALM 139:17-18 TPT

"I will say to the north, Give up,
and to the south, Do not withhold;
bring my sons from afar
and my daughters from the end of the earth,
everyone who is called by my name,
whom I created for my glory,
whom I formed and made."
> ISAIAH 43:6-7 ESV

GOD who made you has something to say to you;
the God who formed you in the womb wants to help you.
> ISAIAH 44:2 MSG

"Before I shaped you in the womb,
I knew all about you.
Before you saw the light of day,
I had holy plans for you:
A prophet to the nations—
that's what I had in mind for you."
JEREMIAH 1:5 MSG

"Aren't two sparrows sold for a penny? Yet not one of them falls to the ground without your Father's consent. But even the hairs of your head have all been counted. So don't be afraid therefore; you are worth more than many sparrows."
MATTHEW 10:29-31 HCSB

"And I tell you that you are Peter, and on this rock I will build my church, and the gates of Hades will not overcome it."
MATTHEW 16:18 NIV

"Consider the ravens: They do not sow or reap, they have no storeroom or barn; yet God feeds them. And how much more valuable you are than birds!"
LUKE 12:24 NIV

"It is through him that we live and function and have our identity; just as your own poets have said, 'Our lineage comes from him.'"
ACTS 17:28 TPT

Could it be any clearer that our former identity is forever deprived of its power? For we were co-crucified with him to dismantle the stronghold of sin within us, so that we would not continue to live one moment longer submitted to sin's power.
ROMANS 6:6 TPT

So if my behavior contradicts my desires to do good, I must conclude that it's not my true identity doing it, but the unwelcome intruder of sin hindering me from being who I really am.
ROMANS 7:20 TPT

But you are not in the flesh but in the Spirit, if indeed the Spirit of God dwells in you. Now if anyone does not have the Spirit of Christ, he is not His. And if Christ is in you, the body is dead because of sin, but the Spirit is life because of righteousness. But if the Spirit of Him who raised Jesus from the dead dwells in you, He who raised Christ from the dead will also give life to your mortal bodies through His Spirit who dwells in you.
ROMANS 8:9-11 NKJV

But in fact God has placed the parts in the body, every one of them, just as he wanted them to be. If they were all one part, where would the body be?
1 CORINTHIANS 12:18-19 NIV

But thanks be to God, who always leads us as captives in Christ's triumphal procession and uses us to spread the aroma of the knowledge of him everywhere. For we are to God the pleasing aroma of Christ among those who are being saved and those who are perishing.
2 CORINTHIANS 2:14-15 NIV

My old self has been crucified with Christ. It is no longer I who live, but Christ lives in me. So I live in this earthly body by trusting in the Son of God, who loved me and gave himself for me.
GALATIANS 2:20 NLT

For we are God's masterpiece. He has created us anew in Christ Jesus, so we can do the good things he planned for us long ago.
EPHESIANS 2:10 NLT

And I am sure of this, that he who began a good work in you will bring it to completion at the day of Jesus Christ.
PHILIPPIANS 1:6 ESV

As you come to him, the living Stone—rejected by humans but chosen by God and precious to him—you also, like living stones, are being built into a spiritual house to be a holy priesthood, offering spiritual sacrifices acceptable to God through Jesus Christ.
1 PETER 2:4-5 NIV

For he has said,
"I will reveal who you really are to my brothers and sisters,
and I will glorify you with praises in the midst of the congregation."
HEBREWS 2:12 TPT

Idolatry

"When you have children and grandchildren and have been in the land a long time, and if you act corruptly, make an idol in the form of anything, and do what is evil in the sight of the LORD your God, provoking Him to anger, I call heaven and earth as witnesses against you today that you will quickly perish from the land you are about to cross the Jordan to possess. You will not live long there, but you will certainly be destroyed."

DEUTERONOMY 4:25-27 HCSB

"You must not make for yourself an idol of any kind, or an image of anything in the heavens or on the earth or in the sea. You must not bow down to them or worship them, for I, the LORD your God, am a jealous God who will not tolerate your affection for any other gods. I lay the sins of the parents upon their children; the entire family is affected—even children in the third and fourth generations of those who reject me."

DEUTERONOMY 5:8-9 NLT

This is what the LORD says: "I am going to bring disaster on this place and its people, according to everything written in the book the king of Judah has read. Because they have forsaken me and burned incense to other gods and aroused my anger by all the idols their hands have made, my anger will burn against this place and will not be quenched."

2 KINGS 22:16-17 NIV

But those who trust in idols,
who say to images, "You are our gods,"
will be turned back in utter shame.

ISAIAH 42:17 NIV

Can any of the worthless foreign gods send us rain?
Does it fall from the sky by itself?
No, you are the one, O LORD our God!
Only you can do such things.
So we will wait for you to help us.

JEREMIAH 14:22 NLT

Jesus

"But from today on, the Son of Man will be enthroned in the place of honor, power, and authority with Almighty God."
LUKE 22:69 TPT

"I am the good shepherd. I know My own sheep, and they know Me, as the Father knows Me, and I know the Father. I lay down My life for the sheep."
JOHN 10:14-15 HCSB

"My own sheep will hear my voice and I know each one, and they will follow me."
JOHN 10:27 TPT

Jesus explained, "I am the Way, I am the Truth, and I am the Life. No one comes next to the Father except through union with me. To know me is to know my Father too."
JOHN 14:6 TPT

"Now everyone in Israel can know for certain that Jesus, whom you crucified, is the one God has made both Lord and the Messiah."
ACTS 2:36 TPT

"We tell you the good news: What God promised our ancestors he has fulfilled for us, their children, by raising up Jesus. As it is written in the second Psalm:
'You are my son;
today I have become your father.'"
ACTS 13:32-33 NIV

For when the time was right, the Anointed One came and died to demonstrate his love for sinners who were entirely helpless, weak, and powerless to save themselves.
ROMANS 5:6 TPT

Just as it is written:
"As surely as I am the Living God, I tell you:
Every knee will bow before me,
and every tongue will confess the truth and glorify me!"
ROMANS 14:11 TPT

But whoever is united with the Lord is one with him in spirit.
1 CORINTHIANS 6:17 NIV

For all of God's promises have been fulfilled in Christ with a resounding "Yes!" And through Christ, our "Amen" (which means "Yes") ascends to God for his glory.
2 CORINTHIANS 1:20 NLT

For Christ's love compels us, since we have reached this conclusion: If One died for all, then all died. And He died for all so that those who live should no longer live for themselves, but for the One who died for them and was raised.
2 CORINTHIANS 5:14-15 HCSB

Therefore God also has highly exalted Him and given Him the name which is above every name, that at the name of Jesus every knee should bow, of those in heaven, and of those on earth, and of those under the earth, and that every tongue should confess that Jesus Christ is Lord, to the glory of God the Father.
PHILIPPIANS 2:9-11 NKJV

Yes, everything else is worthless when compared with the infinite value of knowing Christ Jesus my Lord. For his sake I have discarded everything else, counting it all as garbage, so that I could gain Christ and become one with him.
PHILIPPIANS 3:8-9A NLT

This saying is trustworthy and deserving of full acceptance: "Christ Jesus came into the world to save sinners"—and I am the worst of them.
1 TIMOTHY 1:15 HCSB

For there is one God, and there is one mediator between God and men, the man Christ Jesus, who gave himself as a ransom for all, which is the testimony given at the proper time.
1 TIMOTHY 2:5-6 ESV

For in Scripture it says: "See, I lay a stone in Zion,
a chosen and precious cornerstone,
and the one who trusts in him
will never be put to shame."

1 PETER 2:6 NIV

Who is a liar but he who denies that Jesus is the Christ? He is antichrist who denies the Father and the Son. Whoever denies the Son does not have the Father either; he who acknowledges the Son has the Father also.

1 JOHN 2:22-23 NKJV

This is how you can recognize the Spirit of God: Every spirit that acknowledges that Jesus Christ has come in the flesh is from God, but every spirit that does not acknowledge Jesus is not from God. This is the spirit of the antichrist, which you have heard is coming and even now is already in the world.

1 JOHN 4:2-3 NIV

Then the seventh angel sounded: And there were loud voices in heaven, saying, "The kingdoms of this world have become the kingdoms of our Lord and of His Christ, and He shall reign forever and ever!"

REVELATION 11:15 NKJV

"Look, I am coming quickly!"

REVELATION 22:7 HCSB

He who testifies about these things says, "Yes, I am coming quickly."
Amen! Come, Lord Jesus!

REVELATION 22:20 HCSB

Joy

Light shines a on the righteous
and joy on the upright in heart.
> PSALM 97:11 NIV

The humble will be filled with fresh joy from the LORD.
The poor will rejoice in the Holy One of Israel.
> ISAIAH 29:19 NLT

The desert and the parched land will be glad;
the wilderness will rejoice and blossom.
> ISAIAH 35:1 NIV

"Those who have been ransomed by the LORD will return.
They will enter Jerusalem singing,
crowned with everlasting joy.
Sorrow and mourning will disappear,
and they will be filled with joy and gladness."
> ISAIAH 35:10 NLT

GOD'S ransomed will come back,
come back to Zion cheering, shouting,
Joy eternal wreathing their heads,
exuberant ecstasies transporting them—
and not a sign of moans or groans.
> ISAIAH 51:11 MSG

"So you'll go out in joy,
you'll be led into a whole and complete life.
The mountains and hills will lead the parade,
bursting with song.
All the trees of the forest will join the procession,
exuberant with applause."
> ISAIAH 55:12 MSG

"My servants will sing
out of the joy of their hearts,
but you will cry out
from anguish of heart
and wail in brokenness of spirit."
>   ISAIAH 65:14 NIV

"You'll see all this and burst with joy
—you'll feel ten feet tall—
As it becomes apparent that GOD is on your side
and against his enemies."
>   ISAIAH 66:14 MSG

"Watch them come! They'll come weeping for joy
as I take their hands and lead them,
Lead them to fresh flowing brooks,
lead them along smooth, uncluttered paths.
Yes, it's because I'm Israel's Father
and Ephraim's my firstborn son!"
>   JEREMIAH 31:9 MSG

"They will come and shout for joy on the heights of Zion;
they will rejoice in the bounty of the LORD—
the grain, the new wine and the olive oil,
the young of the flocks and herds.
They will be like a well-watered garden,
and they will sorrow no more."
>   JEREMIAH 31:12 NIV

Judgment

"I lift my hand to heaven and solemnly swear:
As surely as I live forever,
when I sharpen my flashing sword
and my hand grasps it in judgment,
I will take vengeance on my adversaries
and repay those who hate me."

DEUTERONOMY 32:40-41 NIV

God shall judge the righteous and the wicked,
For there is a time there for every purpose and for every work.

ECCLESIASTES 3:17 NKJV

For God will bring every act to judgment, including every hidden thing, whether good or evil.

ECCLESIASTES 12:14 HCSB

For the day of the LORD is near upon all the nations.
As you have done, it shall be done to you;
your deeds shall return on your own head.

OBADIAH 15 ESV

The great day of the LORD is near—
near and coming quickly.
The cry on the day of the LORD is bitter;
the Mighty Warrior shouts his battle cry.

ZEPHANIAH 1:14 NIV

That day will be a day of wrath—
a day of distress and anguish,
a day of trouble and ruin,
a day of darkness and gloom,
a day of clouds and blackness—

ZEPHANIAH 1:15 NIV

Therefore judge nothing before the appointed time; wait until the Lord comes. He will bring to light what is hidden in darkness and will expose the motives of the heart. At that time each will receive their praise from God.
1 CORINTHIANS 4:5 NIV

For we must all appear before the judgment seat of Christ, that each one may receive the things done in the body, according to what he has done, whether good or bad.
2 CORINTHIANS 5:10 NKJV

Those who refuse to know God and refuse to obey the Message will pay for what they've done. Eternal exile from the presence of the Master and his splendid power is their sentence. But on that very same day when he comes, he will be exalted by his followers and celebrated by all who believe—and all because you believed what we told you.
2 THESSALONIANS 1:8-10 MSG

And as we live in God, our love grows more perfect. So we will not be afraid on the day of judgment, but we can face him with confidence because we live like Jesus here in this world.
1 JOHN 4:17 NLT

"But the cowardly, the unbelieving, the vile, the murderers, the sexually immoral, those who practice magic arts, the idolaters and all liars—they will be consigned to the fiery lake of burning sulfur. This is the second death."
REVELATION 21:8 NIV

Justice

"For the LORD your God is God of gods and Lord of lords, the great, the mighty, and the awesome God, who is not partial and takes no bribe. He executes justice for the fatherless and the widow, and loves the sojourner, giving him food and clothing."
DEUTERONOMY 10:17–18 ESV

"You shall not pervert justice; you shall not show partiality, nor take a bribe, for a bribe blinds the eyes of the wise and twists the words of the righteous. You shall follow what is altogether just, that you may live and inherit the land which the LORD your God is giving you."
DEUTERONOMY 16:19–20 ESV

"Cursed is the one who perverts the justice due the stranger, the fatherless, and widow."
DEUTERONOMY 27:19 NKJV

"Celebrate, nations, join the praise of his people.
He avenges the deaths of his servants,
Pays back his enemies with vengeance,
and cleanses his land for his people."
DEUTERONOMY 32:43 MSG

Now let the fear of the LORD be on you. Judge carefully, for with the LORD our God there is no injustice or partiality or bribery.
2 CHRONICLES 19:7 NIV

"He does not let the wicked live
but gives justice to the afflicted."
JOB 36:6 NLT

"He never takes his eyes off the innocent,
but he sets them on thrones with kings
and exalts them forever."
JOB 36:7 NLT

The orphans and the oppressed will be terrified no longer,
for you will bring them justice and no one will trouble them.
> PSALM 10:18 TPT

For the LORD is righteous,
he loves justice;
the upright will see his face.
> PSALM 11:7 NIV

He will make your innocence radiate like the dawn,
and the justice of your cause will shine like the noonday sun.
> PSALM 37:6 NLT

Then how glad the nations will be when you are their King.
They will sing, they will shout,
for you give true justice to the people.
Yes! You, Lord, are the Shepherd of the nations!
> PSALM 67:4 TPT

Let the rivers clap their hands;
Let the hills be joyful together before the LORD,
For He is coming to judge the earth.
With righteousness He shall judge the world,
And the peoples with equity.
> PSALM 98:8-9 NKJV

You're a God who makes things right,
giving justice to the defenseless.
> PSALM 103:6 TPT

I know that the LORD secures justice for the poor
and upholds the cause of the needy.
> PSALM 140:12 NIV

The oppressor will come to an end,
and destruction will cease;
the aggressor will vanish from the land.
In love a throne will be established;
in faithfulness a man will sit on it—
one from the house of David—
one who in judging seeks justice
and speeds the cause of righteousness.
ISAIAH 16:4B-5 NIV

Justice will rule in the wilderness
and righteousness in the fertile field.
ISAIAH 32:16 NLT

"For I, the LORD, love justice;
I hate robbery and wrongdoing.
In my faithfulness I will reward my people
and make an everlasting covenant with them."
ISAIAH 61:8 NLT

But the LORD is still there in the city,
and he does no wrong.
Day by day he hands down justice,
and he does not fail.
But the wicked know no shame.
ZEPHANIAH 3:5 NLT

And we know that God, in his justice, will punish anyone who does such things.
ROMANS 2:2 NLT

Do not take revenge, my dear friends, but leave room for God's wrath, for it is written: "It is mine to avenge; I will repay."
ROMANS 12:19 NIV

Justification

It will be credited to us who believe in Him who raised Jesus our Lord from the dead. He was delivered up for our trespasses and raised for our justification.
ROMANS 4:24–25 HCSB

So then, as through one trespass there is condemnation for everyone, so also through one righteous act there is life-giving justification, for everyone.
ROMANS 5:18 HCSB

Who will bring any charge against those whom God has chosen? It is God who justifies.
ROMANS 8:33 NIV

For it is with your heart that you believe and are justified, and it is with your mouth that you profess your faith and are saved.
ROMANS 10:10 NIV

Kindness

So lift your hands and thank God for his marvelous kindness
and for all his miracles of mercy for those he loves.
How he satisfies the souls of thirsty ones
and fills the hungry with all that is good!
PSALM 107:8-9 TPT

Do the riches of his extraordinary kindness make you take him for granted and despise him? Haven't you experienced how kind and understanding he has been to you? Don't mistake his tolerance for acceptance. Do you realize that all the wealth of his extravagant kindness is meant to melt your heart and lead you into repentance?
ROMANS 2:4 TPT

As my vision continued that night, I saw someone like a son of man coming with the clouds of heaven. He approached the Ancient One and was led into his presence. He was given authority, honor, and sovereignty over all the nations of the world, so that people of every race and nation and language would obey him. His rule is eternal—it will never end. His kingdom will never be destroyed.
DANIEL 7:13-14 NLT

Kingdom

Then the sovereignty, power and greatness of all the kingdoms under heaven will be handed over to the holy people of the Most High. His kingdom will be an everlasting kingdom, and all rulers will worship and obey him.
DANIEL 7:27 NIV

"Repent of your sins and turn to God, for the Kingdom of Heaven is near."
MATTHEW 3:2 NLT

"Then the righteous will shine like the sun in their Father's Kingdom. Anyone with ears to hear should listen and understand!"
MATTHEW 13:43 NLT

"I assure you," He said, "unless you are converted and become like children, you will never enter the kingdom of heaven. Therefore, whoever humbles himself like this child—this one is the greatest in the kingdom of heaven."
MATTHEW 18:3-4 HCSB

Jesus said, "Let the children come to me. Don't stop them! For the Kingdom of Heaven belongs to those who are like these children."
MATTHEW 19:14 NLT

"You have a special place in my Father's heart. Come and experience the full inheritance of the kingdom realm that has been destined for you from before the foundation of the world!"
MATTHEW 25:34 TPT

"The secret of the kingdom of God has been given to you."
MARK 4:11 NIV

"Let the little children come to Me. Don't stop them, for the kingdom of God belongs to such as these. I assure you: Whoever does not welcome the kingdom of God like a little child will never enter it."
MARK 10:14-15 HCSB

"You'll watch outsiders stream in from east, west, north, and south and sit down at the table of God's kingdom. And all the time you'll be outside looking in—and wondering what happened. This is the Great Reversal: the last in line put at the head of the line, and the so-called first ending up last."

LUKE 13:29-30 MSG

Jesus called them back. "Let these children alone. Don't get between them and me. These children are the kingdom's pride and joy. Mark this: Unless you accept God's kingdom in the simplicity of a child, you'll never get in."

LUKE 18:16-17 MSG

Jesus replied, "I tell you the truth, unless you are born again, you cannot see the Kingdom of God."

JOHN 3:3 NLT

Do not be deceived: No sexually immoral people, idolaters, adulterers, or anyone practicing homosexuality, no thieves, greedy people, drunkards, verbally abusive people, or swindlers will inherit God's kingdom.

1 CORINTHIANS 6:9-10 HCSB

Do you see what we've got? An unshakable kingdom! And do you see how thankful we must be? Not only thankful, but brimming with worship, deeply reverent before God. For God is not an indifferent bystander.

HEBREWS 12:28 MSG

Leadership

"But commission Joshua, and encourage and strengthen him, for he will lead this people across and will cause them to inherit the land that you will see."
DEUTERONOMY 3:28 NIV

Then GOD commanded Joshua son of Nun saying, "Be strong. Take courage. You will lead the People of Israel into the land I promised to give them. And I'll be right there with you."
DEUTERONOMY 31:23 MSG

The LORD told Joshua, "Today I will begin to make you a great leader in the eyes of all the Israelites. They will know that I am with you, just as I was with Moses."
JOSHUA 3:7 NLT

"I will raise up for myself a faithful priest, who will do according to what is in my heart and mind. I will firmly establish his priestly house, and they will minister before my anointed one always."
1 SAMUEL 2:35 NIV

Then all the tribes of Israel went to David at Hebron and told him, "We are your own flesh and blood. In the past, when Saul was our king, you were the one who really led the forces of Israel. And the LORD told you, 'You will be the shepherd of my people Israel. You will be Israel's leader.'"
2 SAMUEL 5:1–2 NLT

But the LORD did not want to destroy Judah, for he had made a covenant with David and promised that his descendants would continue to rule, shining like a lamp forever.
2 KINGS 8:19 NLT

LORD God of Israel,
keep what You promised
to Your servant, my father David:
"You will never fail to have a man
to sit before Me on the throne of Israel,
if only your sons guard their way to walk in My Law
as you have walked before Me."

2 CHRONICLES 6:16-17 HCSB

Liberation

"I will say to the prisoners, 'Come out in freedom,'
and to those in darkness, 'Come into the light.'
They will be my sheep, grazing in green pastures
and on hills that were previously bare."
ISAIAH 49:9 NLT

Jesus said to those who believed in him, "When you continue to embrace all that I teach, you prove that you are my true followers. For if you embrace the truth, it will release more freedom into your lives."
JOHN 8:31-32 TPT

Through his powerful declaration of acquittal, God freely gives away his righteousness. His gift of love and favor now cascades over us, all because Jesus, the Anointed One, has liberated us from the guilt, punishment, and power of sin!
ROMANS 3:28 TPT

For the "law" of the life-giving Spirit flowing through the anointing of Jesus has liberated us from the "law" of sin and death.
ROMANS 8:2 TPT

For the one who was a slave when called to faith in the Lord is the Lord's freed person; similarly, the one who was free when called is Christ's slave.
1 CORINTHIANS 7:22 NIV

It is for freedom that Christ has set us free. Stand firm, then, and do not let yourselves be burdened again by a yoke of slavery.
GALATIANS 5:1 NIV

Life

"Honor your father and your mother, as the LORD your God commanded you, that your days may be long, and that it may go well with you in the land that the LORD your God is giving you."

DEUTERONOMY 5:16 ESV

"Oh, that their hearts would be inclined to fear me and keep all my commands always, so that it might go well with them and their children forever!"

DEUTERONOMY 5:29 NIV

"These are the commands, decrees, and regulations that the LORD your God commanded me to teach you. You must obey them in the land you are about to enter and occupy, and you and your children and grandchildren must fear the LORD your God as long as you live. If you obey all his decrees and commands, you will enjoy a long life."

DEUTERONOMY 6:1-2 NLT

"Do what is right; do what is good in GOD'S sight so you'll live a good life and be able to march in and take this pleasant land that GOD so solemnly promised through your ancestors, throwing out your enemies left and right—exactly as GOD said."

DEUTERONOMY 6:18-19 MSG

Man does not live on bread alone but on every word that comes from the mouth of the LORD.

DEUTERONOMY 8:3 NIV

Clean out the pollution of wrongful murder from Israel so that you'll be able to live well and breathe clean air.

DEUTERONOMY 19:13 MSG

Do not have two differing weights in your bag—one heavy, one light. Do not have two differing measures in your house—one large, one small. You must have accurate and honest weights and measures, so that you may live long in the land the LORD your God is giving you. For the LORD your God detests anyone who does these things, anyone who deals dishonestly.

DEUTERONOMY 25:13-16 NIV

This day I call the heavens and the earth as witnesses against you that I have set before you life and death, blessings and curses. Now choose life, so that you and your children may live and that you may love the LORD your God, listen to his voice, and hold fast to him. For the LORD is your life, and he will give you many years in the land he swore to give to your fathers, Abraham, Isaac and Jacob.
DEUTERONOMY 30:19-20 NIV

"Take to heart all these words I am giving as a warning to you today, so that you may command your children to carefully follow all the words of this law. For they are not meaningless words to you but they are your life, and by them you will live long in the land you are crossing the Jordan to possess."
DEUTERONOMY 32:46-47 HCSB

"The LORD gives both death and life;
he brings some down to the grave but raises others up."
1 SAMUEL 2:6 NLT

"And if you walk in obedience to me and keep my decrees and commands as David your father did, I will give you a long life."
1 KINGS 3:14 NIV

For God watches how people live;
he sees everything they do.
JOB 34:21 NLT

My life, my every moment,
my destiny—it's all in your hands.
So I know you can deliver me
from those who persecute me relentlessly.
PSALM 31:14 TPT

For with You is the fountain of life;
In Your light we see light.
PSALM 36:9 NKJV

Commit everything you do to the LORD.
Trust him, and he will help you.
PSALM 37:5 NLT

A single day in your courts
is better than a thousand anywhere else!
I would rather be a gatekeeper in the house of my God
than live the good life in the homes of the wicked.
   PSALM 84:10 NLT

Even in old age they will still produce fruit;
they will remain vital and green.
They will declare, "The LORD is just!
He is my rock!
There is no evil in him!"
   PSALM 92:14-15 NLT

For all my godly lovers will enjoy life to the fullest
and will inherit their destinies.
   PROVERBS 2:21 TPT

The path of the righteous is like the morning sun,
shining ever brighter till the full light of day.
   PROVERBS 4:18 NIV

If you do what I say you will live well.
Guard your life with my revelation-truth,
for my teaching is as precious as your eyesight.
   PROVERBS 7:2 TPT

For by Wisdom your days will be many,
and years will be added to your life.
   PROVERBS 9:11 HCSB

The fear of the LORD prolongs life,
but the years of the wicked are cut short.
   PROVERBS 10:27 HCSB

The way of the godly leads to life;
that path does not lead to death.
   PROVERBS 12:28 NLT

Guard your words and you'll guard your life.
But if you don't control your tongue,
it will ruin everything.
>   PROVERBS 13:3 TPT

The fear of the LORD is a fountain of life,
To turn one away from the snares of death.
>   PROVERBS 14:27 NKJV

There is nothing better for man than to eat, drink, and enjoy, his work. I have seen that even this is from God's hand, because who can eat and who can enjoy life apart from Him?
>   ECCLESIASTES 2:24-25 HCSB

He has made everything beautiful in its time.
>   ECCLESIASTES 3:11A NIV

Though a sinner does evil a hundred times, and his days are prolonged, yet I surely know that it will be well with those who fear God, who fear before Him.
>   ECCLESIASTES 8:12 NKJV

So go ahead. Eat your food with joy, and drink your wine with a happy heart, for God approves of this!
>   ECCLESIASTES 9:7 NLT

"No longer will they build houses and others live in them,
or plant and others eat.
For as the days of a tree,
so will be the days of my people;
my chosen ones will long enjoy
the work of their hands."
>   ISAIAH 65:22 NIV

"But a wicked person who turns his back on that life of sin and keeps all my statutes, living a just and righteous life, he'll live, really live. He won't die. I won't keep a list of all the things he did wrong. He will live."
>   EZEKIEL 18:21-22 MSG

"Look at the proud!
They trust in themselves, and their lives are crooked.
But the righteous will live by their faithfulness to God."
HABAKKUK 2:4 NLT

"If you try to hang on to your life, you will lose it. But if you give up your life for my sake, you will save it."
MATTHEW 16:25 NLT

"For whoever wants to save their life will lose it, but whoever loses their life for me will save it."
LUKE 9:24 NIV

"The thief comes only to steal and kill and destroy; I have come that they may have life, and have it to the full."
JOHN 10:10 NIV

For our struggle is not against flesh and blood, but against the rulers, against the authorities, against the powers of this dark world and against the spiritual forces of evil in the heavenly realms.
EPHESIANS 6:12 NIV

Your old life is dead. Your new life, which is your real life—even though invisible to spectators—is with Christ in God. He is your life.
COLOSSIANS 3:3 MSG

We're being shown how to turn our backs on a godless, indulgent life, and how to take on a God-filled, God-honoring life. This new life is starting right now, and is whetting our appetites for the glorious day when our great God and Savior, Jesus Christ, appears.
TITUS 2:12-13 MSG

For the Scriptures say, "If you want to enjoy life and see many happy days, keep your tongue from speaking evil and your lips from telling lies. Turn away from evil and do good. Search for peace, and work to maintain it."
1 PETER 3:10-11 NLT

Loneliness

"He will not leave you or forsake you."
DEUTERONOMY 31:6B ESV

"The Lord himself goes before you and will be with you; he will never leave you nor forsake you. Do not be afraid; do not be discouraged."
DEUTERONOMY 31:8 NIV

Father to the fatherless, defender of widows—
this is God, whose dwelling is holy.
God places the lonely in families;
he sets the prisoners free and gives them joy.
PSALM 68:5-6A NLT

Love

GOD, your God, refused to listen to Balaam but turned the curse into a blessing—how GOD, your God, loves you!
DEUTERONOMY 23:5 MSG

"The LORD is slow to anger, abounding in love and forgiving sin and rebellion. Yet he does not leave the guilty unpunished; he punishes the children for the sin of the parents to the third and fourth generation."
NUMBERS 14:18-19 NIV

"I will be a father to him, and he will be a son to Me. When he does wrong, I will discipline him with a human rod and with blows from others. But My faithful love will never leave him as I removed it from Saul; I removed him from your way."
2 SAMUEL 7:14-15 HCSB

"O GOD, God of Israel, there is no God like you in the skies above or on the earth below who unswervingly keeps covenant with his servants and relentlessly loves them as they sincerely live in obedience to your way."
1 KINGS 8:23 MSG

Give thanks to the LORD, for he is good;
his love endures forever.
1 CHRONICLES 16:34 NIV

For the king trusts in the LORD.
The unfailing love of the Most High will keep him from stumbling.
PSALM 21:7 NLT

Many are the woes of the wicked,
but the LORD'S unfailing love
surrounds the one who trusts in him.
PSALM 32:10 NIV

Your unfailing love, O LORD, is as vast as the heavens;
your faithfulness reaches beyond the clouds.
> PSALM 36:5 NLT

Your unfailing love is better than life itself;
how I praise you!
> PSALM 63:3 NLT

For the Lord is always good
And ready to receive you.
He's so loving that it will amaze you;
So kind that it will astound you!
And he is famous for his faithfulness toward all.
Everyone knows our God can be trusted,
for he keeps his promises to every generation!
> PSALM 100:5 TPT

But Lord, your endless love stretches from one eternity to the other,
unbroken and unrelenting toward those who fear you
and those who bow facedown in awe before you!
Your faithfulness to keep every gracious promise you've made
passes from parents, to children, to grandchildren, and beyond.
> PSALM 103:17 TPT

Give thanks to the LORD, for He is good;
His faithful love endures forever.
> PSALM 107:1 HCSB

I will give thanks to you, O LORD, among the peoples;
I will sing praises to you among the nations.
For your steadfast love is great above the heavens;
your faithfulness reaches to the clouds.
> PSALM 108:3-4 ESV

Oh give thanks to the LORD, for he is good;
for his steadfast love endures forever!
> PSALM 118:1 ESV

He brought me to the banqueting house,
And his banner over me was love.
> SONG OF SONGS 2:4 ESV

Set me as a seal upon your heart,
as a seal upon your arm,
for love is strong as death,
jealousy is fierce as the grave.
Its flashes are flashes of fire,
the very flame of the LORD.
> SONG OF SONGS 8:6–7 ESV

"Since you were precious in My sight,
You have been honored,
And I have loved you;
Therefore I will give men for you,
And people for your life."
> ISAIAH 43:4 NKJV

"Though the mountains move
and the hills shake,
My love will not be removed from you
and My covenant of peace will not be shaken,"
says your compassionate LORD.
> ISAIAH 54:10 HCSB

GOD told them, "I've never quit loving you and never will.
Expect love, love, and more love!"
> JEREMIAH 31:3 MSG

The LORD says,
"Then I will heal you of your faithlessness;
my love will know no bounds,
for my anger will be gone forever."
> HOSEA 14:4 NLT

"A new command I give you: Love one another. As I have loved you, so you must love one another. By this everyone will know that you are my disciples, if you love one another."
JOHN 13:34–35 NIV

"Those who truly love me are those who obey my commandments. Whoever passionately loves me will be passionately loved by my Father. And I will passionately love you in return and will manifest my life within you."
JOHN 14:21 TPT

"As the Father has loved me, so have I loved you. Abide in my love. If you keep my commandments, you will abide in my love, just as I have kept my Father's commandments and abide in his love."
JOHN 15:9–10 ESV

"You live fully in me and now I live fully in them
so that they will experience perfect unity,
and the world will be convinced that you have sent me.
For they will see that you love each one of them
with the same passionate love that you have for me."
JOHN 17:23 TPT

Now, who of us would dare to die for the sake of a wicked person? We can all understand if someone was willing to die for a truly noble person, yet who has ever heard of someone dying for an evil enemy? But Christ proved God's passionate love for us by dying in our place while we were still lost and ungodly!
ROMANS 5:7–8 TPT

Who could ever separate us from the endless love of God's Anointed One? Absolutely no one! For nothing in the universe has the power to diminish his love toward us. Troubles, pressures, and problems are unable to come between us and heaven's love. What about persecutions, deprivations, dangers, and death threats? No, for they are all impotent to hinder omnipotent love, even though it is written:
All day long we face death threats for your sake, God.
We are considered to be nothing more than sheep to be slaughtered!
ROMANS 8:35–36 TPT

For I am convinced that neither death nor life, neither angels nor demons, neither the present nor the future, nor any powers, neither height nor depth, nor anything else in all creation, will be able to separate us from the love of God that is in Christ Jesus our Lord.
ROMANS 8:38-39 NIV

Love does no harm to a neighbor. Therefore love is the fulfillment of the law.
ROMANS 13:10 NIV

Love never fails.
1 CORINTHIANS 13:8 NIV

Three things will last forever—faith, hope, and love—and the greatest of these is love.
1 CORINTHIANS 13:13 NLT

I pray that you, being rooted and firmly established in love, may be able to comprehend with all the saints what is the length and width, height and depth of God's love, and to know the Messiah's love that surpasses knowledge, so you may be filled with all the fullness of God.
EPHESIANS 3:17-19 HCSB

Above all, maintain an intense love for each other, since love covers a multitude of sins.
1 PETER 4:8 HCSB

Whoever says, "I know him," but does not do what he commands is a liar, and the truth is not in that person. But if anyone obeys his word, love for God is truly made complete in them.
1 JOHN 2:4-5 NIV

Do not love the world or anything in the world. If anyone loves the world, love for the Father is not in them.
1 JOHN 2:15 NIV

We know what real love is because Jesus gave up his life for us. So we also ought to give up our lives for our brothers and sisters.
1 JOHN 3:16 NLT

God showed how much he loved us by sending his one and only Son into the world so that we might have eternal life through him. This is real love—not that we loved God, but that he loved us and sent his Son as a sacrifice to take away our sins.

1 JOHN 4:9-10 NLT

No one has seen God, ever. But if we love one another, God dwells deeply within us, and his love becomes complete in us—perfect love!

1 JOHN 4:12 MSG

Mercy

But the LORD was with Joseph and showed him mercy, and He gave him favor in the sight of the keeper of the prison.

GENESIS 39:21 NKJV

"When you are in distress and all these things have happened to you, then in later days you will return to the LORD your God and obey him. For the LORD your God is a merciful God; he will not abandon or destroy you or forget the covenant with your ancestors, which he confirmed to them by oath."

DEUTERONOMY 4:30-31 NIV

But the Israelites pleaded with the LORD and said, "We have sinned. Punish us as you see fit, only rescue us today from our enemies." Then the Israelites put aside their foreign gods and served the LORD. And he was grieved by their misery.

JUDGES 10:15-16 NLT

"Do not be afraid," Samuel replied. "You have done all this evil; yet do not turn away from the LORD, but serve the LORD with all your heart."

1 SAMUEL 12:21 NIV

GOD said to Solomon, "Since this is the way it is with you, that you have no intention of keeping faith with me and doing what I have commanded, I'm going to rip the kingdom from you and hand it over to someone else. But out of respect for your father David I won't do it in your lifetime. It's your son who will pay—I'll rip it right out of his grasp. Even then I won't take it all; I'll leave him one tribe in honor of my servant David and out of respect for my chosen city Jerusalem."

1 KINGS 11:11 MSG

"For if you return to the LORD, your brethren and your children will be treated with compassion by those who lead them captive, so that they may come back to this land; for the LORD your God is gracious and merciful, and will not turn His face from you if you return to Him."

2 CHRONICLES 30:9 NKJV

He crowns you with love and mercy—a paradise crown.
   PSALM 103:4B MSG

For as the heavens are high above the earth,
So great is His mercy toward those who fear Him;
   PSALM 103:11 NKJV

"But even in those days"—this is the LORD's declaration—"I will not finish you off."
   JEREMIAH 5:18 HCSB

"Is not Israel still my son,
my darling child?" says the LORD.
"I often have to punish him,
but I still love him.
That's why I long for him
and surely will have mercy on him."
   JEREMIAH 31:20 NLT

"But I will have mercy on the house of Judah, and I will save them by the LORD their God. I will not save them by bow or by sword or by war or by horses or by horsemen."
   HOSEA 1:7 ESV

Then I will sow her for Myself in the earth,
And I will have mercy on her who had not obtained mercy;
Then I will say to those who were not My people,
"You are My people!"
And they shall say, "You are my God!"'
   HOSEA 2:23 NKJV

Change your life, not just your clothes.
Come back to GOD, your God.
And here's why: God is kind and merciful.
He takes a deep breath, puts up with a lot,
This most patient God, extravagant in love,
always ready to cancel catastrophe.
   JOEL 2:13 MSG

Those who worship false gods
turn their backs on all God's mercies.
JONAH 2:8 NLT

"Who is a God like You,
Pardoning iniquity
And passing over the transgression of the remnant of His heritage?
He does not retain His anger forever,
Because He delights in mercy."
MICAH 7:18 NKJV

Therefore this is what the LORD says: "I will return to Jerusalem with mercy, and there my house will be rebuilt. And the measuring line will be stretched out over Jerusalem," declares the LORD Almighty.
ZECHARIAH 1:16 NIV

"The merciful are blessed,
for they will be shown mercy."
MATTHEW 5:7 HCSB

On hearing this, Jesus said, "It is not the healthy who need a doctor, but the sick. But go and learn what this means: 'I desire mercy, not sacrifice.' For I have not come to call the righteous, but sinners."
MATTHEW 9:12-13 NIV

"His mercy extends to those who fear him,
from generation to generation."
LUKE 1:50 NIV

God's choice doesn't depend on how badly someone wants it or tries to earn it, but it depends on God's kindness and mercy.
ROMANS 9:16 TPT

Just as you who were at one time disobedient to God have now received mercy as a result of their disobedience, so they too have now become disobedient in order that they too may now receive mercy as a result of God's mercy to you.
ROMANS 11:30-31 NIV

Because of his great love for us, God, who is rich in mercy, made us alive with Christ even when we were dead in transgressions—it is by grace you have been saved.
EPHESIANS 2:4-5 NIV

But—When God our Savior revealed his kindness and love, he saved us, not because of the righteous things we had done, but because of his mercy. He washed away our sins, giving us a new birth and new life through the Holy Spirit.
TITUS 3:4-5 NLT

For I will be merciful to their unrighteousness, and their sins and their lawless deeds I will remember no more.
HEBREWS 8:12 NKJV

There will be no mercy for those who have not shown mercy to others. But if you have been merciful, God will be merciful when he judges you.
JAMES 2:13 NLT

Praise the God and Father of our Lord Jesus Christ. According to His great mercy, He has given us a new birth into a living hoped through the resurrection of Jesus Christ from the dead and into an inheritance that is imperishable, uncorrupted, and unfading, kept in heaven for you.
1 PETER 1:3-4 HCSB

Once you were not a people, but now you are the people of God; once you had not received mercy, but now you have received mercy.
1 PETER 2:10 NIV

New Birth

"Yet to all who did receive him, to those who believed in his name, he gave the right to become children of God children born not of natural descent, nor of human decision or a husband's will, but born of God."
JOHN 1:12-13 NIV

Do you not know that all of us who have been baptized into Christ Jesus were baptized into his death? We were buried therefore with him by baptism into death, in order that, just as Christ was raised from the dead by the glory of the Father, we too might walk in newness of life.
ROMANS 6:3-4 ESV

Spiritually alive, we have access to everything God's Spirit is doing, and can't be judged by unspiritual critics.
1 CORINTHIANS 2:15 MSG

By His own choice, He gave us a new birth by the message of truth so that we would be the firstfruits of His creatures
JAMES 1:18 HCSB

If you know that he is righteous, you know that everyone who does what is right has been born of him.
1 JOHN 2:29 NIV

No one who is born of God will continue to sin, because God's seed remains in them; they cannot go on sinning, because they have been born of God.
1 JOHN 3:9 NIV

Dear friends, let us love one another, because love is from God, and everyone who loves has been born of God and knows God.
1 JOHN 4:7 NIV

Everyone who believes that Jesus is the Christ is born of God, and everyone who loves the father loves his child as well
1 JOHN 5:1 NIV

Obedience

When Abram was ninety-nine years old, the LORD appeared to him and said, "I am God Almighty; walk before me faithfully and be blameless. Then I will make my covenant between me and you and will greatly increase your numbers."
GENESIS 17:1–2 NIV

He said, "If you listen carefully to the LORD your God and do what is right in his eyes, if you pay attention to his commands and keep all his decrees, I will not bring on you any of the diseases I brought on the Egyptians, for I am the LORD, who healed you."
EXODUS 15:26 NIV

"Now if you will obey me and keep my covenant, you will be my own special treasure from among all the peoples on earth; for all the earth belongs to me. And you will be my kingdom of priests, my holy nation.' This is the message you must give to the people of Israel."
EXODUS 19:5–6 MSG

"You shall not make for yourself a carved image, or any likeness of anything that is in heaven above, or that is in the earth beneath, or that is in the water under the earth. You shall not bow down to them or serve them, for I the LORD your God am a jealous God, visiting the iniquity of the fathers on the children to the third and the fourth generation of those who hate me, but showing steadfast love to thousands of those who love me and keep my commandments."
EXODUS 20:4–6 ESV

"Keep my decrees and laws: The person who obeys them lives by them. I am GOD."
LEVITICUS 18:5 MSG

"You must keep my decrees and laws—natives and foreigners both. You must not do any of these abhorrent things. The people who lived in this land before you arrived did all these things and polluted the land. And if you pollute it, the land will vomit you up just as it vomited up the nations that preceded you."
LEVITICUS 18:26–28 MSG

"If you follow my decrees and are careful to obey my commands, I will send you the seasonal rains. The land will then yield its crops, and the trees of the field will produce their fruit. Your threshing season will overlap with the grape harvest, and your grape harvest will overlap with the season of planting grain. You will eat your fill and live securely in your own land."
LEVITICUS 26:3-5 NLT

"So remember this and keep it firmly in mind: The LORD is God both in heaven and on earth, and there is no other. If you obey all the decrees and commands I am giving you today, all will be well with you and your children. I am giving you these instructions so you will enjoy a long life in the land the LORD your God is giving you for all time."
DEUTERONOMY 4:39-40 NLT

"But I lavish unfailing love for a thousand generations on those who love me and obey my commands."
DEUTERONOMY 5:10 NLT

So be careful to do what the LORD your God has commanded you; do not turn aside to the right or to the left. Walk in obedience to all that the LORD your God has commanded you, so that you may live and prosper and prolong your days in the land that you will possess.
DEUTERONOMY 5:32-33 NIV

"Listen closely, Israel, and be careful to obey. Then all will go well with you, and you will have many children in the land flowing with milk and honey, just as the LORD, the God of your ancestors, promised you."
DEUTERONOMY 6:3 NLT

"But He directly pays back and destroys those who hate Him. He will not hesitate to directly pay back the one who hates Him. So keep the command—the statutes and ordinances—that I am giving you to follow today."
DEUTERONOMY 7:10-11 HCSB

"Be careful to obey all the commands I am giving you today. Then you will live and multiply, and you will enter and occupy the land the LORD swore to give your ancestors."
DEUTERONOMY 8:1 NLT

Observe therefore all the commands I am giving you today, so that you may have the strength to go in and take over the land that you are crossing the Jordan to possess, and so that you may live long in the land the LORD swore to your ancestors to give to them and their descendants, a land flowing with milk and honey.
DEUTERONOMY 11:8-9 NIV

Be careful, or you will be enticed to turn away and worship other gods and bow down to them. Then the LORD'S anger will burn against you, and he will shut up the heavens so that it will not rain and the ground will yield no produce, and you will soon perish from the good land the LORD is giving you.
DEUTERONOMY 11:16-17 NIV

If you listen obediently to the Voice of GOD, your God, and heartily obey all his commandments that I command you today, GOD, your God, will place you on high, high above all the nations of the world.
DEUTERONOMY 28:1 MSG

You will experience all these blessings if you obey the LORD your God.
DEUTERONOMY 28:2 NLT

The LORD will establish you as a people holy to himself, as he has sworn to you, if you keep the commandments of the LORD your God and walk in his ways. And all the peoples of the earth shall see that you are called by the name of the LORD, and they shall be afraid of you.
DEUTERONOMY 28:9-10 ESV

This commandment that I'm commanding you today isn't too much for you, it's not out of your reach. No. The word is right here and now—as near as the tongue in your mouth, as near as the heart in your chest. Just do it!
DEUTERONOMY 30:11, 14 MSG

"If you fear the LORD and serve and obey him and do not rebel against his commands, and if both you and the king who reigns over you follow the LORD your God—good! But if you do not obey the LORD, and if you rebel against his commands, his hand will be against you, as it was against your ancestors."
1 SAMUEL 12:14-15 NIV

"Above all, fear the LORD and worship Him faithfully with all your heart; consider the great things He has done for you. However, if you continue to do what is evil, both you and your king will be swept away."
1 SAMUEL 12:24-25 HCSB

But Samuel replied,
"What is more pleasing to the LORD:
your burnt offerings and sacrifices
or your obedience to his voice?
Listen! Obedience is better than sacrifice,
and submission is better than offering the fat of rams."
1 SAMUEL 15:22 NLT

"Now if you walk before Me as your father David walked, in integrity of heart and in uprightness, to do according to all that I have commanded you, and if you keep My statutes and My judgments, then I will establish the throne of your kingdom over Israel forever, as I promised David your father, saying, 'You shall not fail to have a man on the throne of Israel.'"
1 KINGS 9:4-5 NKJV

"If you do whatever I command you and walk in obedience to me and do what is right in my eyes by obeying my decrees and commands, as David my servant did, I will be with you. I will build you a dynasty as enduring as the one I built for David and will give Israel to you."
1 KINGS 11:38 NIV

"I will establish his kingdom forever if he perseveres in keeping My commands and My ordinances as he is today."
1 CHRONICLES 28:7 HCSB

"And as for you, if you will walk before me as David your father walked, doing according to all that I have commanded you and keeping my statutes and my rules, then I will establish your royal throne, as I covenanted with David your father, saying, 'You shall not lack a man to rule Israel.'"
2 CHRONICLES 7:17-18 ESV

He makes them listen to correction
and commands them to repent of their evil.
If they obey and serve him,
they will spend the rest of their days in prosperity
and their years in contentment.
But if they do not listen,
they will perish by the sword
and die without knowledge.
JOB 36:10-12 NIV

"It's the praising life that honors me.
As soon as you set your foot on the Way,
I'll show you my salvation"
PSALM 50:23 MSG

How joyous are those who love the Lord
and bow low before God, ready to obey him!
Your reward will be prosperity, happiness, and well-being.
PSALM 128:1-2 TPT

"Now then, my children, listen to me;
blessed are those who keep my ways."
PROVERBS 8:32 NIV

The integrity of the upright guides them,
but the crookedness of the treacherous destroys them.
PROVERBS 11:3 ESV

When all has been heard, the conclusion of the matter is: fear God and keep His commands, because this is for all humanity.
ECCLESIASTES 12:13 HCSB

If you are willing and obedient,
you will eat the good things of the land;
ISAIAH 1:19 NIV

This is what the LORD says:
"Preserve justice and do what is right,
for My salvation is coming soon,
and My righteousness will be revealed.
Happy is the man who does this,
anyone who maintains this,
who keeps the Sabbath without desecrating it,
and keeps his hand from doing any evil."
   ISAIAH 56:1-2 HCSB

For thus says the LORD:
"To the eunuchs who keep My Sabbaths,
And choose what pleases Me,
And hold fast My covenant,
Even to them I will give in My house
And within My walls a place and a name
Better than that of sons and daughters;
I will give them an everlasting name
That shall not be cut off."
   ISAIAH 56:4-5 NKJV

"Share your food with the hungry,
and give shelter to the homeless.
Give clothes to those who need them,
and do not hide from relatives who need your help.
Then your salvation will come like the dawn,
and your wounds will quickly heal.
Your godliness will lead you forward,
and the glory of the LORD will protect you from behind."
   ISAIAH 58:7-8 NLT

GOD'S Message:
"But just as one bad apple doesn't ruin the whole bushel,
there are still plenty of good apples left.
So I'll preserve those in Israel who obey me.
I won't destroy the whole nation.
I'll bring out my true children from Jacob
and the heirs of my mountains from Judah.
My chosen will inherit the land,
my servants will move in."
ISAIAH 65:8-9 MSG

"Run up and down every street in Jerusalem," says the LORD.
"Look high and low; search throughout the city!
If you can find even one just and honest person,
I will not destroy the city."
JEREMIAH 5:1 NLT

"If you really change your ways and your actions and deal with each other justly, if you do not oppress the foreigner, the fatherless or the widow and do not shed innocent blood in this place, and if you do not follow other gods to your own harm, then I will let you live in this place, in the land I gave your ancestors for ever and ever."
JEREMIAH 7:5-7 NIV

This is what I told them: "Obey me, and I will be your God, and you will be my people. Do everything as I say, and all will be well!"
JEREMIAH 7:23 NLT

Jeremiah said, "You shall not be given to them. Obey now the voice of the LORD in what I say to you, and it shall be well with you, and your life shall be spared."
JEREMIAH 38:20 ESV

"If he has walked in My statutes
And kept My judgments faithfully—
He is just;
He shall surely live!"
Says the Lord GOD.
EZEKIEL 18:9 NKJV

"Then I said to their children in the wilderness: Don't follow the statutes of your fathers, defile yourselves with their idols, or keep their ordinances. I am Yahweh your God. Follow My statutes, keep My ordinances, and practice them."
EZEKIEL 20:18-20 HCSB

I'll put my Spirit in you and make it possible for you to do what I tell you and live by my commands.
EZEKIEL 36:27 MSG

He has told you, O man, what is good;
and what does the LORD require of you
but to do justice, and to love kindness,
and to walk humbly with your God?
MICAH 6:8 ESV

"Blessed rather are those who hear the word of God and obey it."
LUKE 11:28 NIV

Jesus answered, "My teaching is not my own. It comes from the one who sent me. Anyone who chooses to do the will of God will find out whether my teaching comes from God or whether I speak on my own."
JOHN 7:16-17 NIV

"If you really knew God, you would listen, receive, and respond with faith to his words. But since you don't listen and respond to what he says, it proves you don't belong to him and you have no room for him in your hearts."
JOHN 8:47 TPT

"If anyone hears my words but does not keep them, I do not judge that person. For I did not come to judge the world, but to save the world. There is a judge for the one who rejects me and does not accept my words; the very words I have spoken will condemn them at the last day. For I did not speak on my own, but the Father who sent me commanded mea to say all that I have spoken."
JOHN 12:47-49 NIV

"You show that you are my intimate friends when you obey all that I command you."
JOHN 15:14 TPT

Finally brothers, whatever is true, whatever is honorable, whatever is just, whatever is pure, whatever is lovely, whatever is commendable—if there is any moral excellence and if there is any praise—dwell on these things. Do what you have learned and received and heard and seen in me, and the God of peace will be with you.
PHILIPPIANS 4:8-9 HCSB

We know that we have come to know him if we keep his commands.
1 JOHN 2:3 NIV

For everything in the world—the lust of the flesh, the lust of the eyes, and the pride of life—comes not from the Father but from the world. The world and its desires pass away, but whoever does the will of God lives forever.
1 JOHN 2:16-17 NIV

And this is his command: to believe in the name of his Son, Jesus Christ, and to love one another as he commanded us. The one who keeps God's commands lives in him, and he in them. And this is how we know that he lives in us: We know it by the Spirit he gave us.
1 JOHN 3:23-24 NIV

Loving God means keeping his commandments, and his commandments are not burdensome.
1 JOHN 5:3 NLT

Anyone who does not remain in Christ's teaching but goes beyond it, does not have God. The one who remains in that teaching, this one has both the Father and the Son.
2 JOHN 9 HCSB

"The one who keeps the prophetic words of this book is blessed."
REVELATION 22:7 HCSB

"Blessed are those who wash their robes. They will be permitted to enter through the gates of the city and eat the fruit from the tree of life. Outside the city are the dogs—the sorcerers, the sexually immoral, the murderers, the idol worshipers, and all who love to live a lie."
REVELATION 22:14-15 NLT

Patience

Guide me in Your truth and teach me,
for You are the God of my salvation;
I wait for You all day long.
    PSALM 25:5 HCSB

We wait for Yahweh;
He is our help and shield.
For our hearts rejoice in Him
because we trust in His holy name.
    PSALM 33:20-21 MSG

But for you, O LORD, do I wait;
it is you, O Lord my God, who will answer.
    PSALM 38:15 ESV

God, the one and only—
I'll wait as long as he says.
Everything I hope for comes from him,
so why not?
    PSALM 62:5 MSG

Since before time began
no one has ever imagined,
No ear heard, no eye seen, a God like you
who works for those who wait for him.
    ISAIAH 64:4 MSG

The LORD is good to those whose hope is in him,
to the one who seeks him;
it is good to wait quietly
for the salvation of the LORD.
    LAMENTATIONS 3:25-26 NIV

Therefore I will look to the LORD;
I will wait for the God of my salvation;
My God will hear me.
> MICAH 7:7 NKJV

The Lord does not delay His promise, as some understand delay, but is patient with you, not wanting any to perish but all to come to repentance.
> 2 PETER 3:9 HCSB

And remember, our Lord's patience gives people time to be saved.
> 2 PETER 3:15 NLT

Peace

"I'm going to give you peace from all your enemies."
2 SAMUEL 7:11 MSG

"But you will have a son who will be a man of peace and rest, and I will give him rest from all his enemies on every side. His name will be Solomon, and I will grant Israel peace and quiet during his reign."
1 CHRONICLES 22:9 NIV

"For you shall have a covenant with the stones of the field,
And the beasts of the field shall be at peace with you."
JOB 5:23 NKJV

GOD gives his people peace.
PSALM 29:11B MSG

The meek shall inherit the land
and delight themselves in abundant peace.
PSALM 37:11 ESV

But all who listen to me will live in peace,
untroubled by fear of harm.
PROVERBS 1:33 NLT

"He will settle disputes among the nations
and provide arbitration for many peoples.
They will turn their swords into plows
and their spears into pruning knives.
Nations will not take up the sword against other nations,
and they will never again train for war."
ISAIAH 2:4 HCSB

The wolf will live with the lamb,
the leopard will lie down with the goat,
the calf and the lion and the yearling together;
and a little child will lead them.
The cow will feed with the bear,
their young will lie down together,
and the lion will eat straw like the ox.
The infant will play near the cobra's den,
and the young child will put its hand into the viper's nest.
They will neither harm nor destroy
on all my holy mountain,
for the earth will be filled with the knowledge of the LORD
as the waters cover the sea.

ISAIAH 11:6-9 NIV

You will keep in perfect peace
all who trust in you,
all whose thoughts are fixed on you!

ISAIAH 26:3 NLT

And the effect of righteousness will be peace,
and the result of righteousness, quietness and trust forever.

ISAIAH 32:17 ESV

"All your children will be taught by the LORD,
and great will be their peace."

ISAIAH 54:13 NIV

"The wolf and the lamb will feed together,
and the lion will eat straw like the ox,
and dust will be the serpent's food.
They will neither harm nor destroy
on all my holy mountain,"
says the LORD.

ISAIAH 65:25 NIV

"I will make a covenant of peace with them, and cause wild beasts to cease from the land; and they will dwell safely in the wilderness and sleep in the woods."
EZEKIEL 34:25 NKJV

The LORD will mediate between peoples
and will settle disputes between strong nations far away.
They will hammer their swords into plowshares
and their spears into pruning hooks.
Nation will no longer fight against nation,
nor train for war anymore.
MICAH 4:3 NLT

And he will be our peace
when the Assyrians invade our land
and march through our fortresses.
We will raise against them seven shepherds,
even eight commanders.
MICAH 5:5 NIV

"The glory of this present house will be greater than the glory of the former house," says the LORD Almighty. "And in this place I will grant peace,' declares the LORD Almighty."
HAGGAI 2:9 NLT

"God blesses those who work for peace,
for they will be called the children of God."
MATTHEW 5:9 NLT

"Peace I leave with you; my peace I give you. I do not give to you as the world gives. Do not let your hearts be troubled and do not be afraid."
JOHN 14:27 NIV

Therefore, since we have been made right in God's sight by faith, we have peace with God because of what Jesus Christ our Lord has done for us.
ROMANS 5:1 NLT

He brought this Good News of peace to you Gentiles who were far away from him, and peace to the Jews who were near.

EPHESIANS 2:17 NLT

Do not be anxious about anything, but in every situation, by prayer and petition, with thanksgiving, present your requests to God. And the peace of God, which transcends all understanding, will guard your hearts and your minds in Christ Jesus.

PHILIPPIANS 4:6-7 NIV

Persecution

"Blessed are those who are persecuted because of righteousness,
for theirs is the kingdom of heaven."
MATTHEW 5:10 NIV

"God blesses you when people mock you and persecute you and lie about you and say all sorts of evil things against you because you are my followers. Be happy about it! Be very glad! For a great reward awaits you in heaven. And remember, the ancient prophets were persecuted in the same way."
MATTHEW 5:11-12 NLT

"You must be on your guard. You will be handed over to the local councils and flogged in the synagogues. On account of me you will stand before governors and kings as witnesses to them."
MARK 13:9 NIV

"What blessings await you when people hate you and exclude you and mock you and curse you as evil because you follow the Son of Man. When that happens, be happy! Yes, leap for joy! For a great reward awaits you in heaven. And remember, their ancestors treated the ancient prophets that same way."
LUKE 6:22-23 NLT

"And remember this: When people accuse you before every one and forcefully drag you before the religious leaders and authorities, do not be troubled. Don't worry about defending yourself or be concerned about how to answer their accusations. Simply be confident and allow the Spirit of Wisdom access to your heart, and he will reveal in that very moment what you are to say to them."
LUKE 12:11-12 TPT

"And because you follow me, you will be on trial before kings and governmental leaders as an opportunity to testify to them in my name. Yet determine in your hearts not to prepare for your own defense. Simply speak with the words of wisdom that I will give you that moment, and none of your persecutors will be able to withstand the grace and wisdom that comes from your mouths.
LUKE 21:12-15 TPT

"Remember what I told you: 'A servant is not greater than his master.' If they persecuted me, they will persecute you also. If they obeyed my teaching, they will obey yours also. They will treat you this way because of my name, for they do not know the one who sent me."
JOHN 15:20-21 NIV

And God will use this persecution to show his justice and to make you worthy of his Kingdom, for which you are suffering. In his justice he will pay back those who persecute you.
2 THESSALONIANS 1:5-6 NLT

Indeed, all who desire to live a godly life in Christ Jesus will be persecuted, while evil people and impostors will go on from bad to worse, deceiving and being deceived.
2 TIMOTHY 3:12-13 ESV

If you are insulted because of the name of Christ, you are blessed, for the Spirit of glory and of God rests on you.
1 PETER 4:14 NIV

Perseverance

For if we are faithful to the end, trusting God just as firmly as when we first believed, we will share in all that belongs to Christ.
HEBREWS 3:14 HCSB

For you have need of endurance, so that after you have done the will of God, you may receive the promise:
"For yet a little while,
And He who is coming will come and will not tarry.
Now the just shall live by faith;
But if anyone draws back,
My soul has no pleasure in him."
HEBREWS 10:36-38 NKJV

But the one who looks intently into the perfect law of freedom and perseveres in it, and is not a forgetful hearer but one who does good works—this person will be blessed in what he does.
JAMES 1:25 HCSB

"Whoever has ears, let them hear what the Spirit says to the churches. To the one who is victorious, I will give the right to eat from the tree of life, which is in the paradise of God."
REVELATION 2:7 NIV

"Do not be afraid of what you are about to suffer. I tell you, the devil will put some of you in prison to test you, and you will suffer persecution for ten days. Be faithful, even to the point of death, and I will give you life as your victor's crown."
REVELATION 2:10 NIV

"Whoever has ears, let them hear what the Spirit says to the churches. The one who is victorious will not be hurt at all by the second death."
REVELATION 2:11 NIV

"Whoever has ears, let them hear what the Spirit says to the churches. To the one who is victorious, I will give some of the hidden manna. I will also give that person a white stone with a new named written on it, known only to the one who receives it."
REVELATION 2:17 NIV

"To all who are victorious, who obey me to the very end,
To them I will give authority over all the nations."
REVELATION 2:26 NLT

"All who are victorious will be clothed in white. I will never erase their names from the Book of Life, but I will announce before my Father and his angels that they are mine."
REVELATION 3:5 NLT

"Because you have obeyed my command to persevere, I will protect you from the great time of testing that will come upon the whole world to test those who belong to this world."
REVELATION 3:10 NLT

"I'll make each conqueror a pillar in the sanctuary of my God, a permanent position of honor. Then I'll write names on you, the pillars: the Name of my God, the Name of God's City—the new Jerusalem coming down out of Heaven—and my new Name."
REVELATION 3:12 MSG

"To the one who is victorious, I will give the right to sit with me on my throne, just as I was victorious and sat down with my Father on his throne."
REVELATION 3:21 NIV

Plans

He frustrates the devices of the crafty,
So that their hands cannot carry out their plans.

JOB 5:12 NKJV

Before you do anything,
put your trust totally in God and not in yourself.
Then every plan you make will succeed.

PROVERBS 16:3 TPT

We plan the way we want to live,
but only GOD makes us able to live it.

PROVERBS 16:9 MSG

A person may have many ideas concerning God's plan for his life,
But only the designs of his purpose will succeed in the end.

PROVERBS 19:21 TPT

The LORD of Hosts Himself has planned it;
therefore, who can stand in its way?
It is His hand that is outstretched,
so who can turn it back?

ISAIAH 14:27 HCSB

This is what the LORD says: "When seventy years are completed for Babylon, I will come to you and fulfill my good promise to bring you back to this place. For I know the plans I have for you," declares the LORD, "plans to prosper you and not to harm you, plans to give you hope and a future."

JEREMIAH 29:10-11 NIV

He said, Praise the name of God forever and ever,
for he has all wisdom and power.
He controls the course of world events;
he removes kings and sets up other kings.

DANIEL 2:20-21 NLT

Indeed, the Sovereign LORD never does anything
until he reveals his plans to his servants the prophets.
The lion has roared—
so who isn't frightened?
The Sovereign LORD has spoken—
so who can refuse to proclaim his message?

AMOS 3:7-8 NIV

Poverty

"The LORD makes some poor and others rich;
he brings some down and lifts others up.
He lifts the poor from the dust
and the needy from the garbage dump.
He sets them among princes,
placing them in seats of honor.
For all the earth is the LORD's,
and he has set the world in order."

    1 SAMUEL 2:7-8 NLT

The Lord is always the safest place for the poor
when the workers of wickedness oppress them.

    PSALM 14:6 TPT

The Lord will preserve and protect [the poor and helpless].
They'll be honored and esteemed
while their enemies are defeated.

    PSALM 41:2 TPT

For GOD listens to the poor,
He doesn't walk out on the wretched.

    PSALM 69:33 MSG

He will spare the poor and needy,
And will save the souls of the needy.

    PSALM 72:13 NKJV

"God blesses you who are poor,
for the Kingdom of God is yours."

    LUKE 6:20 NLT

Power

"I am the sprouting vine and you're my branches. As you live in union with me as your source, fruitfulness will stream from within you—but when you live separated from me you are powerless."

JOHN 15:5 TPT

He said to them: "It is not for you to know the times or dates the Father has set by his own authority. But you will receive power when the Holy Spirit comes on you; and you will be my witnesses in Jerusalem, and in all Judea and Samaria, and to the ends of the earth."

ACTS 1:7-8 NIV

We now have this light shining in our hearts, but we ourselves are like fragile clay jars containing this great treasure. This makes it clear that our great power is from God, not from ourselves.

2 CORINTHIANS 4:7 NLT

For though we live in the body, we do not wage war in an unspiritual way, since the weapons of our warfare are not worldly, but are powerful through God for the demolition of strongholds. We demolish arguments and every high-minded thing that is raised up against the knowledge of God, taking every thought captive to obey Christ.

2 CORINTHIANS 10:3-5 HCSB

[Christ] was crucified in weakness, but He lives by God's power. For we also are weak in Him, yet toward you we will lived with Him by God's power.

2 CORINTHIANS 13:4 HCSB

I also pray that you will understand the incredible greatness of God's power for us who believe him. This is the same mighty power that raised Christ from the dead and seated him in the place of honor at God's right hand in the heavenly realms.

EPHESIANS 1:19-20 NLT

Never doubt God's mighty power to work in you and accomplish all this. He will achieve infinitely more than your greatest request, your most unbelievable dream, and exceed your wildest imagination! He will outdo them all, for his miraculous power constantly energizes you.

EPHESIANS 3:20 TPT

For God will never give you the spirit of cowardly fear, but the Holy Spirit who gives you mighty power, love, and sound judgment!

2 TIMOTHY 1:7 TPT

His divine power has given us everything we need for a godly life through our knowledge of him who called us by his own glory and goodness.

2 PETER 1:3 NIV

Prayer

What other nation is so great as to have their gods near them the way the LORD our God is near us whenever we pray to him?

DEUTERONOMY 4:7 NIV

Then Eli answered and said, "Go in peace, and the God of Israel grant your petition which you have asked of Him."

1 SAMUEL 1:17 NKJV

He was the one who prayed to the God of Israel, "Oh, that you would bless me and expand my territory! Please be with me in all that I do, and keep me from all trouble and pain!" And God granted him his request.

1 CHRONICLES 4:10 NLT

"Now my eyes will be open and my ears attentive to the prayers offered in this place. I have chosen and consecrated this temple so that my Name may be there forever. My eyes and my heart will always be there."

2 CHRONICLES 7:15-16 NIV

You'll pray to him and he'll listen;
he'll help you do what you've promised.
You'll decide what you want and it will happen;
your life will be bathed in light.

JOB 22:26-27 MSG

But know that the LORD has set apart the godly for himself;
the LORD hears when I call to him.

PSALM 4:3 ESV

In the morning, LORD, you hear my voice;
in the morning I lay my requests before you
and wait expectantly.

PSALM 5:3 NIV

The LORD has heard my plea;
the LORD will answer my prayer.
>   PSALM 6:9 NLT

To you, LORD, I call;
you are my Rock,
do not turn a deaf ear to me.
For if you remain silent,
I will be like those who go down to the pit.
>   PSALM 28:1 NIV

Evening, morning and noon
I cry out in distress,
and he hears my voice.
>   PSALM 55:17 NIV

God himself will hear me!
God-Enthroned through everlasting ages,
the God of Unchanging Faithfulness,
he will put them in their place,
all those who refuse to love and revere him!
>   PSALM 55:19 TPT

You faithfully answer our prayers with awesome deeds,
O God our savior.
>   PSALM 65:5 NLT

Whenever trouble strikes I will keep crying out to you,
for I know your help is on the way.
>   PSALM 86:7 TPT

"I will answer your cry for help every time you pray,
and you will find and feel my presence
even in your time of pressure and trouble.
I will be your glorious Hero and give you a feast!"
>   PSALM 91:15 TPT

He will listen to the prayers of the destitute.
He will not reject their pleas.

PSALM 102:17 NLT

I cry aloud to the LORD;
I plead aloud to the LORD for mercy.
I pour out my complaint before Him;
I reveal my trouble to Him.
Although my spirit is weak within me,
You know my way.

PSALM 142:1–3 HCSB

The LORD is near to all who call upon Him,
To all who call upon Him in truth.

PSALM 145:18 NKJV

The sacrifice of the wicked is detestable to the LORD,
but the prayer of the upright is His delight.

PROVERBS 15:8 HCSB

The LORD is far from the wicked,
but he hears the prayer of the righteous.

PROVERBS 15:29 NIV

Oh yes, people of Zion, citizens of Jerusalem, your time of tears is over. Cry for help and you'll find it's grace and more grace. The moment he hears, he'll answer.

ISAIAH 30:19 MSG

"Go and tell Hezekiah that this is what the LORD God of your ancestor David says: I have heard your prayer; I have seen your tears. Look, I am going to add 15 years to your life. And I will deliver you and this city from the power of the king of Assyria; I will defend this city."

ISAIAH 38:5–6 HCSB

"At that time, when you call, the LORD will answer;
when you cry out, He will say, 'Here I am.'
If you get rid of the yoke among you,
the finger-pointing and malicious speaking."
ISAIAH 58:9 HCSB

"Even before they call, I will answer;
while they are still speaking, I will hear."
ISAIAH 65:24 HCSB

"Then you will call on me and come and pray to me, and I will listen to you. You will seek me and find me when you seek me with all your heart."
JEREMIAH 29:12-13 NIV

"Call to me and I will answer you. I'll tell you marvelous and wondrous things that you could never figure out on your own."
JEREMIAH 33:3 MSG

"I cried out to the LORD in my great trouble,
and he answered me.
I called to you from the land of the dead,
and LORD, you heard me!"
JONAH 2:2 NLT

"They will call on My name,
and I will answer them.
I will say: They are My people,
and they will say: Yahweh is our God."
ZECHARIAH 13:9 HCSB

"But when you pray, go into your private room, shut your door, and pray to your Father who is in secret. And your Father who sees in secret will reward you."
MATTHEW 6:6 HCSB

"For your Father knows exactly what you need even before you ask him!"
MATTHEW 6:8 NLT

"Ask and it will be given to you; seek and you will find; knock and the door will be opened to you. For everyone who asks receives; the one who seeks finds; and to the one who knocks, the door will be opened."
MATTHEW 7:7-8 NIV

"When two of you get together on anything at all on earth and make a prayer of it, my Father in heaven goes into action. And when two or three of you are together because of me, you can be sure that I'll be there."
MATTHEW 18:19-20 MSG

"I tell you, you can pray for anything, and if you believe that you've received it, it will be yours."
MARK 11:24 NLT

"So it is with your prayers. Ask and you'll receive. Seek and you'll discover. Knock on heaven's door, and it will one day open for you. Every persistent person will get what he asks for. Every persistent seeker will discover what he needs. And everyone who knocks persistently will one day find an open door."
LUKE 11:9-10 TPT

"You can ask for anything in my name, and I will do it, so that the Son can bring glory to the Father."
JOHN 14:13 NLT

"But if you remain in me and my words remain in you, you may ask for anything you want, and it will be granted!"
JOHN 15:7 NLT

"I assure you: Anything you ask the Father in My name, He will give you. Until now you have asked for nothing in My name. Ask and you will receive, so that your joy may be complete."
JOHN 16:23-24 HCSB

In him and through faith in him we may approach God with freedom and confidence.
EPHESIANS 3:12 NIV

You desire and do not have. You murder and covet and cannot obtain. You fight and war. You do not have because you do not ask. You ask and don't receive because you ask with wrong motives, so that you may spend it on your evil desires.
JAMES 4:2-3 HCSB

Confess and acknowledge how you have offended one another and then pray for one another to be instantly healed, for tremendous power is released through the passionate, heartfelt prayer of a godly believer!
JAMES 5:16 TPT

Husbands, in the same way, live with your wives with an understanding of their weaker nature yet showing them honor as co-heirs of the grace of life, so that your prayers will not be hindered.
1 PETER 3:7 HCSB

"The eyes of the Lord watch over those who do right,
and his ears are open to their prayers.
But the Lord turns his face
against those who do evil."
1 PETER 3:12 NLT

Dear friends, if we don't feel guilty, we can come to God with bold confidence. And we will receive from him whatever we ask because we obey him and do the things that please him.
1 JOHN 3:21-22 NLT

Now this is the confidence we have before Him: Whenever we ask anything according to His will, He hears us.
1 JOHN 5:14 HCSB

Presence

From heaven the LORD looks down
and sees all mankind;
from his dwelling place he watches
all who live on earth—
he who forms the hearts of all,
who considers everything they do.
>   PSALM 33:13-15 NIV

But the LORD watches over those who fear him,
those who rely on his unfailing love.
>   PSALM 33:18 NLT

"I will be with you
when you pass through the waters,
and when you pass through the rivers,
they will not overwhelm you.
You will not be scorched
when you walk through the fire,
and the flame will not burn you."
>   ISAIAH 43:2 HCSB

"See, I have engraved you on the palms of my hands;
your walls are ever before me."
>   ISAIAH 49:16 NIV

"They will fight against you but will not overcome you, for I am with you and will rescue you," declares the LORD.
>   JEREMIAH 1:19 NIV

"My dwelling place will be with them; I will be their God, and they will be my people. Then the nations will know that I the LORD make Israel holy, when my sanctuary is among them forever."
>   EZEKIEL 37:27-28 NIV

"I will pour out My Spirit on all humanity;
then your sons and your daughters will prophesy,
your old men will have dreams,
and your young men will see visions.
I will even pour out My Spirit
on the male and female slaves in those days."

JOEL 2:28-29 HCSB

Then Haggai, GOD'S messenger, preached GOD'S Message to the people: "I am with you!"

HAGGAI 1:13 MSG

"This is the promise I made to you when you came out of Egypt, and My Spirit is present among you; don't be afraid."

HAGGAI 2:5 HCSB

"Shout and be glad, Daughter Zion. For I am coming, and I will live among you," declares the LORD. "Many nations will be joined with the LORD in that day and will become my people. I will live among you and you will know that the LORD Almighty has sent me to you. The LORD will inherit Judah as his portion in the holy land and will again choose Jerusalem. Be still before the LORD, all mankind, because he has roused himself from his holy dwelling."

ZECHARIAH 2:10-13 NIV

Thus says the LORD:
"I will return to Zion,
And dwell in the midst of Jerusalem.
Jerusalem shall be called the City of Truth,
The Mountain of the LORD of hosts,
The Holy Mountain."

ZECHARIAH 8:3 NKJV

King David said this about him:
"I see that the LORD is always with me.
I will not be shaken, for he is right beside me.
No wonder my heart is glad,
and my tongue shouts his praises!
My body rests in hope.
For you will not leave my soul among the dead
or allow your Holy One to rot in the grave.
You have shown me the way of life,
and you will fill me with the joy of your presence."
ACTS 2:25-28 NLT

From one man He has made every nationality to live over the whole earth and has determined their appointed times and the boundaries of where they live. He did this so they might seek God, and perhaps they might reach out and find Him, though He is not far from each one of us.
ACTS 17:26-27 HCSB

Rejoice in the Lord always. I will say it again: Rejoice! Let your gentleness be evident to all. The Lord is near.
PHILIPPIANS 4:4-5 NIV

Prophecy

Listen to my words:
"When there is a prophet among you,
I, the LORD, reveal myself to them in visions,
I speak to them in dreams.
But this is not true of my servant Moses;
he is faithful in all my house.
With him I speak face to face,
clearly and not in riddles;
he sees the form of the LORD.
Why then were you not afraid
to speak against my servant Moses?"
   NUMBERS 12:6-8 NIV

"But the prophet who presumes to speak a word in my name that I have not commanded him to speak, or who speaks in the name of other gods, that same prophet shall die."
   DEUTERONOMY 18:20 ESV

"When a prophet speaks in the name of the LORD, if the word does not come to pass or come true, that is a word that the LORD has not spoken; the prophet has spoken it presumptuously. You need not be afraid of him."
   DEUTERONOMY 18:22 ESV

"The Spirit of the LORD will control you, you will prophesy with them, and you will be transformed into a different person. When these signs have happened to you, do whatever your circumstances require, because God is with you."
   1 SAMUEL 10:6-7 HCSB

"In the Last Days," God says,
"I will pour out my Spirit
on every kind of people:
Your sons will prophesy,
also your daughters;
Your young men will see visions,
your old men dream dreams.
When the time comes,
I'll pour out my Spirit
On those who serve me, men and women both,
and they'll prophesy.
I'll set wonders in the sky above
and signs on the earth below,"
ACTS 2:17-19 NLT

Above all, you must realize that no prophecy in Scripture ever came from the prophet's own understanding, or from human initiative. No, those prophets were moved by the Holy Spirit, and they spoke from God.
2 PETER 1:20-21 NLT

Prosperity

"I will look on you with favor and make you fruitful and increase your numbers, and I will keep my covenant with you. You will still be eating last year's harvest when you will have to move it out to make room for the new. I will put my dwelling place among you, and I will not abhor you. I will walk among you and be your God, and you will be my people."

LEVITICUS 26:9-12 NIV

"Be careful to obey all these things I command you, so that you and your children after you may prosper forever, because you will be doing what is good and right in the sight of the LORD your God."

DEUTERONOMY 12:28 HCSB

"The LORD your God will make you prosper abundantly in all the work of your hands with children, the offspring of your livestock, and your land's produce. Indeed, the LORD will again delight in your prosperity, as He delighted in that of your fathers, when you obey the LORD your God by keeping His commands and statutes that are written in this book of the law and return to Him with all your heart and all your soul."

DEUTERONOMY 30:9-10 HCSB

"This Book of the Law shall not depart from your mouth, but you shall meditate on it day and night, so that you may be careful to do according to all that is written in it. For then you will make your way prosperous, and then you will have good success."

JOSHUA 1:8 ESV

Then the Spirit of God came on Zechariah son of Jehoiad the priest. He stood before the people and said, "This is what God says: 'Why do you disobey the LORD'S commands? You will not prosper. Because you have forsaken the LORD, he has forsaken you.'"

2 CHRONICLES 24:20 NIV

The God of heaven will make us prosper, and we his servants will arise and build, but you have no portion or right or claim in Jerusalem.

NEHEMIAH 2:20 ESV

Submit to God and be at peace with him;
in this way prosperity will come to you.

JOB 22:21 NIV

He is like a tree
planted by streams of water
that yields its fruit in its season,
and its leaf does not wither.
In all that he does, he prospers.
The wicked are not so,
but are like chaff that the wind drives away.

PSALM 1:3 ESV

They will spend their days in prosperity,
and their descendants will inherit the land.

PSALM 25:13 NIV

Worship in awe and wonder, all you who've been made holy!
For all who fear him will feast with plenty.

PSALM 34:9 TPT

Does anyone want to live a life
that is long and prosperous?
Then keep your tongue from speaking evil
and your lips from telling lies!
Turn away from evil and do good.
Search for peace, and work to maintain it.

PSALM 34:12-14 NLT

The righteous will flourish like a palm tree,
they will grow like a cedar of Lebanon;
planted in the house of the LORD,
they will flourish in the courts of our God.

PSALM 92:12-13 NIV

My son, don't forget my teaching,
but let your heart keep my commands;
for they will bring you
many days, a full life, and well-being.
PROVERBS 3:1–2 HCSB

Wisdom extends to you long life in one hand
with wealth and promotion in the other.
Out of her mouth flows righteousness,
and her words release both law and mercy.
PROVERBS 3:16 TPT

I love those who love [wisdom]
and those who seek [wisdom] find me.
With [wisdom] are riches and honor,
enduring wealth and prosperity.
PROVERBS 8:18 NIV

Laying your life down in tender surrender before the Lord
will bring life, prosperity, and honor as your reward.
PROVERBS 22:4 TPT

This is what the LORD Almighty, the God of Israel, says: "When I bring them back from captivity, the people in the land of Judah and in its towns will once again use these words: 'The LORD bless you, you prosperous city, you sacred mountain.'"
JEREMIAH 31:23 NIV

"This is what the LORD says: As I have brought all this great calamity on this people, so I will give them all the prosperity I have promised them."
JEREMIAH 32:42 NIV

Everyone will live in peace and prosperity,
enjoying their own grapevines and fig trees,
for there will be nothing to fear.
The LORD of Heaven's Armies
has made this promise
MICAH 4:4 NLT

Proclaim further: This is what the LORD Almighty says: "My towns will again overflow with prosperity, and the LORD will again comfort Zion and choose Jerusalem."
ZECHARIAH 1:7 NIV

"But now I will not treat the remnant of my people as I treated them before," says the LORD of Heaven's Armies. "For I am planting seeds of peace and prosperity among you. The grapevines will be heavy with fruit. The earth will produce its crops, and the heavens will release the dew. Once more I will cause the remnant in Judah and Israel to inherit these blessings."
ZECHARIAH 8:11-12 NLT

Yes, you will be enriched in every way so that you can always be generous. And when we take your gifts to those who need them, they will thank God.
2 CORINTHIANS 9:11 NLT

Protection

Then the Lord replied to him, "In that case, whoever kills Cain will suffer vengeance seven times over." And He placed a mark on Cain so that whoever found him would not kill him.

GENESIS 4:15 HCSB

Then God said to Noah, "I have decided to put an end to every creature, for the earth is filled with wickedness because of them; therefore I am going to destroy them along with the earth.

"Make yourself an ark of gopher wood. Make rooms in the ark, and cover it with pitch inside and outside. This is how you are to make it: The ark will be 450 feet long, 75 feet wide, and 45 feet high. You are to make a roof, finishing the sides of the ark to within 18 inches of the roof. You are to put a door in the side of the ark. Make it with lower, middle, and upper decks."

"Understand that I am bringing a flood-floodwaters on the earth to destroy every creature under heaven with the breath of life in it. Everything on earth will die. But I will establish My covenant with you, and you will enter the ark with your sons, your wife, and your sons' wives."

GENESIS 6:13-18 HCSB

Then Noah built an altar to the Lord and, taking some of all the clean animals and clean birds, he sacrificed burnt offerings on it. The Lord smelled the pleasing aroma and said in his heart: "Never again will I curse the ground because of humans, even though every inclination of the human heart is evil from childhood. And never again will I destroy all living creatures, as I have done.

"As long as the earth endures,
seedtime and harvest,
cold and heat,
summer and winter,
day and night
will never cease."

GENESIS 8:20-22 NIV

After this, the word of the LORD came to Abram in a vision:
"Do not be afraid, Abram.
I am your shield,
your very great reward."

GENESIS 15:1 NIV

And Moses built an altar and named it, "The LORD Is My Banner." He said, "Indeed, my hand is lifted up toward the LORD's throne. The LORD will be at war with Amalek from generation to generation."

EXODUS 17:15 HCSB

"I will give you peace in the land, and you will be able to sleep with no cause for fear. I will rid the land of wild animals and keep your enemies out of your land. In fact, you will chase down your enemies and slaughter them with your swords. Five of you will chase a hundred, and a hundred of you will chase ten thousand! All your enemies will fall beneath your sword."

LEVITICUS 26:6-8 NLT

"All your life, no one will be able to hold out against you. In the same way I was with Moses, I'll be with you. I won't give up on you; I won't leave you. "

JOSHUA 1:5 MSG

"For who is God, except the LORD?
And who is a rock, except our God?"

2 SAMUEL 22:32 NKJV

For I was ashamed to ask the king for soldiers and horsemen to accompany us and protect us from enemies along the way. After all, we had told the king, "Our God's hand of protection is on all who worship him, but his fierce anger rages against those who abandon him."

EZRA 8:22 NLT

For the LORD watches over the way of the righteous,
but the way of the wicked leads to ruin.

PSALM 1:6 HCSB

But let all who take refuge in you rejoice;
let them sing joyful praises forever.
Spread your protection over them,
that all who love your name may be filled with joy.
>   PSALM 5:11 NLT

Therefore, LORD, we know you will protect the oppressed,
preserving them forever from this lying generation,
even though the wicked strut about,
and evil is praised throughout the land.
>   PSALM 12:7 NLT

My heart and soul explode with joy—full of glory!
Even my body will rest confident and secure.
For you will not abandon me to the realm of death
nor will you allow your Holy One to experience corruption.
>   PSALM 16:9-10 TPT

Pull me from the trap my enemies set for me,
for I find protection in you alone.
>   PSALM 31:4 NLT

Love the LORD, all you godly ones!
For the LORD protects those who are loyal to him,
but he harshly punishes the arrogant.
>   PSALM 31:23 NLT

The angel of the LORD encamps
around those who fear him, and delivers them.
>   PSALM 34:7 ESV

He's your bodyguard, shielding every bone;
not even a finger gets broken.
>   PSALM 34:20 MSG

The wicked lie in wait for the righteous,
intent on putting them to death;
but the LORD will not leave them in the power of the wicked
or let them be condemned when brought to trial.
>   PSALM 37:32-33 NIV

He only is my rock and my salvation;
He is my defense;
I shall not be moved.
>   PSALM 62:6 NKJV

O LORD, I have come to you for protection;
don't let me be disgraced.
>   PSALM 71:1 NLT

When we live our lives within the shadow
of the God Most High, our secret Hiding Place,
we will always be shielded from harm!
How then could evil prevail against us, or disease infect us?
>   PSALM 91:9-10 TPT

For here is what the Lord has spoken to me:
"Because you have delighted in me as my great lover,
I will greatly protect you.
I will set you in a high place,
safe and secure before my face."
>   PSALM 91:14 TPT

O priests, descendants of Aaron, trust the LORD!
He is your helper and your shield.
>   PSALM 115:10 NLT

He will guard and guide me, never letting me stumble or fall.
God is my Keeper; he will never forget or ignore me.
He will never slumber nor sleep;
He is the Guardian-God for his people, Israel.
>   PSALM 121:3-4 TPT

The LORD protects you;
the LORD is a shelter right by your side.
The sun will not strike you by day
or the moon by night.
>   PSALM 121:5-6 HCSB

Those who trust in the Lord are as unshakeable,
as unmovable as Mighty Mount Zion!
Just as the mountains surround Jerusalem,
so the Lord's wrap-around presence surrounds his people,
protecting them now and forever.
>   PSALM 125:1-2 TPT

The LORD preserves all who love Him,
But all the wicked He will destroy.
>   PSALM 145:20 NKJV

The LORD protects the foreigners among us.
>   PSALM 146:9 NLT

The fear of man is a snare,
but the one who trusts in the LORD is protected.
>   PROVERBS 29:25 HCSB

He is a shield to all who come to him for protection.
>   PROVERBS 30:5 NLT

"He protects His flock like a shepherd;
He gathers the lambs in His arms
and carries them in the fold of His garment.
He gently leads those that are nursing."
>   ISAIAH 40:11 HCSB

But you will not leave in haste
or go in flight;
for the LORD will go before you,
the God of Israel will be your rear guard.
>   ISAIAH 52:12 NIV

"No weapon formed against you will succeed,
and you will refute any accusation
raised against you in court.
This is the heritage of the LORD's servants,
and their righteousness is from Me."

ISAIAH 54:17 HCSB

The LORD of Heaven's Armies will protect his people,
and they will defeat their enemies by hurling great stones.
They will shout in battle as though drunk with wine.
They will be filled with blood like a bowl,
drenched with blood like the corners of the altar.

ZECHARIAH 9:15 NLT

"Everyone then who hears these words of mine and does them will be like a wise man who built his house on the rock. And the rain fell, and the floods came, and the winds blew and beat on that house, but it did not fall, because it had been founded on the rock."

MATTHEW 7:24-25 ESV

Put on the full suit of armor that God wears when he goes into battle, so that you will be protected as you fight against the evil strategies of the accuser!

EPHESIANS 6:11 TPT

Provision

Then God said, "Look! I have given you every seed-bearing plant throughout the earth and all the fruit trees for your food. And I have given every green plant as food for all the wild animals, the birds in the sky, and the small animals that scurry along the ground—everything that has life." And that is what happened.
GENESIS 1:29-30 NLT

Then God blessed Noah and his sons, saying to them, "Be fruitful and increase in number and fill the earth. The fear and dread of you will fall on all the beasts of the earth, and on all the birds in the sky, on every creature that moves along the ground, and on all the fish in the sea; they are given into your hands. Everything that lives and moves about will be food for you. Just as I gave you the green plants, I now give you everything."
GENESIS 9:1-3 NIV

Then the LORD appeared to Abram and said, "To your descendants I will give this land." And there he built an altar to the LORD, who had appeared to him.
GENESIS 12:7 NKJV

And the LORD said to Abram, after Lot had separated from him: "Lift your eyes now and look from the place where you are—northward, southward, eastward, and westward; for all the land which you see I give to you and your descendants forever. And I will make your descendants as the dust of the earth; so that if a man could number the dust of the earth, then your descendants also could be numbered. Arise, walk in the land through its length and its width, for I give it to you."
GENESIS 13:14-17 NKJV

So the LORD made a covenant with Abram that day and said, "I have given this land to your descendants, all the way from the border of Egypt to the great Euphrates River."
GENESIS 15:18 NLT

The LORD appeared to Isaac and said, "Do not go down to Egypt; live in the land where I tell you to live. Stay in this land for a while, and I will be with you and will bless you. For to you and your descendants I will give all these lands and will confirm the oath I swore to your father Abraham. I will make your descendants as numerous as the stars in the sky and will give them all these lands, and through your offspring all nations on earth will be blessed, because Abraham obeyed me and did everything I required of him, keeping my commands, my decrees and my instructions."

GENESIS 26:1-5 NIV

Then GOD was right before him, saying, "I am GOD, the God of Abraham your father and the God of Isaac. I'm giving the ground on which you are sleeping to you and to your descendants. Your descendants will be as the dust of the Earth; they'll stretch from west to east and from north to south. All the families of the Earth will bless themselves in you and your descendants. Yes. I'll stay with you, I'll protect you wherever you go, and I'll bring you back to this very ground. I'll stick with you until I've done everything I promised you."

GENESIS 28:13-15 MSG

"And I will set your bounds from the Red Sea to the sea, Philistia, and from the desert to the River. For I will deliver the inhabitants of the land into your hand, and you shall drive them out before you."

EXODUS 23:31 NKJV

GOD spoke to Aaron, "I am personally putting you in charge of my contributions, all the holy gifts I get from the People of Israel. I am turning them over to you and your children for your personal use. This is the standing rule. You and your sons get what's left from the offerings, whatever hasn't been totally burned up on the Altar— the leftovers from Grain-Offerings, Absolution-Offerings, and Compensation-Offerings. Eat it reverently; it is most holy; every male may eat it. Treat it as holy."

NUMBERS 18:8-10 MSG

"You also get the Wave-Offerings from the People of Israel. I present them to you and your sons and daughters as a gift. This is the standing rule. Anyone in your household who is ritually clean may eat it."

NUMBERS 18:11 MSG

"I also give you the harvest gifts brought by the people as offerings to the LORD the best of the olive oil, new wine, and grain. All the first crops of their land that the people present to the LORD belong to you. Any member of your family who is ceremonially clean may eat this food."
NUMBERS 18:12-13 NLT

"Everything in Israel that is devoted to the LORD is yours."
NUMBERS 18:14 NIV

"The meat of these animals will be yours, just like the breast and right thigh that are presented by lifting them up as a special offering before the altar. Yes, I am giving you all these holy offerings that the people of Israel bring to the LORD. They are for you and your sons and daughters, to be eaten as your permanent share. This is an eternal and unbreakable covenant between the LORD and you, and it also applies to your descendants."
NUMBERS 18:18-19 NLT

"To the Levites I have given every tithe in Israel for an inheritance, in return for their service that they do, their service in the tent of meeting."
NUMBERS 18:21 ESV

"Instead, I give to the Levites as their inheritance the tithes that the Israelites present as an offering to the LORD. That is why I said concerning them: 'They will have no inheritance among the Israelites.'"
NUMBERS 18:24 NIV

"Tell the Levites, When you offer the best part, the rest will be treated the same as grain from the threshing floor or wine from the wine vat that others give. You and your households are free to eat the rest of it anytime and anyplace—it's your wages for your work at the Tent of Meeting. By offering the best part, you'll avoid guilt, you won't desecrate the holy offerings of the People of Israel, and you won't die."
NUMBERS 18:30-32 MSG

The LORD said to Moses, "Take the staff, and you and your brother Aaron gather the assembly together. Speak to that rock before their eyes and it will pour out its water. You will bring water out of the rock for the community so they and their livestock can drink."
NUMBERS 20:7-8 NIV

From there they went to Beer, which is the well where the LORD said to Moses, "Gather the people together, and I will give them water."
NUMBERS 21:16 NKJV

The LORD spoke to Moses, saying, "Among these the land shall be divided for inheritance according to the number of names. To a large tribe you shall give a large inheritance, and to a small tribe you shall give a small inheritance; every tribe shall be given its inheritance in proportion to its list. But the land shall be divided by lot. According to the names of the tribes of their fathers they shall inherit. Their inheritance shall be divided according to lot between the larger and the smaller."
NUMBERS 26:52-56 ESV

Then Moses said to them: "If you do this thing, if you arm yourselves before the LORD for the war, and all your armed men cross over the Jordan before the LORD until He has driven out His enemies from before Him, and the land is subdued before the LORD, then afterward you may return and be blameless before the LORD and before Israel; and this land shall be your possession before the LORD."
NUMBERS 32:20-22 NKJV

The LORD spoke to Moses in the plains of Moab by the Jordan across from Jericho, "Tell the Israelites: When you cross the Jordan into the land of Canaan, you must drive out all the inhabitants of the land before you, destroy all their stone images and cast images, and demolish all their high places. You are to take possession of the land and settle in it because I have given you the land to possess."
NUMBERS 33:50-53 HCSB

And the LORD spoke to Moses in the plains of Moab by the Jordan across from Jericho, saying: "Command the children of Israel that they give the Levites cities to dwell in from the inheritance of their possession, and you shall also give the Levites common-land around the cities. They shall have the cities to dwell in; and their common-land shall be for their cattle, for their herds, and for all their animals."
NUMBERS 35:1-3 NKJV

"Six of the towns you give the Levites will be cities of refuge, to which a person who has killed someone may flee. In addition, give them forty-two other towns. These six towns will be a place of refuge for Israelites and for foreigners residing among them, so that anyone who has killed another accidentally can flee there."
NUMBERS 35:6, 15 NIV

"Look, I've given you this land. Now go in and take it. It's the land GOD promised to give your ancestors Abraham, Isaac, and Jacob and their children after them."
DEUTERONOMY 1:8 MSG

When GOD heard what you said, he exploded in anger. He swore, "Not a single person of this evil generation is going to get so much as a look at the good land that I promised to give to your parents. Not one—except for Caleb son of Jephunneh. He'll see it. I'll give him and his descendants the land he walked on because he was all for following GOD, heart and soul."
DEUTERONOMY 1:34-36 MSG

"And the LORD was also angry with me because of you. He said to me, 'Moses, not even you will enter the Promised Land! Instead, your assistant, Joshua son of Nun, will lead the people into the land. Encourage him, for he will lead Israel as they take possession of it. I will give the land to your little ones—your innocent children. You were afraid they would be captured, but they will be the ones who occupy it."
DEUTERONOMY 1:37-39 NLT

"For I must die in this land; I must not go over the Jordan. But you shall go over and take possession of that good land."
DEUTERONOMY 4:22 ESV

When the LORD your God enlarges your border as He has promised you, and you say, "Let me eat meat," because you long to eat meat, you may eat as much meat as your heart desires.
DEUTERONOMY 12:20 NKJV

"You are about to enter the land the LORD your God is giving you."
DEUTERONOMY 17:14A NLT

"These are the parts the priests may claim as their share from the cattle, sheep, and goats that the people bring as offerings: the shoulder, the cheeks, and the stomach. You must also give to the priests the first share of the grain, the new wine, the olive oil, and the wool at shearing time. For the LORD your God chose the tribe of Levi out of all your tribes to minister in the LORD's name forever."
DEUTERONOMY 18:3-5 NLT

"Go to Moab, to the mountains east of the river, and climb Mount Nebo, which is across from Jericho. Look out across the land of Canaan, the land I am giving to the people of Israel as their own special possession."
DEUTERONOMY 32:49 NLT

"I will give you every place where you set your foot, as I promised Moses."
JOSHUA 1:3 NIV

"Go through the camp and tell the people, 'Get your provisions ready. Three days from now you will cross the Jordan here to go in and take possession of the land the LORD your God is giving you for your own.'"
JOSHUA 1:11 NIV

Thus the LORD gave to Israel all the land that he swore to give to their fathers. And they took possession of it, and they settled there.
JOSHUA 21:43 ESV

"You will become pregnant and give birth to a son, and his hair must never be cut. For he will be dedicated to God as a Nazirite from birth. He will begin to rescue Israel from the Philistines."
JUDGES 13:5 NLT

And all the people who were at the gate, and the elders, said, "We are witnesses. The LORD make the woman who is coming to your house like Rachel and Leah, the two who built the house of Israel; and may you prosper in Ephrathah and be famous in Bethlehem. May your house be like the house of Perez, whom Tamar bore to Judah, because of the offspring which the LORD will give you from this young woman."
RUTH 4:11-12 NKJV

"I will establish a place for My people Israel and plant them, so that they may live there and not be disturbed again. Evildoers will not afflict them as they have done ever since the day I ordered judges to be over My people Israel."
2 SAMUEL 7:10-11A HCSB

"Since you have asked for this and not for long life or wealth for yourself, nor have asked for the death of your enemies but for discernment in administering justice, I will do what you have asked. I will give you a wise and discerning heart, so that there will never have been anyone like you, nor will there ever be. Moreover, I will give you what you have not asked for—both wealth and honor—so that in your lifetime you will have no equal among kings."

1 KINGS 3:11-13 NIV

"And this shall be the sign for you: this year eat what grows of itself, and in the second year what springs of the same. Then in the third year sow and reap and plant vineyards, and eat their fruit."

2 KINGS 19:29 ESV

"I give you the land of Canaan,
this is your inheritance;
Even though you're not much to look at,
a few straggling strangers."

1 CHRONICLES 16:18-19 MSG

Furthermore, I declare to you that the LORD Himself will build a house for you. When your time comes to be with your fathers, I will raise up after you your descendant, who is one of your own sons, and I will establish his kingdom. He will build a house for Me, and I will establish his throne forever. I will be a father to him, and he will be a son to Me. I will not take away My faithful love from him as I took it from the one who was before you. I will appoint him over My house and My kingdom forever, and his throne will be established forever.

1 CHRONICLES 17:10-14 HCSB

God said to Solomon, "Because your greatest desire is to help your people, and you did not ask for wealth, riches, fame, or even the death of your enemies or a long life, but rather you asked for wisdom and knowledge to properly govern my people—I will certainly give you the wisdom and knowledge you requested. But I will also give you wealth, riches, and fame such as no other king has had before you or will ever have in the future!"

2 CHRONICLES 1:11-12 NLT

He gives rain to the earth
and sends water to the fields.
   JOB 5:10 HCSB

LORD, you alone are my portion and my cup;
you make my lot secure.
The boundary lines have fallen for me in pleasant places;
surely I have a delightful inheritance.
   PSALM 16:5 NIV

The LORD is my shepherd;
I have all that I need.
   PSALM 23:1 NLT

Even the strong and the wealthy grow weak and hungry,
but those who passionately pursue the Lord
will never lack any good thing.
   PSALM 34:10 TPT

Take delight in the LORD,
and he will give you your heart's desires.
   PSALM 37:4 NLT

Even in a time of disaster he will watch over [the innocent],
and they will always have more than enough
no matter what happens.
   PSALM 37:19 TPT

Wait for the LORD and keep His way,
and He will exalt you to inherit the land.
You will watch when the wicked are destroyed.
   PSALM 37:34 HCSB

Those who walk along his paths with integrity
will never lack one thing they need,
For he provides it all!
O Lord of Heaven's Armies,
what euphoria fills those who forever trust in you!
PSALM 84:12 TPT

He provides food for those who fear him;
he remembers his covenant forever.
PSALM 111:5 NIV

He gives food to every creature.
His love is eternal.
PSALM 136:25 HCSB

Springs of water will burst out in the wilderness,
streams flow in the desert.
Hot sands will become a cool oasis,
thirsty ground a splashing fountain.
Even lowly jackals will have water to drink,
and barren grasslands flourish richly.
ISAIAH 35:6–7 MSG

"The poor and homeless are desperate for water,
their tongues parched and no water to be found.
But I'm there to be found, I'm there for them,
and I, God of Israel, will not leave them thirsty."
ISAIAH 41:17 MSG

"Nobody hungry, nobody thirsty,
shade from the sun, shelter from the wind,
For the Compassionate One guides them,
takes them to the best springs."
ISAIAH 49:10 MSG

"Come, all you who are thirsty,
come to the waters;
and you who have no money,
come, buy and eat!
Come, buy wine and milk
without money and without cost.
Why spend money on what is not bread,
and your labor on what does not satisfy?
Listen, listen to me, and eat what is good,
and you will delight in the richest of fare."

ISAIAH 55:1-2 NIV

"My servants will eat,
but you will go hungry;
my servants will drink,
but you will go thirsty;
my servants will rejoice,
but you will be put to shame."

ISAIAH 65:13 NIV

"In that day Jerusalem will be known as 'The Throne of the LORD.' All nations will come there to honor the LORD. They will no longer stubbornly follow their own evil desires. In those days the people of Judah and Israel will return together from exile in the north. They will return to the land I gave their ancestors as an inheritance forever."

JEREMIAH 3:17-18 NLT

Therefore say: "This is what the Sovereign LORD says: I will gather you from the nations and bring you back from the countries where you have been scattered, and I will give you back the land of Israel again."

EZEKIEL 11:17 NIV

"For I will take you from the nations and gather you from all the countries, and will bring you into your own land."

EZEKIEL 36:24 HCSB

"My servant David will be king over them, and they will all have one shepherd. They will follow my laws and be careful to keep my decrees. They will live in the land I gave to my servant Jacob, the land where your ancestors lived. They and their children and their children's children will live there forever, and David my servant will be their prince forever."

EZEKIEL 37:24–25 NIV

But the saints of the Most High shall receive the kingdom, and possess the kingdom forever, even forever and ever.

DANIEL 7:18 HCSB

"As for you, go your way till the end. You will rest, and then at the end of the days you will rise to receive your allotted inheritance."

DANIEL 12:13 NIV

"In that day the mountains will drip with sweet wine,
and the hills will flow with milk.
Water will fill the streambeds of Judah,
and a fountain will burst forth from the LORD's Temple,
watering the arid valley of acacias."

JOEL 3:18 NLT

"Can any of you add a single cubit to his height by worrying? And why do you worry about clothes? Learn how the wildflowers of the field grow: they don't labor or spin thread. Yet I tell you that not even Solomon in all his splendor was adorned like one of these! If that's how God clothes the grass of the field, which is here today and thrown into the furnace tomorrow, won't He do much more for you—you of little faith?"

MATTHEW 6:27–30 HCSB

"But seek first the kingdom of God and His righteousness, and all these things will be provided for you."

MATTHEW 6:33 HCSB

"If you then, who are evil, know how to give good gifts to your children, how much more will your Father in heaven give good things to those who ask Him!"

MATTHEW 7:11 HCSB

"Those who hunger for him will always be filled,
but the smug and self-satisfied he will send away empty."
LUKE 1:53 TPT

"What father among you, if his son asks for a fish, will instead of a fish give him a serpent; or if he asks for an egg, will give him a scorpion? If you then, who are evil, know how to give good gifts to your children, how much more will the heavenly Father give the Holy Spirit to those who ask him!"
LUKE 11:11-13 ESV

"Each and every day he will supply your needs as you seek his kingdom passionately, above all else."
LUKE 12:31 TPT

For God has proved his love by giving us his greatest treasure, the gift of his Son. And since God freely offered him up as the sacrifice for us all, he certainly won't withhold from us anything else he has to give.
ROMANS 8:32 TPT

And God will generously provide all you need. Then you will always have everything you need and plenty left over to share with others.
2 CORINTHIANS 9:8 NLT

And my God will supply every need of yours according to his riches in glory in Christ Jesus.
PHILIPPIANS 4:19 ESV

Every good and perfect gift is from above, coming down from the Father of the heavenly lights, who does not change like shifting shadows.
JAMES 1:17 NIV

Punishment

"For I will pass through the land of Egypt on that night, and will strike all the firstborn in the land of Egypt, both man and beast; and against all the gods of Egypt I will execute judgment: I am the LORD. Now the blood shall be a sign for you on the houses where you are. And when I see the blood, I will pass over you; and the plague shall not be on you to destroy you when I strike the land of Egypt."
    EXODUS 12:12-13 NKJV

"You must not misuse the name of the LORD your God. The LORD will not let you go unpunished if you misuse his name."
    EXODUS 20:7 NLT

"For the land is defiled; therefore I visit the punishment of its iniquity upon it, and the land vomits out its inhabitants."
    LEVITICUS 18:28 NKJV

The LORD said to Moses, "Give the people of Israel these instructions, which apply both to native Israelites and to the foreigners living in Israel. If any of them offer their children as a sacrifice to Molech, they must be put to death. The people of the community must stone them to death. I myself will turn against them and cut them off from the community, because they have defiled my sanctuary and brought shame on my holy name by offering their children to Molech."
    LEVITICUS 20:1-3 NLT

"If a person turns to mediums and necromancers, whoring after them, I will set my face against that person and will cut him off from among his people."
    LEVITICUS 20:6 ESV

"But if you refuse to obey me and won't observe my commandments, despising my decrees and holding my laws in contempt by your disobedience, making a shambles of my covenant, I'll step in and pour on the trouble: debilitating disease, high fevers, blindness, your life leaking out bit by bit. You'll plant seed but your enemies will eat the crops. I'll turn my back on you and stand by while your enemies defeat you. People who hate you will govern you. You'll run scared even when there's no one chasing you."
    LEVITICUS 26:14-17 MSG

"Because your men explored the land for forty days, you must wander in the wilderness for forty years—a year for each day, suffering the consequences of your sins. Then you will discover what it is like to have me for an enemy. I, the LORD, have spoken! I will certainly do these things to every member of the community who has conspired against me. They will be destroyed here in this wilderness, and here they will die!"
NUMBERS 14:34-35 NLT

GOD said to Aaron, "You and your sons, along with your father's family, are responsible for taking care of sins having to do with the Sanctuary; you and your sons are also responsible for sins involving the priesthood. So enlist your brothers of the tribe of Levi to join you and assist you and your sons in your duties in the Tent of Testimony. They will report to you as they go about their duties related to the Tent, but they must not have anything to do with the holy things of the Altar under penalty of death—both they and you will die! They are to work with you in taking care of the Tent of Meeting, whatever work is involved in the Tent. Outsiders are not allowed to help you."
NUMBERS 18:1-4 MSG

"Starting now, the rest of the People of Israel cannot wander in and out of the Tent of Meeting; they'll be penalized for their sin and the penalty is death. It's the Levites and only the Levites who are to work in the Tent of Meeting and they are responsible for anything that goes wrong."
NUMBERS 18:22-23 MSG

"The LORD was angry with me on your account. He swore that I would not cross the Jordan and enter the good land the LORD your God is giving you as an inheritance."
DEUTERONOMY 4:21 HCSB

"No one among you is to make his son or daughter pass through the fire, practice divination, tell fortunes, interpret omens, practice sorcery, cast spells, consult a medium or a familiar spirit, or inquire of the dead. Everyone who does these things is detestable to the LORD, and the LORD your God is driving out the nations before you because of these detestable things."
DEUTERONOMY 18:10-12 HCSB

"GOD'S curse on anyone who moves his neighbor's boundary marker."
DEUTERONOMY 27:17 MSG

"Cursed be anyone who misleads a blind man on the road."
DEUTERONOMY 27:18 ESV

"Cursed is anyone who has sexual intercourse with an animal."
DEUTERONOMY 27:21 NLT

"Cursed is the one who attacks his neighbor secretly."
DEUTERONOMY 27:24 NKJV

"Cursed be anyone who takes a bribe to shed innocent blood."
DEUTERONOMY 27:25 ESV

"Cursed is the one who does not confirm all the words of this law."
DEUTERONOMY 27:26 NKJV

"Here's what will happen if you don't obediently listen to the Voice of GOD, your God, and diligently keep all the commandments and guidelines that I'm commanding you today. All these curses will come down hard on you:
GOD'S curse in the city,
    GOD'S curse in the country;
    GOD'S curse on your basket and bread bowl;
    GOD'S curse on your children,
    the crops of your land,
    the young of your livestock,
    the calves of your herds,
    the lambs of your flocks.
    GOD'S curse in your coming in,
    GOD'S curse in your going out."
DEUTERONOMY 28:15–19 MSG

"Israel has sinned. They have violated My covenant that I appointed for them. They have taken some of what was set apart. They have stolen, deceived, and put the things with their own belongings. This is why the Israelites cannot stand against their enemies. They will turn their backs and run from their enemies, because they have been set apart for destruction. I will no longer be with you unless you remove from you what is set apart."

JOSHUA 7:11-12 HCSB

"But if you turn away from him and cling to the customs of the survivors of these nations remaining among you, and if you intermarry with them, then know for certain that the LORD your God will no longer drive them out of your land. Instead, they will be a snare and a trap to you, a whip for your backs and thorny brambles in your eyes, and you will vanish from this good land the LORD your God has given you."

JOSHUA 23:12-13 NLT

"If you forsake the LORD and serve foreign gods, he will turn and bring disaster on you and make an end of you, after he has been good to you."

JOSHUA 24:20 NIV

So the anger of the LORD was kindled against Israel, and he said, "Because this people have transgressed my covenant that I commanded their fathers and have not obeyed my voice, I will no longer drive out before them any of the nations that Joshua left when he died, in order to test Israel by them, whether they will take care to walk in the way of the LORD as their fathers did, or not."

JUDGES 2:20-22 ESV

So the LORD said to the children of Israel, "Did I not deliver you from the Egyptians and from the Amorites and from the people of Ammon and from the Philistines? Also the Sidonians and Amalekites and Maonites oppressed you; and you cried out to Me, and I delivered you from their hand. Yet you have forsaken Me and served other gods. Therefore I will deliver you no more."

JUDGES 10:11-13 NKJV

"Stop acting so proud and haughty!
Don't speak with such arrogance!
For the LORD is a God who knows what you have done;
he will judge your actions."

1 SAMUEL 2:3 NLT

"Those who oppose the LORD will be shattered;
He will thunder in the heavens against them.
The LORD will judge the ends of the earth."
1 SAMUEL 2:10A HCSB

Therefore the LORD, the God of Israel, declares: "I promised that members of your family would minister before me forever." But now the LORD declares: "Far be it from me! Those who honor me I will honor, but those who despise me will be disdained. The time is coming when I will cut short your strength and the strength of your priestly house, so that no one in it will reach old age."
1 SAMUEL 2:30-31 NIV

The LORD said to Samuel, "I am about to do something in Israel that everyone who hears about it will shudder. On that day I will carry out against Eli everything I said about his family, from beginning to end. I told him that I am going to judge his family forever because of the iniquity he knows about: his sons are defiling the sanctuary, and he has not stopped them. Therefore, I have sworn to Eli's family: The iniquity of Eli's family will never be wiped out by either sacrifice or offering."
1 SAMUEL 3:11-14 HCSB

Now therefore, the sword shall never depart from your house, because you have despised Me, and have taken the wife of Uriah the Hittite to be your wife. Thus says the LORD: "Behold, I will raise up adversity against you from your own house; and I will take your wives before your eyes and give them to your neighbor, and he shall lie with your wives in the sight of this sun. For you did it secretly, but I will do this thing before all Israel, before the sun."
2 SAMUEL 12:10-12 NKJV

Now the word of the LORD came to Jehu son of Hanani against Baasha: "Because I raised you up from the dust and made you ruler over My people Israel, but you have walked in the way of Jeroboam and have caused My people Israel to sin, provoking Me with their sins, take note: I will sweep away Baasha and his house, and I will make your house like the house of Jeroboam son of Nebat."
1 KINGS 16:1-3 HCSB

And Elijah the Tishbite, of the inhabitants of Gilead, said to Ahab, "As the LORD God of Israel lives, before whom I stand, there shall not be dew nor rain these years, except at my word."

1 KINGS 17:1 NKJV

"And because of your raging against me
and your arrogance, which I have heard for myself,
I will put my hook in your nose
and my bit in your mouth.
I will make you return
by the same road on which you came."

2 KINGS 19:28 NLT

"This is what the LORD says: I am going to bring disaster on this city and its people. All the curses written in the scroll that was read to the king of Judah will come true. For my people have abandoned me and offered sacrifices to pagan gods, and I am very angry with them for everything they have done. My anger will be poured out on this place, and it will not be quenched."

2 CHRONICLES 34:24-25 NLT

Consider now: Who, being innocent, has ever perished?
Where were the upright ever destroyed?
As I have observed, those who plow evil
and those who sow trouble reap it.

JOB 4:7-8 NIV

The LORD says: "I will not relent from punishing Judah for three crimes, even four, because they have rejected the instruction of the LORD and have not kept His statutes. The lies that their ancestors followed have led them astray."

AMOS 2:4 HCSB

But those governed by selfishness and self-promotion, whose hearts are unresponsive to God's truth and would rather embrace unrighteousness, will experience the fullness of wrath.

ROMANS 2:8 TPT

Purity

"The person who touches any human corpse will be unclean for seven days. He is to purify himself with the water on the third day and the seventh day; then he will be clean. But if he does not purify himself on the third and seventh days, he will not be clean. Anyone who touches a body of a person who has died, and does not purify himself, defiles the tabernacle of the LORD. That person will be cut off from Israel. He remains unclean because the water for impurity has not been sprinkled on him, and his uncleanness is still on him."

NUMBERS 19:11-13 HCSB

"Whoever in the open field touches one who is slain by a sword or who has died, or a bone of a man, or a grave, shall be unclean seven days."

NUMBERS 19:16 NKJV

"With the pure You will show Yourself pure;
And with the devious You will show Yourself shrewd."

2 SAMUEL 22:27 NKJV

To the pure you show yourself pure,
but to the wicked you show yourself hostile.

PSALM 18:26 NLT

Who, then, ascends into the presence of the Lord?
And who has the privilege of entering into God's holy place?
Those who are clean—whose works and ways are pure;
whose hearts are true and sealed by the truth;
those who never deceive, whose words are sure.

PSALM 24:3-4 TPT

How can a young person stay on the path of purity?
By living according to your word.

PSALM 119:9 NIV

The Lord detests the lifestyle of the wicked,
but he loves those who pursue purity.
PROVERBS 15:9 TPT

"I will purify them from all the wrongs they have committed against Me, and I will forgive all the wrongs they have committed against Me, rebelling against Me."
JEREMIAH 33:8 HCSB

"Blessed are the pure in heart,
for they will see God."
MATTHEW 5:8 NIV

"What goes into someone's mouth does not defile them, but what comes out of their mouth, that is what defiles them."
MATTHEW 15:11 NIV

Jesus called the crowd together again and said, "Listen now, all of you—take this to heart. It's not what you swallow that pollutes your life; it's what you vomit—that's the real pollution."
MARK 7:14-15 MSG

God wants you to live a pure life. Keep yourselves from sexual promiscuity.
1 THESSALONIANS 4:3 MSG

Purpose

"He is the one who will build a house for my Name. He will be my son, and I will be his father. And I will establish the throne of his kingdom over Israel forever."

1 CHRONICLES 22:10 NIV

"The LORD has kept the promise he made. I have succeeded David my father and now I sit on the throne of Israel, just as the LORD promised, and I have built the temple for the Name of the LORD, the God of Israel. There I have placed the ark, in which is the covenant of the LORD that he made with the people of Israel."

2 CHRONICLES 6:10-11 NIV

Mordecai sent her this message: "Don't think that just because you live in the king's house you're the one Jew who will get out of this alive. If you persist in staying silent at a time like this, help and deliverance will arrive for the Jews from someplace else; but you and your family will be wiped out. Who knows? Maybe you were made queen for just such a time as this."

ESTHER 4:13-14 MSG

His destiny-plan for the earth stands sure.
His forever-plan remains in place and will never fail.

PSALM 33:11 TPT

I call to God Most High,
to God who fulfills His purpose for me.

PSALM 52:2 HCSB

The LORD will fulfill His purpose for me.
LORD, Your love is eternal;
do not abandon the work of Your hands.

PSALM 138:8 HCSB

The Lord works everything together
to accomplish his purpose.
Even the wicked are included in his plans—
he sets them aside for the day of disaster.
> PROVERBS 16:4 TPT

Yet LORD, You are our Father;
we are the clay, and You are our potter;
we all are the work of Your hands.
> ISAIAH 64:8 HCSB

Then the LORD reached out his hand and touched my mouth and said to me, "I have put my words in your mouth. See, today I appoint you over nations and kingdoms to uproot and tear down, to destroy and overthrow, to build and to plant."
> JEREMIAH 1:9-10 NIV

"I will give you the keys of the kingdom of heaven; whatever you bind on earth will be bound in heaven, and whatever you loose on earth will be loosed in heaven."
> MATTHEW 16:19 NIV

The earth and sky will wear out and fade away before one word I speak loses its power or fails to accomplish its purpose.
> MATTHEW 24:35 TPT

He said to them, "I watched Satan fall from heaven like a lightning flash. Look, I have given you the authority to trample on snakes and scorpions and over all the power of the enemy; nothing will ever harm you."
> LUKE 10:18-19 HCSB

So we are convinced that every detail of our lives is continually woven together to fit into God's perfect plan of bringing what is good into our lives, for we are his lovers who have been invited to fulfill his designed purpose
> ROMANS 8:28 TPT

Yes, the body has many different parts, not just one part. If the foot says, "I am not a part of the body because I am not a hand," that does not make it any less a part of the body. And if the ear says, "I am not part of the body because I am not an eye," would that make it any less a part of the body?

1 CORINTHIANS 12:14-16 NLT

In a large house there are articles not only of gold and silver, but also of wood and clay; some are for special purposes and some for common use. Those who cleanse themselves from the latter will be instruments for special purposes, made holy, useful to the Master and prepared to do any good work.

2 TIMOTHY 2:20-21 NIV

Reconciliation

More than that, we also rejoice in God through our Lord Jesus Christ, through whom we have now received reconciliation.
ROMANS 5:11 ESV

Everything is from God, who reconciled us to Himself through Christ and gave us the ministry of reconciliation.
2 CORINTHIANS 5:18 HCSB

Once you were alienated from God and were enemies in your minds because of your evil behavior. But now he has reconciled you by Christ's physical body through death to present you holy in his sight, without blemish and free from accusation.
COLOSSIANS 1:21-22 NIV

Redemption

"Therefore tell the Israelites: I am Yahweh, and I will deliver you from the forced labor of the Egyptians and free you from slavery to them. I will redeem you with an outstretched arm and great acts of judgment. I will take you as My people, and I will be your God. You will know that I am Yahweh your God, who delivered you from the forced labor of the Egyptians. I will bring you to the land that I swore, to give to Abraham, Isaac, and Jacob, and I will give it to you as a possession. I am Yahweh."

EXODUS 6:6-8 HCSB

"It was not because you were more in number than any other people that the LORD set his love on you and chose you, for you were the fewest of all peoples, but it is because the LORD loves you and is keeping the oath that he swore to your fathers, that the LORD has brought you out with a mighty hand and redeemed you from the house of slavery, from the hand of Pharaoh king of Egypt."

DEUTERONOMY 7:7-8 ESV

He redeems you from hell—saves your life!

PSALM 103:4 MSG

Now this is what the LORD says—
the One who created you, Jacob,
and the One who formed you, Israel—
"Do not fear, for I have redeemed you;
I have called you by your name; you are Mine."

ISAIAH 43:1 HCSB

He gave Himself for us to redeem us from all lawlessness and to cleanse for Himself a people for His own possession, eager to do good works.

TITUS 2:14 HCSB

So Christ has now become the High Priest over all the good things that have come. He has entered that greater, more perfect Tabernacle in heaven, which was not made by human hands and is not part of this created world. With his own blood—not the blood of goats and calves—he entered the Most Holy Place once for all time and secured our redemption forever.

HEBREWS 9:11-12 NLT

You are worthy to take the scroll
and to open its seals,
because You were slaughtered,
and You redeemed people
for God by Your blood
from every tribe and language
and people and nation.
You made them a kingdom
and priests to our God,
and they will reign on the earth.

REVELATION 5:9-10 HCSB

Refuge

He is a shield for all those who take refuge in him.
2 SAMUEL 22:31 HCSB

"This God is my strong refuge
and has made my way blameless."
2 SAMUEL 22:33 ESV

Blessed are all who take refuge in him.
PSALM 2:12 NIV

The LORD is a refuge for the oppressed,
a refuge in times of trouble.
PSALM 9:9 HCSB

He shields all who take refuge in him.
PSALM 18:30 NIV

The LORD is their strength,
And He is the saving refuge of His anointed.
PSALM 28:8 NKJV

You're my cave to hide in,
my cliff to climb.
Be my safe leader,
be my true mountain guide.
PSALM 31:3 MSG

GOD'S my island hideaway,
keeps danger far from the shore,
throws garlands of hosannas around my neck.
PSALM 32:7 MSG

Taste and see that the LORD is good;
blessed is the one who takes refuge in him.
>   PSALM 34:8 NIV

O God, how extravagant is your cherishing love!
All mankind can find a hiding place,
under the shadow of your wings.
>   PSALM 36:7 TPT

But I will sing of your strength,
in the morning I will sing of your love;
for you are my fortress,
my refuge in times of trouble.
>   PSALM 59:16 NIV

From the ends of the earth,
I cry to you for help
when my heart is overwhelmed.
Lead me to the towering rock of safety,
for you are my safe refuge,
a fortress where my enemies cannot reach me.
>   PSALM 61:2-3 NLT

In God is my salvation and my glory;
The rock of my strength,
And my refuge, is in God.
>   PSALM 62:7 NKJV

This I declare about the LORD:
He alone is my refuge, my place of safety;
he is my God, and I trust him.
>   PSALM 91:2 NLT

Far better to take refuge in GOD
than trust in people;
Far better to take refuge in GOD
than trust in celebrities.
   PSALM 118:8-9 MSG

He is my shield, and I take refuge in Him;
He subdues my people under me.
   PSALM 144:2 HCSB

The way of the LORD is a refuge for the blameless,
but it is the ruin of those who do evil.
   PROVERBS 10:29 NIV

"When you cry out for help,
let your collection of idols save you!
The wind will carry all of them off,
a mere breath will blow them away.
But whoever takes refuge in me
will inherit the land
and possess my holy mountain."
   ISAIAH 57:13 NIV

"The LORD's voice will roar from Zion
and thunder from Jerusalem,
and the heavens and the earth will shake.
But the LORD will be a refuge for his people,
a strong fortress for the people of Israel."
   JOEL 3:16 NLT

Relationship

So in Christ Jesus you are all children of God through faith.
GALATIANS 3:26 NIV

Although you were once distant and far away from God, now you have been brought delightfully close to him through the sacred blood of Jesus—you have actually been united to Christ!
EPHESIANS 2:13 TPT

That's plain enough, isn't it? You're no longer wandering exiles. This kingdom of faith is now your home country. You're no longer strangers or outsiders. You belong here, with as much right to the name Christian as anyone. God is building a home. He's using us all—irrespective of how we got here—in what he is building.
EPHESIANS 2:19 MSG

Through these he has given us his very great and precious promises, so that through them you may participate in the divine nature, having escaped the corruption in the world caused by evil desires.
2 PETER 1:4 NIV

Religion

"For I desire mercy, not sacrifice,
and acknowledgment of God rather than burnt offerings."

HOSEA 6:6 NIV

"I hate, I despise your feast days,
And I do not savor your sacred assemblies.
Though you offer Me burnt offerings and your grain offerings,
I will not accept them,
Nor will I regard your fattened peace offerings."

AMOS 5:21-22 NKJV

And he answered, "If you had a sheep that fell into a well on the Sabbath, wouldn't you work to pull it out? Of course you would. And how much more valuable is a person than a sheep! Yes, the law permits a person to do good on the Sabbath."

MATTHEW 12:11-12 NLT

And he said to them, "The Sabbath was made for man, not man for the Sabbath. So the Son of Man is lord even of the Sabbath."

MARK 2:27-28 ESV

I know and am convinced on the authority of the Lord Jesus that no food, in and of itself, is wrong to eat. But if someone believes it is wrong, then for that person it is wrong.

ROMANS 14:14 NLT

"Do not handle! Do not taste! Do not touch!" These rules, which have to do with things that are all destined to perish with use, are based on merely human commands and teachings. Such regulations indeed have an appearance of wisdom, with their self-imposed worship, their false humility and their harsh treatment of the body, but they lack any value in restraining sensual indulgence.

COLOSSIANS 2:21-23 NIV

Pure and genuine religion in the sight of God the Father means caring for orphans and widows in their distress and refusing to let the world corrupt you.

JAMES 1:27 NLT

Remembrance

So when God destroyed the cities of the plain, he remembered Abraham, and he brought Lot out of the catastrophe that overthrew the cities where Lot had lived.
GENESIS 19:29 NIV

The LORD remembers us and will bless us.
He will bless the house of Israel;
He will bless the house of Aaron;
PSALM 115:12 HCSB

"For I will bring them from the north
and from the distant corners of the earth.
I will not forget the blind and lame,
the expectant mothers and women in labor.
A great company will return!"
JEREMIAH 31:8 NLT

"When my life was fainting away,
I remembered the LORD,
and my prayer came to you,
into your holy temple."
JONAH 2:7 ESV

Renewal

The LORD your God will change your heart and the hearts of all your descendants, so that you will love him with all your heart and soul and so you may live!

DEUTERONOMY 30:6 NLT

Then the women said to Naomi, "Praise the LORD, who has not left you without a family redeemer today. May his name become well known in Israel. He will renew your life and sustain you in your old age. Indeed, your daughter-in-law, who loves you and is better to you than seven sons, has given birth to him."

RUTH 4:14-15 HCSB

"The surviving remnant of the house of Israel will again take root downward and bear fruit upward. For a remnant will go out from Jerusalem and survivors, from Mount Zion. The zeal of the LORD of Hosts will accomplish this."

2 KINGS 19:30-31 NLT

He will once again fill your mouth with laughter
and your lips with shouts of joy.

JOB 8:21 NLT

The ways of wisdom are sweet,
always drawing you into the place of wholeness.
Seeking for her brings the discovery of untold blessings,
for she is the healing tree of life to those who taste her fruits.

PROVERBS 3:17-18 TPT

"We will replace the broken bricks of our ruins with finished stone,
and replant the felled sycamore-fig trees with cedars."

ISAIAH 9:10 NLT

And on that Day also, what's left of Israel, the ragtag survivors of Jacob, will no longer be fascinated by abusive, battering Assyria. They'll lean on GOD, The Holy—yes, truly. The ragtag remnant—what's left of Jacob—will come back to the Strong God.

ISAIAH 10:20-21 MSG

The LORD will strike Egypt, and then he will bring healing. For the Egyptians will turn to the LORD, and he will listen to their pleas and heal them.
ISAIAH 19:22 NLT

They will rebuild the ancient ruins
and restore the places long devastated;
they will renew the ruined cities
that have been devastated for generations.
ISAIAH 61:4 NIV

"For I will create a new heaven and a new earth;
the past events will not be remembered or come to mind."
ISAIAH 65:17 HCSB

Thus says the LORD of hosts, the God of Israel: "Take these deeds, both this purchase deed which is sealed and this deed which is open, and put them in an earthen vessel, that they may last many days." For thus says the LORD of hosts, the God of Israel: "Houses and fields and vineyards shall be possessed again in this land."
JEREMIAH 32:14-15 NKJV

This is what the LORD says: "You say about this place, 'It is a desolate waste, without people or animals.' Yet in the towns of Judah and the streets of Jerusalem that are deserted, inhabited by neither people nor animals, there will be heard once more."
JEREMIAH 33:10 NIV

"I'll give you a new heart. I'll put a new spirit in you. I'll cut out your stone heart and replace it with a red-blooded, firm-muscled heart. Then you'll obey my statutes and be careful to obey my commands. You'll be my people! I'll be your God!"
EZEKIEL 11:19-20 MSG

"They will say, 'This land that was laid waste has become like the garden of Eden; the cities that were lying in ruins, desolate and destroyed, are now fortified and inhabited.' Then the nations around you that remain will know that I the LORD have rebuilt what was destroyed and have replanted what was desolate. I the LORD have spoken, and I will do it."
EZEKIEL 36:35-36 NIV

"For someday the people will follow me.
I, the LORD, will roar like a lion.
And when I roar,
my people will return trembling from the west.
Like a flock of birds, they will come from Egypt.
Trembling like doves, they will return from Assyria.
And I will bring them home again,"
says the LORD.
>   HOSEA 11:10-11 NLT

"I will be to Israel
like a refreshing dew from heaven.
Israel will blossom like the lily;
it will send roots deep into the soil
like the cedars in Lebanon.
Its branches will spread out like beautiful olive trees,
as fragrant as the cedars of Lebanon.
My people will again live under my shade.
They will flourish like grain and blossom like grapevines.
They will be as fragrant as the wines of Lebanon."
>   HOSEA 14:5 NLT

"In that day," declares the LORD,
"I will gather the lame;
I will assemble the exiles
and those I have brought to grief.
I will make the lame my remnant,
those driven away a strong nation."
>   MICAH 4:6-7 NIV

"Those who are left will be the lowly and humble,
for it is they who trust in the name of the LORD.
The remnant of Israel will do no wrong;
they will never tell lies or deceive one another.
They will eat and sleep in safety,
and no one will make them afraid."
>   ZEPHANIAH 3:12-13 NLT

Thus says the LORD of hosts:
"Old men and old women shall again sit
In the streets of Jerusalem,
Each one with his staff in his hand
Because of great age.
The streets of the city
Shall be full of boys and girls
Playing in its streets."
ZECHARIAH 8:4-5 NKJV

Therefore we do not give up. Even though our outer person is being destroyed, our inner person is being renewed day by day.
2 CORINTHIANS 4:16 HCSB

He who was seated on the throne said, "I am making everything new!" Then he said, "Write this down, for these words are trustworthy and true."
REVELATION 21:5 NIV

No longer will there be a curse upon anything. For the throne of God and of the Lamb will be there, and his servants will worship him. And they will see his face, and his name will be written on their foreheads. And there will be no night there—no need for lamps or sun—for the Lord God will shine on them. And they will reign forever and ever.
REVELATION 22:3-4 NLT

Repentance

"Because you took seriously the doom of judgment I spoke against this place and people, and because you responded in humble repentance, tearing your robe in dismay and weeping before me, I'm taking you seriously."

2 KINGS 22:19 MSG

When GOD saw that they were humbly repentant, the word of GOD came to Shemaiah: "Because they are humble, I'll not destroy them—I'll give them a break; I won't use Shishak to express my wrath against Jerusalem."

2 CHRONICLES 12:7 MSG

As for you, if you redirect your heart
and lift up your hands to Him in prayer—
if there is iniquity in your hand, remove it,
and don't allow injustice to dwell in your tents—
then you will hold your head high, free from fault.
You will be firmly established and unafraid.

JOB 11:13-15 HCSB

When he prays to God,
he will be accepted.
And God will receive him with joy
and restore him to good standing.

JOB 33:26 NLT

The Lord is so close to all whose hearts are crushed by pain,
and he is always ready to restore the repentant one.

PSALM 34:18 TPT

The sacrifice you desire is a broken spirit.
You will not reject a broken and repentant heart, O God.

PSALM 51:17 NLT

Repent at my rebuke!
Then I will pour out my thoughts to you,
I will make known to you my teachings.
> PROVERBS 1:23 NIV

This is what the Sovereign LORD, the Holy One of Israel, says:
"In repentance and rest is your salvation,
in quietness and trust is your strength,
but you would have none of it."
> ISAIAH 30:15 NIV

"Return, you faithless children.
I will heal your unfaithfulness."
> JEREMIAH 3:22 HCSB

Therefore this is what the LORD says:
"If you repent, I will restore you
that you may serve me;
if you utter worthy, not worthless, words,
you will be my spokesman.
Let this people turn to you,
but you must not turn to them."
> JEREMIAH 15:19 NIV

"For I take no pleasure in the death of anyone," declares the Sovereign LORD. "Repent and live!"
> EZEKIEL 18:32 NIV

"Tell them: As I live"—the declaration of the Lord GOD—"I take no pleasure in the death of the wicked, but rather that the wicked person should turn from his way and live. Repent, repent of your evil ways! Why will you die, house of Israel?"
> EZEKIEL 33:11 HCSB

"Therefore say to them, 'Thus declares the LORD of hosts: "Return to me," says the LORD of hosts, "and I will return to you," says the LORD of hosts.
> ZECHARIAH 1:3 ESV

"Yet from the days of your fathers
You have gone away from My ordinances
And have not kept them.
Return to Me, and I will return to you,"
Says the LORD of hosts.
MALACHI 3:7 NKJV

From that time on Jesus began to preach, "Repent, for the kingdom of heaven has come near."
MATTHEW 4:17 NIV

"Imagine a woman who has ten coins and loses one. Won't she light a lamp and scour the house, looking in every nook and cranny until she finds it? And when she finds it you can be sure she'll call her friends and neighbors: 'Celebrate with me! I found my lost coin!' Count on it—that's the kind of party God's angels throw every time one lost soul turns to God."
LUKE 15:8-10 MSG

For godly sorrow produces repentance leading to salvation, not to be regretted; but the sorrow of the world produces death.
2 CORINTHIANS 7:10 NKJV

"Remember, therefore, what you have received and heard; hold it fast, and repent. But if you do not wake up, I will come like a thief, and you will not know at what time I will come to you."
REVELATION 3:3 NIV

Rescue

The LORD said, "I have indeed seen the misery of my people in Egypt. I have heard them crying out because of their slave drivers, and I am concerned about their suffering. So I have come down to rescue them from the hand of the Egyptians and to bring them up out of that land into a good and spacious land, a land flowing with milk and honey—the home of the Canaanites, Hittites, Amorites, Perizzites, Hivites and Jebusites. And now the cry of the Israelites has reached me, and I have seen the way the Egyptians are oppressing them. So now, go. I am sending you to Pharaoh to bring my people the Israelites out of Egypt."

EXODUS 3:7-10 NIV

"The LORD who rescued me from the paw of the lion and the paw of the bear will rescue me from the hand of this Philistine."

1 SAMUEL 17:37 NIV

"I will call upon the LORD, who is worthy to be praised;
So shall I be saved from my enemies."

2 SAMUEL 22:4 NKJV

He saves the needy from the sword,
From the mouth of the mighty,
And from their hand.

JOB 5:15 NKJV

From six disasters he will rescue you;
even in the seventh, he will keep you from evil.

JOB 5:19 NLT

In famine he will redeem you from death,
and in war from the power of the sword.

JOB 5:20 ESV

But the Lord says, "Now I will arise! I will defend the poor,
those who were plundered, the oppressed,
and the needy who groan for help.
I will arise to rescue and protect them!"
  PSALM 12:5 TPT

You rescue the humble,
but you humiliate the proud.
  PSALM 18:27 NLT

He rescues [those who fear the Lord] from death
and keeps them alive in times of famine.
  PSALM 33:19 NLT

Yet when holy lovers of God
cry out to him with all their hearts,
the Lord will hear them and come
to rescue them from all their troubles.
  PSALM 34:17 TPT

Then call on me when you are in trouble,
and I will rescue you,
and you will give me glory.
  PSALM 50:15 NLT

Our God is a mighty God who saves us over and over!
For the Lord, Yahweh, rescues us
from the ways of death many times.
  PSALM 68:20 TPT

[The needy] will be rescued from tyranny and torture,
for their lifeblood is precious in his eyes.
  PSALM 72:14 TPT

For he stands at the right hand of the needy,
to save their lives from those who would condemn them.
  PSALM 109:30-31 NIV

He picks up the poor from out of the dirt,
rescues the wretched who've been thrown out with the trash,
Seats them among the honored guests,
a place of honor among the brightest and best.
PSALM 113:7-8 MSG

Wisdom will save you from evil people,
from those whose words are twisted.
PROVERBS 2:12 NLT

In that day there will be an altar to the LORD in the heart of Egypt, and there will be a monument to the LORD at its border. It will be a sign and a witness that the LORD of Heaven's Armies is worshiped in the land of Egypt. When the people cry to the LORD for help against those who oppress them, he will send them a savior who will rescue them.
ISAIAH 19:19-20 NLT

For this is what the LORD says:
"Even the captives of a mighty man will be taken,
and the prey of a tyrant will be delivered;
I will contend with the one who contends with you,
and I will save your children."
ISAIAH 49:25 HCSB

Sing to the LORD!
Praise the LORD!
For though I was poor and needy,
he rescued me from my oppressors.
JEREMIAH 20:13 NLT

"So then, the days are coming," declares the LORD, "when people will no longer say, 'As surely as the LORD lives, who brought the Israelites up out of Egypt,' but they will say, 'As surely as the LORD lives, who brought the descendants of Israel up out of the land of the north and out of all the countries where he had banished them.' Then they will live in their own land."
JEREMIAH 23:7-8 NIV

"I will be found by you," declares the LORD, "and will bring you back from captivity. I will gather you from all the nations and places where I have banished you," declares the LORD, "and will bring you back to the place from which I carried you into exile."
JEREMIAH 29:14 NIV

"I will tend My flock and let them lie down." This is the declaration of the Lord GOD. "I will seek the lost, bring back the strays, bandage the injured, and strengthen the weak, but I will destroy the fat and the strong. I will shepherd them with justice."
EZEKIEL 34:15-16 HCSB

"If you throw us in the fire, the God we serve can rescue us from your roaring furnace and anything else you might cook up, O king. But even if he doesn't, it wouldn't make a bit of difference, O king. We still wouldn't serve your gods or worship the gold statue you set up."
DANIEL 3:17 MSG

"At that time Michael, the archangel who stands guard over your nation, will arise. Then there will be a time of anguish greater than any since nations first came into existence. But at that time every one of your people whose name is written in the book will be rescued."
DANIEL 12:1 NLT

"Those who have been rescued will go up to Mount Zion in Jerusalem
to rule over the mountains of Edom.
And the LORD himself will be king!"
OBADIAH 21 NLT

"Shepherd-rule will extend as far as needed,
to Assyria and all other Nimrod-bullies.
Our shepherd-ruler will save us from old or new enemies,
from anyone who invades or violates our land."
MICAH 5:6 MSG

"I will remove from you
all who mourn over the loss of your appointed festivals,
which is a burden and reproach for you.
At that time I will deal
with all who oppressed you.
I will rescue the lame;
I will gather the exiles.
I will give them praise and honor
in every land where they have suffered shame."
ZEPHANIAH 3:18-19 NIV

"Among the other nations, Judah and Israel became symbols of a cursed nation. But no longer! Now I will rescue you and make you both a symbol and a source of blessing. So don't be afraid. Be strong, and get on with rebuilding the Temple!"
ZECHARIAH 8:13 NLT

Their GOD will save the day. He'll rescue them.
They'll become like sheep, gentle and soft,
Or like gemstones in a crown,
catching all the colors of the sun.
Then how they'll shine! shimmer! glow!
the young men robust, the young women lovely!
ZECHARIAH 9:16-17 MSG

"Look at it this way. If someone has a hundred sheep and one of them wanders off, doesn't he leave the ninety-nine and go after the one? And if he finds it, doesn't he make far more over it than over the ninety-nine who stay put? Your Father in heaven feels the same way. He doesn't want to lose even one of these simple believers."
MATTHEW 18:12-14 MSG

"He has rescued us from the power of our enemies!
This fulfills the sacred oath he made with our father Abraham.
Now we can boldly worship God with holy lives,
living in purity as priests in his presence every day!"
LUKE 1:73-75 TPT

Jesus continued, "In the same way, there will be a glorious celebration in heaven over the rescue of one lost sinner who repents, comes back home, and returns to the fold—more so than for all the righteous people who never strayed away."
LUKE 15:7 TPT

"God did not send his Son into the world to judge and condemn the world, but to be its Savior and rescue it!"
JOHN 3:17 TPT

What a wretched man I am! Who will rescue me from this dying body? I thank God through Jesus Christ our Lord! So then, with my mind I myself am a slave to the law of God, but with my flesh, to the law of sin.
ROMANS 7:24-25 HCSB

So then faith eliminates the distinction between Jew and non-Jew, for he is the same Lord Jehovah for all people. And he has enough treasures to lavish generously upon all who call on him. And it's true:
"Everyone who calls on the name of the Lord Yahweh
will be rescued and experience new life."
ROMANS 10:12-13 TPT

May God our Father and the Lord Jesus Christ give you grace and peace. Jesus gave his life for our sins, just as God our Father planned, in order to rescue us from this evil world in which we live.
GALATIANS 1:3-4 NLT

He has rescued us from the domain of darkness and transferred us into the kingdom of the Son He loves.
COLOSSIANS 1:13 HCSB

If that animal blood and the other rituals of purification were effective in cleaning up certain matters of our religion and behavior, think how much more the blood of Christ cleans up our whole lives, inside and out.
HEBREWS 9:13-14 MSG

My dear friends, if you know people who have wandered off from God's truth, don't write them off. Go after them. Get them back and you will have rescued precious lives from destruction and prevented an epidemic of wandering away from God.
JAMES 5:19-20 MSG

For you were like sheep going astray, but have now returned to the Shepherd and Overseer of your souls.
1 PETER 2:25 NKJV

So God knows how to rescue the godly from evil trials. And he knows how to hold the feet of the wicked to the fire until Judgment Day.
2 PETER 2:9 MSG

Rest

"Therefore the children of Israel shall keep the Sabbath, to observe the Sabbath throughout their generations as a perpetual covenant. It is a sign between Me and the children of Israel forever; for in six days the LORD made the heavens and the earth, and on the seventh day He rested and was refreshed."

EXODUS 31:16–17 NKJV

Remember what Moses the LORD's servant commanded you when he said, "The LORD your God will give you rest, and He will give you this land."

JOSHUA 1:13 HCSB

And the LORD gave them rest on every side just as he had sworn to their fathers. Not one of all their enemies had withstood them, for the LORD had given all their enemies into their hands.

JOSHUA 21:44 ESV

"Blessed be the LORD, who has given rest to His people Israel, according to all that He promised. There has not failed one word of all His good promise, which He promised through His servant Moses."

1 KINGS 8:56 NKJV

Those who live in the shelter of the Most High
will find rest in the shadow of the Almighty.

PSALM 91:1 NLT

You give them relief from troubled times
until a pit is dug to capture the wicked.

PSALM 94:13 NLT

This is what the LORD says:
"Stand at the crossroads and look;
ask for the ancient paths,
ask where the good way is, and walk in it,
and you will find rest for your souls."

JEREMIAH 6:16 NIV

"In that day," says the LORD, "I will be the God of all the families of Israel, and they will be my people. This is what the LORD says:
"Those who survive the coming destruction
will find blessings even in the barren land,
for I will give rest to the people of Israel."
JEREMIAH 31:1 NLT

Thus says the LORD of hosts:
"The children of Israel were oppressed,
Along with the children of Judah;
All who took them captive have held them fast;
They have refused to let them go.
Their Redeemer is strong;
The LORD of hosts is His name.
He will thoroughly plead their case,
That He may give rest to the land,
And disquiet the inhabitants of Babylon."
JEREMIAH 50:33-34 NKJV

For as long, then, as that promise of resting in him pulls us on to God's goal for us, we need to be careful that we're not disqualified.
HEBREWS 4:1 MSG

Restoration

When all these blessings and curses I have set before you come on you and you take them to heart wherever the LORD your God disperses you among the nations, and when you and your children return to the LORD your God and obey him with all your heart and with all your soul according to everything I command you today, then the LORD your God will restore your fortunes a and have compassion on you and gather you again from all the nations where he scattered you.
DEUTERONOMY 30:1-3 NIV

No matter how far away you end up, GOD, your God, will get you out of there and bring you back to the land your ancestors once possessed. It will be yours again. He will give you a good life and make you more numerous than your ancestors.
DEUTERONOMY 30:3-5 MSG

Then the LORD said to Joshua, "Today I have rolled away the shame of your slavery in Egypt." So that place has been called Gilgal to this day.
JOSHUA 5:9 NLT

But now, for a brief moment, the LORD our God has been gracious in leaving us a remnant and giving us a firm place in his sanctuary, and so our God gives light to our eyes and a little relief in our bondage. Though we are slaves, our God has not forsaken us in our bondage. He has shown us kindness in the sight of the kings of Persia: He has granted us new life to rebuild the house of our God and repair its ruins, and he has given us a wall of protection in Judah and Jerusalem.
EZRA 9:8-9 NIV

"But if you earnestly seek God
and ask the Almighty for mercy,
if you are pure and upright,
then He will move even now on your behalf
and restore the home where your righteousness dwells.
Then, even if your beginnings were modest,
your final days will be full of prosperity."
JOB 8:5-7 HCSB

"If you return to the Almighty, you will be restored—
so clean up your life.
If you give up your lust for money
and throw your precious gold into the river,
the Almighty himself will be your treasure.
He will be your precious silver!"
    JOB 22:23-27 NLT

You will restore me to even greater honor
and comfort me once again.
    PSALM 71:21 NLT

"I'll give you the back of my hand,
purge the junk from your life, clean you up.
I'll set honest judges and wise counselors among you
just like it was back in the beginning."
    ISAIAH 1:25-26 MSG

And that's when GOD'S Branch will sprout green and lush. The produce of the country will give Israel's survivors something to be proud of again. Oh, they'll hold their heads high! Everyone left behind in Zion, all the discards and rejects in Jerusalem, will be reclassified as "holy"—alive and therefore precious.
    ISAIAH 4:2-3 MSG

The Lord GOD will wipe away the tears
from every face
and remove His people's disgrace
from the whole earth,
for the LORD has spoken.
    ISAIAH 25:8 HCSB

"Afflicted city, lashed by storms and not comforted,
I will rebuild you with stones of turquoise,
your foundations with lapis lazuli.
I will make your battlements of rubies,
your gates of sparkling jewels,
and all your walls of precious stones."
    ISAIAH 54:11-12 NIV

The high and lofty one who lives in eternity,
the Holy One, says this:
"I live in the high and holy place
with those whose spirits are contrite and humble.
I restore the crushed spirit of the humble
and revive the courage of those with repentant hearts."
ISAIAH 57:15 NLT

For behold, the days are coming, says the LORD, "that I will bring back from captivity My people Israel and Judah," says the LORD. "And I will cause them to return to the land that I gave to their fathers, and they shall possess it."
JEREMIAH 30:3 NKJV

"I will rebuild you, my virgin Israel.
You will again be happy
and dance merrily with your tambourines.
Again you will plant your vineyards on the mountains of Samaria
and eat from your own gardens there."
JEREMIAH 31:4-5 NLT

"The days are coming," declares the LORD, "when this city will be rebuilt for me from the Tower of Hananel to the Corner Gate. The measuring line will stretch from there straight to the hill of Gareb and then turn to Goah. The whole valley where dead bodies and ashes are thrown, and all the terraces out to the Kidron Valley on the east as far as the corner of the Horse Gate, will be holy to the LORD. The city will never again be uprooted or demolished."
JEREMIAH 31:38-40 NIV

"Once more fields will be bought in this land of which you say, 'It is a desolate waste, without people or animals, for it has been given into the hands of the Babylonians.' Fields will be bought for silver, and deeds will be signed, sealed and witnessed in the territory of Benjamin, in the villages around Jerusalem, in the towns of Judah and in the towns of the hill country, of the western foothills and of the Negev, because I will restored their fortunes, declares the LORD."
JEREMIAH 32:43-44 NIV

"But do not be afraid, Jacob, my servant;
do not be dismayed, Israel.
For I will bring you home again from distant lands,
and your children will return from their exile.
Israel will return to a life of peace and quiet,
and no one will terrorize them."
JEREMIAH 46:27 NLT

"But the time is coming," says the LORD, "when people who are taking an oath will no longer say, 'As surely as the LORD lives, who rescued the people of Israel from the land of Egypt.' Instead, they will say, 'As surely as the LORD lives, who brought the people of Israel back to their own land from the land of the north and from all the countries to which he had exiled them.' For I will bring them back to this land that I gave their ancestors."
JEREMIAH 16:14-15 NLT

The punishment of your iniquity, O daughter of Zion, is accomplished;
he will keep you in exile no longer;
LAMENTATIONS 4:22 ESV

"When I bring you from the peoples and gather you from the countries where you have been scattered, I will accept you as a pleasing aroma. And I will demonstrate My holiness through you in the sight of the nations. When I lead you into the land of Israel, the land I swore to give your fathers, you will know that I am Yahweh."
EZEKIEL 20:41-42 HCSB

This is what the Sovereign LORD says: "The people of Israel will again live in their own land, the land I gave my servant Jacob. For I will gather them from the distant lands where I have scattered them. I will reveal to the nations of the world my holiness among my people."
EZEKIEL 28:25 NLT

"I will also sprinkle clean water on you, and you will be clean. I will cleanse you from all your impurities and all your idols."
EZEKIEL 36:25 HCSB

This is what the Sovereign LORD says: "When I cleanse you from your sins, I will repopulate your cities, and the ruins will be rebuilt. The fields that used to lie empty and desolate in plain view of everyone will again be farmed."

EZEKIEL 36:33-34 NLT

This is what the Sovereign LORD says: "Look! I am going to put breath into you and make you live again! I will put flesh and muscles on you and cover you with skin. I will put breath into you, and you will come to life. Then you will know that I am the LORD."

EZEKIEL 37:5-6 NLT

"Therefore, prophesy. Tell them, 'GOD, the Master, says: I'll dig up your graves and bring you out alive—O my people! Then I'll take you straight to the land of Israel. When I dig up graves and bring you out as my people, you'll realize that I am GOD. I'll breathe my life into you and you'll live. Then I'll lead you straight back to your land and you'll realize that I am GOD. I've said it and I'll do it. GOD'S Decree.'"

EZEKIEL 37:12-14 MSG

Yet the time will come when Israel's people will be like the sands of the seashore—too many to count! Then, at the place where they were told, "You are not my people," it will be said, "You are children of the living God." Then the people of Judah and Israel will unite together. They will choose one leader for themselves, and they will return from exile together. What a day that will be—the day of Jezreel—when God will again plant his people in his land.

HOSEA 1:10-11 NLT

Although they have sold themselves among the nations,
I will now gather them together.
They will begin to waste away
under the oppression of the mighty king.

HOSEA 8:10 NIV

"So I will restore to you the years that the swarming locust has eaten,
The crawling locust,
The consuming locust,
And the chewing locust,
My great army which I sent among you."

JOEL 2:25 NKJV

"In that day I will restore the fallen house of David.
I will repair its damaged walls.
From the ruins I will rebuild it
and restore its former glory.
And Israel will possess what is left of Edom
and all the nations I have called to be mine."
    AMOS 9:11-12 NLT

"I will bring back the captives of My people Israel;
They shall build the waste cities and inhabit them;
They shall plant vineyards and drink wine from them;
They shall also make gardens and eat fruit from them.
I will plant them in their land,
And no longer shall they be pulled up
From the land I have given them,"
Says the LORD your God.
    AMOS 9:13-15 NKJV

I will indeed gather all of you, Jacob;
I will collect the remnant of Israel.
I will bring them together like sheep in a pen,
like a flock in the middle of its fold.
It will be noisy with people.
    MICAH 2:12 HCSB

The LORD will restore the splendor of Jacob
like the splendor of Israel,
though destroyers have laid them waste
and have ruined their vines.
    NAHUM 2:2 NIV

"Well, if that's what you want, stick around."
GOD'S Decree.
"Your day in court is coming,
but remember I'll be there to bring evidence.
I'll bring all the nations to the courtroom,
round up all the kingdoms,
And let them feel the brunt of my anger,
my raging wrath.
My zeal is a fire
that will purge and purify the earth."
    ZEPHANIAH 3:8 MSG

"At that time I will gather you;
at that time I will bring you home.
I will give you honor and praise
among all the peoples of the earth
when I restore your fortunes
before your very eyes,"
says the LORD.
    ZEPHANIAH 3:20 NIV

Return to a stronghold,
you prisoners who have hope;
today I declare that I will restore double to you.
    ZECHARIAH 9:12 HCSB

"I will strengthen Judah
and save the tribes of Joseph.
I will restore them
because I have compassion on them.
They will be as though
I had not rejected them,
for I am the LORD their God
and I will answer them."
    ZECHARIAH 10:6 NIV

"And the prophet's words are fulfilled:
'After these things I will return to you
and raise up the tabernacle of David that has fallen into ruin.
I will restore and rebuild what David experienced
so that all of humanity will be able to encounter the Lord
including the Gentiles whom I have called
to be my very own,' says the Lord.
'For I have made known my works from eternity!'"
ACTS 15:16-18 TPT

I saw the Holy City, the new Jerusalem, coming down out of heaven from God, prepared as a bride beautifully dressed for her husband. And I heard a loud voice from the throne saying, "Look! God's dwelling place is now among the people, and he will dwell with them. They will be his people, and God himself will be with them and be their God. He will wipe every tear from their eyes. There will be no more death or mourning or crying or pain, for the old order of things has passed away."
REVELATION 21:2-4 NIV

Resurrection

"For just as the Father raises the dead and gives them life, even so the Son gives life to whom he is pleased to give it."
JOHN 5:21 NIV

"For I have come down from heaven not to do my will but to do the will of him who sent me. And this is the will of him who sent me, that I shall lose none of all those he has given me, but raise them up at the last day."
JOHN 6:38-39 NIV

"God raised [Jesus] from the dead so that he will never be subject to decay. As God has said,
'I will give you the holy and sure blessings promised to David.'"
ACTS 13:34 NIV

If we are permanently grafted into him to experience a death like his, then we are permanently grafted into him to experience a resurrection like his and the new life that it imparts.
ROMANS 6:5 TPT

If we get included in Christ's sin-conquering death, we also get included in his life-saving resurrection.
ROMANS 6:8 MSG

For as in Adam all die, so also in Christ all will be made alive. But each in his own order: Christ, the firstfruits; afterward, at His coming, those who belong to Christ.
1 CORINTHIANS 15:22-23 HCSB

Our earthly bodies are planted in the ground when we die, but they will be raised to live forever. Our bodies are buried in brokenness, but they will be raised in glory. They are buried in weakness, but they will be raised in strength. They are buried as natural human bodies, but they will be raised as spiritual bodies. For just as there are natural bodies, there are also spiritual bodies.
1 CORINTHIANS 15:42-44 NLT

Listen, I tell you a mystery: We will not all sleep, but we will all be changed—in a flash, in the twinkling of an eye, at the last trumpet. For the trumpet will sound, the dead will be raised imperishable, and we will be changed.

1 CORINTHIANS 15:51-52 NIV

And what we believe is that the One who raised up the Master Jesus will just as certainly raise us up with you, alive.

2 CORINTHIANS 4:14 MSG

I want to know Christ and experience the mighty power that raised him from the dead. I want to suffer with him, sharing in his death, so that one way or another I will experience the resurrection from the dead!

PHILIPPIANS 3:10-11 NLT

We tell you this directly from the Lord: We who are still living when the Lord returns will not meet him ahead of those who have died. For the Lord himself will come down from heaven with a commanding shout, with the voice of the archangel, and with the trumpet call of God. First, the Christians who have died will rise from their graves.

1 THESSALONIANS 4:15-16 NLT

You can trust these words: If we were joined with him in his death, then we are joined with him in his life!

2 TIMOTHY 2:11 TPT

Revelation

I will hear what God the LORD will speak,
For He will speak peace
To His people and to His saints;
But let them not turn back to folly.
>   PSALM 85:8 NKJV

Your word is a lamp to my feet
And a light to my path.
>   PSALM 119:105 NKJV

Tell them therefore, "Thus says the Lord GOD: 'I will lay this proverb to rest, and they shall no more use it as a proverb in Israel." But say to them, "The days are at hand, and the fulfillment of every vision. For no more shall there be any false vision or flattering divination within the house of Israel. For I am the LORD. I speak, and the word which I speak will come to pass; it will no more be postponed; for in your days, O rebellious house, I will say the word and perform it," says the Lord GOD.
>   EZEKIEL 12:23-25 NKJV

He gives wisdom to the wise
and knowledge to the scholars.
He reveals deep and mysterious things
and knows what lies hidden in darkness,
though he is surrounded by light.
>   DANIEL 2:21-22 NLT

"You've been given insight into God's kingdom. You know how it works. Not everybody has this gift, this insight; it hasn't been given to them."
>   MATTHEW 13:11 MSG

"Lord, now You are letting Your servant depart in peace,
According to Your word;
For my eyes have seen Your salvation
Which You have prepared before the face of all peoples,
A light to bring revelation to the Gentiles,
And the glory of Your people Israel."

LUKE 2:29-32 NKJV

"You have been given a teachable heart to perceive the secret, hidden mysteries of God's kingdom realm. But to those who don't have a listening heart, my words are merely stories. Even though they have eyes, they are blind to the true meaning of what I say, and even though they listen, they won't receive full revelation."

LUKE 8:10 TPT

As it is written:
"What no eye has seen,
what no ear has heard,
and what no human mind has conceived"—
the things God has prepared for those who love him—
These are the things God has revealed to us by his Spirit.

1 CORINTHIANS 2:9-10 NIV

It started when God said, "Light up the darkness!" and our lives filled up with light as we saw and understood God in the face of Christ, all bright and beautiful.

2 CORINTHIANS 4:6 MSG

He made known to us the mystery of His will, according to His good pleasure that He planned in Him

EPHESIANS 1:9 HCSB

Throughout our history God has spoken to our ancestors by his prophets in many different ways. The revelation he gave them was only a fragment at a time, building one truth upon another. But to us living in these last days, God now speaks to us openly in the language of a Son, the appointed Heir of everything, for through him God created the panorama of all things and all time.

HEBREWS 1:1-2 TPT

For, "All people are like grass,
and all their glory is like the flowers of the field;
the grass withers and the flowers fall,
but the word of the Lord endures forever."
> 1 PETER 1:24-25 NIV

I testify to everyone who hears the prophetic words of this book: If anyone adds to them, God will add to him the plagues that are written in this book. And if anyone takes away from the words of this prophetic book, God will take away his share of the tree of life and the holy city, written in this book.
> REVELATION 22:18-19 HCSB

Reward

GOD reward you well for what you've done—and with a generous bonus besides from GOD, to whom you've come seeking protection under his wings.

RUTH 2:12 MSG

"For He repays man according to his work,
And makes man to find a reward according to his way."

JOB 34:11 NKJV

"All the love you need is found in me!"
And the Almighty said,
"The greater your passion for more—
the greater reward I will give you!"

PSALM 62:12 TPT

Wise living gets rewarded with honor;
stupid living gets the booby prize.

PROVERBS 3:35 MSG

"But I, the LORD, search all hearts
and examine secret motives.
I give all people their due rewards,
according to what their actions deserve."

JEREMIAH 17:10 NLT

"Watch out! Don't do your good deeds publicly, to be admired by others, for you will lose the reward from your Father in heaven."

MATTHEW 6:1 NLT

"So when you give to the needy, do not announce it with trumpets, as the hypocrites do in the synagogues and on the streets, to be honored by others. Truly I tell you, they have received their reward in full. But when you give to the needy, do not let your left hand know what your right hand is doing, so that your giving may be in secret. Then your Father, who sees what is done in secret, will reward you."

MATTHEW 6:2-4 NIV

"When you fast, do not look somber as the hypocrites do, for they disfigure their faces to show others they are fasting. Truly I tell you, they have received their reward in full. But when you fast, put oil on your head and wash your face, so that it will not be obvious to others that you are fasting, but only to your Father, who is unseen; and your Father, who sees what is done in secret, will reward you."

MATTHEW 6:17-18 NIV

"Anyone who welcomes you welcomes me, and anyone who welcomes me welcomes the one who sent me. Whoever welcomes a prophet as a prophet will receive a prophet's reward, and whoever welcomes a righteous person as a righteous person will receive a righteous person's reward. And if anyone gives even a cup of cold water to one of these little ones who is my disciple, truly I tell you, that person will certainly not lose their reward."

MATTHEW 10:40-42 NIV

"I assure you: In the Messianic Age, when the Son of Man sits on His glorious throne, you who have followed Me will also sit on 12 thrones, judging the 12 tribes of Israel. And everyone who has left houses, brothers or sisters, father or mother, children, or fields because of My name will receive 100 times more and will inherit eternal life."

MATTHEW 19:28-29 HCSB

Jesus said, "Mark my words, no one who sacrifices house, brothers, sisters, mother, father, children, land—whatever—because of me and the Message will lose out. They'll get it all back, but multiplied many times in homes, brothers, sisters, mothers, children, and land—but also in troubles. And then the bonus of eternal life!"

MARK 10:29-30 MSG

If anyone's work that he has built survives, he will receive a reward. If anyone's work is burned up, it will be lost, but he will be saved; yet it will be like an escape through fire.

1 CORINTHIANS 3:14-15 HCSB

And since you've been united to Jesus Christ the Messiah, you are now Abraham's "child" and inherit all the promises of the kingdom-realm!

GALATIANS 3:29 TPT

Shepherd God's flock among you, not overseeing out of compulsion but freely, according to God's will; not for the money but eagerly; not lording it over those entrusted to you, but being examples to the flock. And when the chief Shepherd appears, you will receive the unfading crown of glory.
> 1 PETER 5:2-4

"The nations were angry,
and your wrath has come.
The time has come for judging the dead,
and for rewarding your servants the prophets
and your people who revere your name,
both great and small—
and for destroying those who destroy the earth."
> REVELATION 11:18 NIV

"Look, I am coming soon, bringing my reward with me to repay all people according to their deeds."
> REVELATION 22:12 NLT

Righteousness

"The LORD rewards everyone for their righteousness and faithfulness. The LORD delivered you into my hands today, but I would not lay a hand on the LORD'S anointed."

1 SAMUEL 26:23 NIV

This gospel unveils a continual revelation of God's righteousness—a perfect righteousness given to us when we believe.

ROMANS 1:17 TPT

But now, independently of the law, the righteousness of God is tangible and brought to light through Jesus, the Anointed One. This is the righteousness that the Scriptures prophesied would come. It is God's righteousness made visible through the faithfulness of Jesus Christ. And now all who believe in him receive that gift. For there is really no difference between us.

ROMANS 3:21-22 TPT

He did not waver in unbelief at God's promise but was strengthened in his faith and gave glory to God, because he was fully convinced that what He had promised He was also able to perform. Therefore, it was credited to him for righteousness. Now it was credited to him was not written for Abraham alone, but also for us.

ROMANS 4:20-24 HCSB

And there is still much more to say of his unfailing love for us! For through the blood of Jesus we have heard the powerful declaration, "You are now righteous in my sight."

ROMANS 5:9 TPT

For just as through one man's disobedience the many were made sinners, so also through the one man's obedience the many will be made righteous.

ROMANS 5:19 HCSB

Having determined our destiny ahead of time, he called us to himself and transferred his perfect righteousness to everyone he called. And those who carry his perfect righteousness he co-glorified with his Son!

ROMANS 8:30 TPT

For Christ has already accomplished the purpose for which the law was given. As a result, all who believe in him are made right with God.
ROMANS 10:4 NLT

I no longer count on my own righteousness through obeying the law; rather, I become righteous through faith in Christ. For God's way of making us right with himself depends on faith.
PHILIPPIANS 3:9 NLT

I have fought an excellent fight. I have finished my full course and I've kept my heart full of faith. There's a crown of righteousness waiting in heaven for me, and I know that my Lord will reward me on his day of righteous judgment. And this crown is not only waiting for me, but for all who love and long for his unveiling.
2 TIMOTHY 4:7-8 TPT

But we are looking forward to the new heavens and new earth he has promised, a world filled with God's righteousness.
2 PETER 3:13 NLT

Sacrifice

Because of the sacrifice of Jesus, you will never experience the wrath of God.
ROMANS 5:9 TPT

For God made Christ, who never sinned, to be the offering for our sin, so that we could be made right with God through Christ.
2 CORINTHIANS 5:21 NLT

Unlike those other high priests, he does not need to offer sacrifices every day. They did this for their own sins first and then for the sins of the people. But Jesus did this once for all when he offered himself as the sacrifice for the people's sins.
HEBREWS 7:27 NLT

Yet every day priests still serve, ritually offering the same sacrifices again and again—sacrifices that can never take away sins' guilt. But when this Priest had offered the one supreme sacrifice for sins for all time he sat down on a throne at the right hand of God, waiting until all his whispering enemies are subdued and turn into his footstool. And by his one perfect sacrifice he made us perfectly holy and complete for all time!
HEBREWS 10:11-14 TPT

Sadness

I've learned that his anger is short-lived,
but his loving favor lasts a lifetime!
We may weep through the night,
but at daybreak it will turn into shouts of ecstatic joy.

PSALM 30:5 TPT

Yahweh is the God who continually saves me.
I weep before you night and day.

PSALM 88:1 TPT

"Be glad; rejoice forever in my creation!
And look! I will create Jerusalem as a place of happiness.
Her people will be a source of joy.
I will rejoice over Jerusalem
and delight in my people.
And the sound of weeping and crying
will be heard in it no more."

ISAIAH 65:18-19 NLT

"Blessed are those who mourn,
for they will be comforted."

MATTHEW 5:4 NIV

"God blesses you who weep now,
for in due time you will laugh."

LUKE 6:21 NLT

Safety

"Follow my decrees and be careful to obey my laws, and you will live safely in the land. Then the land will yield its fruit, and you will eat your fill and live there in safety."

LEVITICUS 25:18–19 NIV

"The beloved of the LORD shall dwell in safety by Him,
Who shelters him all the day long;
And he shall dwell between His shoulders."

DEUTERONOMY 33:12 NKJV

"The eternal God is your refuge,
And underneath are the everlasting arms;
He will thrust out the enemy from before you,
And will say, 'Destroy!'"

DEUTERONOMY 33:27 NKJV

Gideon said to God, "If you will save Israel by my hand as you have promised—look, I will place a wool fleece on the threshing floor. If there is dew only on the fleece and all the ground is dry, then I will know that you will save Israel by my hand, as you said." And that is what happened. Gideon rose early the next day; he squeezed the fleece and wrung out the dew—a bowlful of water.

JUDGES 6:36–38 NIV

"You will be safe from slander
and have no fear when destruction comes."

JOB 5:21 NLT

"You will know that your home is safe.
When you survey your possessions, nothing will be missing."

JOB 5:24 NLT

I will both lie down in peace, and sleep;
For You alone, O LORD, make me dwell in safety.

PSALM 4:8 NKJV

You're as real to me as Bedrock beneath my feet,
like a Castle on a cliff, my forever firm Fortress,
my Mountain of hiding, my Pathway of escape,
my Tower of rescue where none can reach me,
my secret Strength and Shield around me,
you are Salvation's Ray of Brightness
shining on the hillside,
always the Champion of my cause.
PSALM 18:2 TPT

It is God who arms me with strength
and keeps my way secure.
PSALM 18:32 NIV

He offers a resting place for me in his luxurious love.
His tracks take me to an oasis of peace, the quiet brook of bliss.
PSALM 23:2 TPT

In the shelter of your presence you hide [those who fear you]
from all human intrigues;
you keep them safe in your dwelling
from accusing tongues.
PSALM 31:20 NIV

For one day the wicked will be destroyed,
but those who trust in the Lord
will live safe and sound with blessings overflowing.
PSALM 37:9 TPT

Turn from evil and do good,
and you will live in the land forever.
For the LORD loves justice,
and he will never abandon the godly.
He will keep them safe forever,
but the children of the wicked will die.
PSALM 37:27-28 NLT

God is a safe place to hide,
ready to help when we need him.
PSALM 46:1 MSG

There's no doubt about it;
God holds our lives safely in his hands.
He's the One who keeps us faithfully following him.
PSALM 66:9 TPT

You're the only place of protection for me.
I keep coming back to hide myself in you,
for you are like a mountain-cliff-fortress where I'm kept safe.
PSALM 71:3 TPT

You'll even walk unharmed
among the fiercest powers of darkness,
trampling every one of them beneath your feet!
PSALM 91:13 TPT

GOD loves all who hate evil,
And those who love him he keeps safe,
Snatches them from the grip of the wicked.
PSALM 97:10 MSG

Calamity is not allowed to overwhelm the righteous,
but there's nothing but trouble waiting for the wicked.
PROVERBS 12:21 TPT

The name of the LORD is a strong tower;
the righteous man runs into it and is safe.
PROVERBS 18:10 ESV

The one whose walk is blameless is kept safe,
but the one whose ways are perverse will fall into the pit.
PROVERBS 28:18 NIV

My people will live in a peaceful neighborhood—
in safe houses, in quiet gardens.
ISAIAH 32:18 MSG

"They will live safely in Israel and build homes and plant vineyards. And when I punish the neighboring nations that treated them with contempt, they will know that I am the LORD their God."
EZEKIEL 28:26 NLT

"And they shall no longer be a prey for the nations, nor shall beasts of the land devour them; but they shall dwell safely, and no one shall make them afraid."
EZEKIEL 34:28 NKJV

"In that day I will make a covenant for them
with the beasts of the field, the birds in the sky
and the creatures that move along the ground.
Bow and sword and battle
I will abolish from the land,
so that all may lie down in safety."
HOSEA 2:18 NIV

"Then you will know that I, the LORD your God,
live in Zion, my holy mountain.
Jerusalem will be holy forever,
and foreign armies will never conquer her again."
JOEL 3:17 NLT

Salvation

Now the day before Saul's arrival, the LORD had informed Samuel, "At this time tomorrow I will send you a man from the land of Benjamin. Anoint him ruler over My people Israel. He will save them from the hand of the Philistines because I have seen the affliction of My people, for their cry has come to Me."
1 SAMUEL 9:15-16 HCSB

"You save a humble people,
but your eyes are on the haughty to bring them down."
2 SAMUEL 22:28 ESV

The LORD lives—may my rock be praised!
God, the rock of my salvation, is exalted.
2 SAMUEL 22:47 HCSB

"Great salvation he brings to his king,
and shows steadfast love to his anointed,
to David and his offspring forever."
2 SAMUEL 22:51 ESV

When others are humiliated and you say, "Lift them up,
God will save the humble."
JOB 22:29 HCSB

My shield is with God,
who saves the upright in heart.
PSALM 7:10 HCSB

He's the Source of my salvation to defend me every day.
I fear no one!
PSALM 27:1B TPT

The salvation of the righteous comes from the LORD;
he is their stronghold in time of trouble.
PSALM 37:39 NIV

But I call to God,
and the LORD will save me.
>   PSALM 55:16 ESV

He alone is my rock and my salvation,
my fortress; I shall not be greatly shaken.
>   PSALM 62:2 ESV

God will save Zion
And build the cities of Judah,
That they may dwell there and possess it.
Also, the descendants of His servants shall inherit it,
And those who love His name shall dwell in it.
>   PSALM 69:35-36 NKJV

Surely his salvation is near to those who fear him,
that glory may dwell in our land.
>   PSALM 85:9 ESV

"You will be satisfied with a full life
and with all that I do for you.
For you will enjoy the fullness of my salvation!"
>   PSALM 91:16 TPT

The LORD guards the inexperienced;
I was helpless, and He saved me.
>   PSALM 116:6 NKJV

Wisdom will save you from the immoral woman,
from the seductive words of the promiscuous woman.
>   PROVERBS 2:16 NLT

Isaiah said, Listen, house of David! Is it not enough for you to try the patience of men? Will you also try the patience of my God? Therefore, the Lord Himself will give you a sign: The virgin will conceive, have a son, and name him Immanuel.
>   ISAIAH 7:13-14 HCSB

For to us a child is born,
to us a son is given,
and the government will be on his shoulders.
And he will be called
Wonderful Counselor, Mighty God,
Everlasting Father, Prince of Peace.
Of the greatness of his government and peace
there will be no end.
He will reign on David's throne
and over his kingdom,
establishing and upholding it
with justice and righteousness
from that time on and forever.
The zeal of the LORD Almighty
will accomplish this.

ISAIAH 9:6-7 NIV

Out of the stump of David's family will grow a shoot—
yes, a new Branch bearing fruit from the old root.
And the Spirit of the LORD will rest on him—
the Spirit of wisdom and understanding,
the Spirit of counsel and might,
the Spirit of knowledge and the fear of the LORD.
He will delight in obeying the LORD.
He will not judge by appearance
nor make a decision based on hearsay.

ISAIAH 11:1-3 NLT

The LORD will save me,
and we will play my music on stringed instruments
all the days of our lives,
at the house of the LORD.

ISAIAH 38:20 ESV

"But Israel shall be saved by the LORD
With an everlasting salvation;
You shall not be ashamed or disgraced
Forever and ever."
    ISAIAH 45:17 NKJV

"In the LORD all the offspring of Israel
shall be justified and shall glory."
    ISAIAH 45:25 ESV

"Look up to the heavens,
and look at the earth beneath;
for the heavens will vanish like smoke,
the earth will wear out like a garment,
and its inhabitants will die like gnats.
But My salvation will last forever,
and My righteousness will never be shattered."
    ISAIAH 51:6 HCSB

"For the moth will eat them up like a garment,
And the worm will eat them like wool;
But My righteousness will be forever,
And My salvation from generation to generation."
    ISAIAH 51:8 NKJV

The LORD will lay bare his holy arm
in the sight of all the nations,
and all the ends of the earth will see
the salvation of our God.
    ISAIAH 52:10 NIV

All of us, like sheep, have strayed away.
We have left God's paths to follow our own.
Yet the LORD laid on him
the sins of us all.
    ISAIAH 53:6 NLT

"Surely, falsehood comes from the hills,
commotion from the mountains,
but the salvation of Israel
is only in the LORD our God."
JEREMIAH 3:23 HCSB

"I will gather the remnant of My flock from all the lands where I have banished them, and I will return them to their grazing land. They will become fruitful and numerous. I will raise up shepherds over them who will shepherd them. They will no longer be afraid or dismayed, nor will any be missing." This is the LORD's declaration.
JEREMIAH 23:3-4 HCSB

"For I will be with you—
this is the LORD's declaration—
to save you!
I will bring destruction on all the nations
where I have scattered you;
however, I will not bring destruction on you.
I will discipline you justly,
and I will by no means leave you unpunished."
JEREMIAH 30:11 HCSB

"Now, son of man, say to your people: The righteousness of the righteous person will not save him on the day of his transgression; neither will the wickedness of the wicked person cause him to stumble on the day he turns from his wickedness. The righteous person won't be able to survive by his righteousness on the day he sins."
EZEKIEL 33:12 HCSB

I will save My flock, and they will no longer be prey for you. I will judge between one sheep and another.
EZEKIEL 34:22 HCSB

But I will sacrifice to You
With the voice of thanksgiving;
I will pay what I have vowed.
Salvation is of the LORD.
JONAH 2:9 NKJV

This is what the LORD Almighty says: "I will save my people from the countries of the east and the west. I will bring them back to live in Jerusalem; they will be my people, and I will be faithful and righteous to them as their God."
ZECHARIAH 8:7-8 NIV

"Truly I tell you, it is hard for someone who is rich to enter the kingdom of heaven." Jesus looked at them and said, "With man this is impossible, but with God all things are possible."
MATTHEW 19:23, 26 NIV

"He has raised up a horn of salvation for us
in the house of His servant David,
just as He spoke by the mouth
of His holy prophets in ancient times;
salvation from our enemies
and from the clutches of those who hate us.
He has dealt mercifully with our fathers
and remembered His holy covenant."
LUKE 1:69-72 NKJV

Jesus overheard their complaining and said, "Who goes to the doctor for a cure? Those who are well or those who are sick? I have not come to call the 'righteous,' but to call those who fail to measure up and bring them to repentance."
LUKE 5:31-32 TPT

"I can assure you of this: If you don't hold back, but freely declare in public that I am the Son of Man, the Messiah, I will freely declare to all the angels of God that you are mine. But if you publicly pretend that you don't know me, I will deny you before the angels of God."
LUKE 12:8-9 TPT

Jesus saw his disappointment, and looking right at him he said, "It is next to impossible for those who have everything to enter into the kingdom realm of God. Nothing could be harder! It could be compared to trying to stuff a rope through the eye of a needle."
Those who heard this said, "Then who can be saved?"
Jesus responded, "What appears humanly impossible is more than possible with God. For God can do what man cannot."
LUKE 18:24-27 TPT

Jesus said to him, "This shows that today life has come to you and your household, for you are a true son of Abraham. The Son of Man has come to seek out and to give life to those who are lost."
LUKE 19:9-10 TPT

"I am the gate; whoever enters through me will be saved. They will come in and go out, and find pasture."
JOHN 10:9 NIV

"Blood and fire and billowing smoke,
the sun turning black and the moon blood-red,
Before the Day of the Lord arrives,
the Day tremendous and marvelous;
And whoever calls out for help
to me, God, will be saved."
ACTS 2:19-21 MSG

"Jesus is 'the stone you masons threw out, which is now the cornerstone.' Salvation comes no other way; no other name has been or will be given to us by which we can be saved, only this one."
ACTS 4:11-12 MSG

When they heard this, their objections were put to rest and they all glorified God, saying, "Look what God has done! He's giving the gift of repentance that leads to life to people who aren't even Jews."
ACTS 11:18 TPT

"So listen well. This wonderful salvation given by God is now being presented to the non-Jewish nations, and they will believe and receive it!"
ACTS 28:28 TPT

I refuse to be ashamed of sharing the wonderful message of God's liberating power unleashed in us through Christ! For I am thrilled to preach that everyone who believes is saved—the Jew first, and then people everywhere!
ROMANS 1:16 TPT

If you declare with your mouth, "Jesus is Lord," and believe in your heart that God raised him from the dead, you will be saved.
ROMANS 10:9 NIV

It is time for us to wake up! For our full salvation is nearer now than when we first believed.
ROMANS 13:11B TPT

When you heard the message of truth, the gospel of your salvation, and when you believed in Him, you were also sealed with the promised Holy Spirit.
EPHESIANS 1:13 HCSB

Salvation is not a reward for the good things we have done, so none of us can boast about it.
EPHESIANS 2:9 NLT

God didn't set us up for an angry rejection but for salvation by our Master, Jesus Christ.
1 THESSALONIANS 5:9 MSG

He gave us resurrection life and drew us to himself by his holy calling on our lives. And it wasn't because of any good we have done, but by his divine pleasure and marvelous grace that confirmed our union with the anointed Jesus, even before time began!
2 TIMOTHY 1:9 TPT

Though He was God's Son, He learned obedience through what He suffered. After He was perfected, He became the source of eternal salvation for all who obey Him.
HEBREWS 5:8-9 HCSB

But Jesus permanently holds his priestly office, since he lives forever and will never have a successor! So he is able to save fully from now throughout eternity, everyone who comes to God through him, because he lives to pray continually for them.
HEBREWS 7:24-25 TPT

Just as people are destined to die once, and after that to face judgment, so Christ was sacrificed once to take away the sins of many; and he will appear a second time, not to bear sin, but to bring salvation to those who are waiting for him.
HEBREWS 9:27-28 NIV

Wives, in the same way submit yourselves to your own husbands so that, if any of them do not believe the word, they may be won over without words by the behavior of their wives, when they see the purity and reverence of your lives.
1 PETER 3:1-2 NIV

They cried out in a loud voice:
"Salvation belongs to our God,
who sits on the throne,
and to the Lamb."
REVELATION 7:10 NIV

And the Spirit and the bride say, "Come!" And let him who hears say, "Come!" And let him who thirsts come. Whoever desires, let him take the water of life freely.
REVELATION 22:17 NKJV

Satisfaction

If you carefully obey my commands I am giving you today, to love the LORD your God and worship Him with all your heart and all your soul, I will provide rain for your land in the proper time, the autumn and spring rains, and you will harvest your grain, new wine, and oil. I will provide grass in your fields for your livestock. You will eat and be satisfied.

DEUTERONOMY 11:13-15 HCSB

My soul will be satisfied as with fat and rich food,
and my mouth will praise you with joyful lips.

PSALM 63:5 ESV

The harvest of the earth is here!
God, the very God we worship
keeps us satisfied at his banquet of blessings,
and the blessings keep coming!

PSALM 67:6-7 TPT

He satisfies you with goodness;
your youth is renewed like the eagle.

PSALM 103:5 HCSB

You open Your hand
and satisfy the desire of every living thing.

PSALM 145:16 HCSB

He grants peace to your borders
and satisfies you with the finest of wheat.

PSALM 147:14 NIV

The fear of the LORD leads to life,
And he who has it will abide in satisfaction;
He will not be visited with evil.

PROVERBS 19:23 NKJV

"And I will bring Israel home again to its own land,
to feed in the fields of Carmel and Bashan,
and to be satisfied once more
in the hill country of Ephraim and Gilead."
JEREMIAH 50:19 NLT

The LORD replied to them:
"I am sending you grain, new wine and olive oil,
enough to satisfy you fully;
never again will I make you
an object of scorn to the nations."
JOEL 2:19 NIV

"You shall eat in plenty and be satisfied,
And praise the name of the LORD your God,
Who has dealt wondrously with you;
And My people shall never be put to shame."
JOEL 2:26 NKJV

"God blesses those who hunger and thirst for justice,
for they will be satisfied."
MATTHEW 5:6 NLT

"If you drink from Jacob's well you'll be thirsty again and again, but if anyone drinks the living water I give them, they will never thirst again and will be forever satisfied! For when you drink the water I give you it becomes a gushing fountain of the Holy Spirit, springing up and flooding you with endless life!"
JOHN 4:13-14 TPT

Jesus said to them, "I am the Bread of Life. Come every day to me and you will never be hungry. Believe in me and you will never be thirsty."
JOHN 6:35 TPT

Jesus stood and shouted out to the crowds—"All you thirsty ones, come to me! Come to me and drink! Believe in me, so that rivers of living water will burst out from within you; flowing from your innermost being, just like the Scripture says!"
JOHN 7:37-38 TPT

Savior

"I am the LORD your God,
the Holy One of Israel, your Savior;
I give Egypt for your ransom,
Cush and Seba in your stead."

ISAIAH 43:3 NIV

Surely he took up our pain
and bore our suffering,
yet we considered him punished by God,
stricken by him, and afflicted.

ISAIAH 53:4 NIV

But he was pierced for our rebellion,
crushed for our sins.
He was beaten so we could be whole.
He was whipped so we could be healed.

ISAIAH 53:5 NLT

After he has suffered,
he will see the light of life and be satisfied;
by his knowledge my righteous servant will justify many,
and he will bear their iniquities.

ISAIAH 53:11 NIV

Therefore I will give him a portion among the great,
and he will divide the spoils with the strong,
because he poured out his life unto death,
and was numbered with the transgressors.
For he bore the sin of many,
and made intercession for the transgressors.

ISAIAH 53:12 NIV

"The days are coming," declares the LORD,
"when I will raise up for David a righteous Branch,
a King who will reign wisely
and do what is just and right in the land.
In his days Judah will be saved
and Israel will live in safety.
This is the name by which he will be called:
The LORD Our Righteous Savior."
JEREMIAH 23:5-6 NIV

"In those days and at that time
I will make a righteous Branch sprout from David's line;
he will do what is just and right in the land.
In those days Judah will be saved
and Jerusalem will live in safety.
This is the name by which it will be called:
The LORD Our Righteous Savior."
JEREMIAH 33:15-16 NIV

But you, Bethlehem, David's country,
the runt of the litter—
From you will come the leader
who will shepherd-rule Israel.
He'll be no upstart, no pretender.
His family tree is ancient and distinguished.
MICAH 5:2 MSG

"And you, O Bethlehem in the land of Judah,
are not least among the ruling cities of Judah,
for a ruler will come from you
who will be the shepherd for my people Israel."
MATTHEW 2:6 NIV

"I baptize you with water for repentance, but the One who is coming after me is more powerful than I. I am not worthy to removed His sandals. He Himself will baptize you with the Holy Spirit and fire."
MATTHEW 3:11 HCSB

When Jesus heard this, He told them, "Those who are well don't need a doctor, but the sick do need one. I didn't come to call the righteous, but sinners."

MARK 2:17 HCSB

Then the high priest asked him, "Are you the Messiah, the Son of the Blessed One?" Jesus said, "I AM. And you will see the Son of Man seated in the place of power at God's right hand and coming on the clouds of heaven."

MARK 14:61-62 NLT

"You will conceive and give birth to a son, and you will name him Jesus. He will be very great and will be called the Son of the Most High. The Lord God will give him the throne of his ancestor David. And he will reign over Israel forever; his Kingdom will never end!"

LUKE 1:31-33 NLT

The angel said, "Don't be afraid. I'm here to announce a great and joyful event that is meant for everybody, worldwide: A Savior has just been born in David's town, a Savior who is Messiah and Master."

LUKE 2:10-11 MSG

Scripture

The hidden things belong to the LORD our God, but the revealed things belong to us and our children forever, so that we may follow all the words of this law.
DEUTERONOMY 29:29 HCSB

"Don't suppose for a minute that I have come to demolish the Scriptures—either God's Law or the Prophets. I'm not here to demolish but to complete. I am going to put it all together, pull it all together in a vast panorama. God's Law is more real and lasting than the stars in the sky and the ground at your feet. Long after stars burn out and earth wears out, God's Law will be alive and working."
MATTHEW 5:17-18 MSG

All Scripture is God-breathed and is useful for teaching, rebuking, correcting and training in righteousness, so that the servant of God a may be thoroughly equipped for every good work.
2 TIMOTHY 3:16-17 NIV

For we have the living Word of God, which is full of energy, and it pierces more sharply than a soldier's sword. It will even penetrate to the very core of our being where soul and spirit, bone and marrow meet—splitting them in two! It scrutinizes and reveals the true thoughts and motives of our hearts.
HEBREWS 4:12 TPT

Security

"When you cross the Jordan and live in the land the LORD your God is giving you to inherit, and He gives you rest from all the enemies around you and you live in security."
>   DEUTERONOMY 12:10 HCSB

"So Israel will live in safety;
Jacob will dwell secure
in a land of grain and new wine,
where the heavens drop dew."
>   DEUTERONOMY 33:28 NIV

He makes my feet like the feet of a deer
and sets me securely on the heights.
>   PSALM 18:33 HCSB

Though many wish to fight
and the tide of battle turns against me,
by your power I will be safe and secure;
peace will be my portion.
>   PSALM 55:18 TPT

Don't fear a thing!
Whether by night or by day,
demonic danger will not trouble you,
nor the powers of evil launched against you.
For God will keep you safe and secure;
they won't lay a hand on you!
>   PSALM 91:6 TPT

The LORD is your security.
He will keep your foot from being caught in a trap.
>   PROVERBS 3:26 NLT

The righteous will never be removed,
but the wicked will not dwell in the land.
>   PROVERBS 10:30 ESV

"You will be secure under a government that is just and fair.
Your enemies will stay far away.
You will live in peace,
and terror will not come near.
If any nation comes to fight you,
it is not because I sent them.
Whoever attacks you will go down in defeat."
>   ISAIAH 54:14–15 NLT

"I will make you a wall to this people,
a fortified wall of bronze;
they will fight against you
but will not overcome you,
for I am with you
to rescue and save you,"
>   JEREMIAH 15:20 NIV

We know that God's children do not make a practice of sinning, for God's Son holds them securely, and the evil one cannot touch them.
>   1 JOHN 5:18 NLT

Self-Control

A person without self-control
is like a city with broken-down walls.
PROVERBS 25:28 NLT

Make every effort to supplement your faith with goodness, goodness with knowledge, knowledge with self-control, self-control with endurance, endurance with godliness, godliness with brotherly affection, and brotherly affection with love. For if these qualities are yours and are increasing, they will keep you from being useless or unfruitful in the knowledge of our Lord Jesus Christ.
2 PETER 1:5-8 HCSB

Shame

Those who look to him are radiant;
their faces are never covered with shame.
> PSALM 34:5 NIV

"Do not be afraid, for you will not be put to shame;
don't be humiliated, for you will not be disgraced.
For you will forget the shame of your youth,
and you will no longer remember
the disgrace of your widowhood."
> ISAIAH 54:4 HCSB

Instead of your shame
you will receive a double portion,
and instead of disgrace
you will rejoice in your inheritance.
And so you will inherit a double portion in your land,
and everlasting joy will be yours.
> ISAIAH 61:7 NIV

"On that day you will no longer need to be ashamed,
for you will no longer be rebels against me.
I will remove all proud and arrogant people from among you.
There will be no more haughtiness on my holy mountain."
> ZEPHANIAH 3:11 NLT

Sin

"Because you've done this, you're cursed,
cursed beyond all cattle and wild animals,
Cursed to slink on your belly
and eat dirt all your life.
I'm declaring war between you and the Woman,
between your offspring and hers.
He'll wound your head,
you'll wound his heel."

GENESIS 3:14-15 MSG

"If you do well, won't you be accepted? And if you don't do well, sin is lying in wait for you, ready to pounce; it's out to get you, you've got to master it."

GENESIS 4:7 MSG

But God came to Abimelech in a dream that night and told him, "You're as good as dead—that woman you took, she's a married woman."

Now Abimelech had not yet slept with her, hadn't so much as touched her. He said, "Master, would you kill an innocent man? Didn't he tell me, 'She's my sister'? And didn't she herself say, 'He's my brother'? I had no idea I was doing anything wrong when I did this."

God said to him in the dream, "Yes, I know your intentions were pure, that's why I kept you from sinning against me; I was the one who kept you from going to bed with her. So now give the man's wife back to him. He's a prophet and will pray for you—pray for your life. If you don't give her back, know that it's certain death both for you and everyone in your family."

GENESIS 20:3-7 MSG

But the LORD said to Moses, "Whoever has sinned against me, I will blot out of my book. But now go, lead the people to the place about which I have spoken to you; behold, my angel shall go before you. Nevertheless, in the day when I visit, I will visit their sin upon them."

EXODUS 32:33-34 ESV

"If anyone sins and does what is forbidden in any of the LORD'S commands, even though they do not know it, they are guilty and will be held responsible."
LEVITICUS 5:17 NIV

"Then the people of Israel will no longer stray from me, nor will they defile themselves anymore with all their sins. They will be my people, and I will be their God, declares the Sovereign LORD."
EZEKIEL 14:11 NIV

"But if a righteous person turns from their righteousness and commits sin and does the same detestable things the wicked person does, will they live? None of the righteous things that person has done will be remembered. Because of the unfaithfulness they are guilty of and because of the sins they have committed, they will die."
EZEKIEL 18:24 NIV

"Don't you see that whatever enters the mouth goes into the stomach and then out of the body? But the things that come out of a person's mouth come from the heart, and these defile them."
MATTHEW 15:17-18 NIV

For all have sinned and fall short of the glory of God.
ROMANS 3:23 HCSB

We have passed away from sin once and for all, as a dead man passes away from this life. So how could we live under sin's rule a moment longer?
ROMANS 6:2 TPT

Count yourselves dead to sin but alive to God in Christ Jesus.
ROMANS 6:11 NIV

If we deliberately keep on sinning after we have received the knowledge of the truth, no sacrifice for sins is left, but only a fearful expectation of judgment and of raging fire that will consume the enemies of God.
HEBREWS 10:26-27 NIV

But if we walk in the light, God himself being the light, we also experience a shared life with one another, as the sacrificed blood of Jesus, God's Son, purges all our sin.

1 JOHN 1:7 MSG

But you know that he appeared so that he might take away our sins. And in him is no sin.

1 JOHN 3:5 NIV

Sovereignty

"I'm convinced: You can do anything and everything.
Nothing and no one can upset your plans."

JOB 42:2 MSG

With his breath he scatters the schemes of nations who oppose him;
they will never succeed.

PSALM 33:10 TPT

Unless the LORD builds a house,
the work of the builders is wasted.
Unless the LORD protects a city,
guarding it with sentries will do no good.

PSALM 127:1 NLT

"My word that comes from My mouth
will not return to Me empty,
but it will accomplish what I please
and will prosper in what I send it to do."

ISAIAH 55:11 HCSB

"And in the days of these kings the God of heaven will set up a kingdom which shall never be destroyed; and the kingdom shall not be left to other people; it shall break in pieces and consume all these kingdoms, and it shall stand forever."

DANIEL 2:44 NKJV

"The decision is announced by messengers, the holy ones declare the verdict, so that the living may know that the Most High is sovereign over all kingdoms on earth and gives them to anyone he wishes and sets over them the lowliest of people."

DANIEL 4:17 NIV

"His sovereign rule lasts and lasts,
his kingdom never declines and falls.
Life on this earth doesn't add up to much,
but God's heavenly army keeps everything going.
No one can interrupt his work,
no one can call his rule into question."

DANIEL 4:34-35 MSG

The One who made the Pleiades and Orion,
who turns darkness into dawn
and darkens day into night,
who summons the waters of the sea
and pours them out over the face of the earth—
Yahweh is His name.

AMOS 5:8 HCSB

Dear friends, don't let this one thing escape you: With the Lord one day is like a thousand years, and a thousand years like one day.

2 PETER 3:8 HCSB

Spiritual Gifts

God's marvelous grace imparts to each one of us varying gifts and ministries that are uniquely ours.

ROMANS 12:6 TPT

Now you have every spiritual gift you need as you eagerly wait for the return of our Lord Jesus Christ.

1 CORINTHIANS 1:7 NLT

To one there is given through the Spirit a message of wisdom, to another a message of knowledge by means of the same Spirit, to another faith by the same Spirit, to another gifts of healing by that one Spirit, to another miraculous powers, to another prophecy, to another distinguishing between spirits, to another speaking in different kinds of tongues, and to still another the interpretation of tongues. All these are the work of one and the same Spirit, and he distributes them to each one, just as he determines.

1 CORINTHIANS 12:8-10 NIV

Stability

"He makes my feet like the feet of a deer
and sets me securely on the heights."
2 SAMUEL 22:34 HCSB

"And I will provide a homeland for my people Israel, planting them in a secure place where they will never be disturbed."
1 CHRONICLES 17:9A NLT

Surely the righteous will never be shaken;
they will be remembered forever.
PSALM 112:6 NIV

Whoever fears the LORD has a secure fortress,
and for their children it will be a refuge.
PROVERBS 14:26 NIV

"Today I have made you a fortified city, an iron pillar and a bronze wall to stand against the whole land—against the kings of Judah, its officials, its priests and the people of the land."
JEREMIAH 1:18 NIV

Therefore put on the full armor of God, so that when the day of evil comes, you may be able to stand your ground, and after you have done everything, to stand.
EPHESIANS 6:13 NIV

Strength

"God brought them out of Egypt;
they have the strength of a wild ox."
>   NUMBERS 23:22 NIV

"God brought them out of Egypt;
they have the strength of a wild ox.
They devour hostile nations
and break their bones in pieces;
with their arrows they pierce them.
Like a lion they crouch and lie down,
like a lioness—who dares to rouse them?"
>   NUMBERS 24:8-9 NIV

The weapons of the strong are smashed to pieces,
while the weak are infused with fresh strength.
>   1 SAMUEL 2:4 MSG

"He will give strength to His king,
And exalt the horn of His anointed."
>   1 SAMUEL 2:10B NKJV

"Be strong, and let us fight bravely for our people and the cities of our God. The LORD will do what is good in his sight."
>   2 SAMUEL 10:12 NIV

"The God of my strength, in whom I will trust;
My shield and the horn of my salvation,
My stronghold and my refuge;
My Savior, You save me from violence."
>   2 SAMUEL 22:3 NKJV

In your strength I can crush an army;
with my God I can scale any wall.
>   2 SAMUEL 22:30 NLT

Glory in his holy name;
let the hearts of those who seek the LORD rejoice!
Seek the LORD and his strength;
seek his presence continually!
 1 CHRONICLES 16:10-11 ESV

"Go and enjoy choice food and sweet drinks, and send some to those who have nothing prepared. This day is holy to our Lord. Do not grieve, for the joy of the LORD is your strength."
 NEHEMIAH 8:10 NIV

In your strength I can crush an army;
with my God I can scale any wall.
 PSALM 18:29 NLT

You empower me for victory with your wrap-around presence.
Your power within makes me strong to subdue,
and by stooping down in gentleness
you strengthened me, and made me great!
 PSALM 18:35 TPT

Lord, because of your strength the king is strong.
Look how he rejoices in you!
He bursts out with a joyful song because of your victory!
 PSALM 21:1 TPT

You are my Strength and my Shield from every danger.
When I fully trust in you, help is on the way.
I jump for joy and burst forth with ecstatic, passionate praise!
I will sing songs of what you mean to me!
 PSALM 28:7 TPT

The LORD gives strength to his people.
 PSALM 29:11 NIV

I will keep watch for You, my strength,
because God is my stronghold.
> PSALM 59:9 HCSB

You are my strength, I sing praise to you;
you, God, are my fortress,
my God on whom I can rely.
> PSALM 59:17 NIV

God said to me once and for all,
"All the strength and power you need flows from me!"
> PSALM 62:11 TPT

God, You are awe-inspiring in Your sanctuaries.
The God of Israel gives power and strength to His people.
May God be praised!
> PSALM 68:35 HCSB

My flesh and my heart fail;
But God is the strength of my heart and my portion forever.
> PSALM 73:26 NKJV

Sing aloud to God our strength;
Make a joyful shout to the God of Jacob.
> PSALM 81:10 NKJV

The LORD is my strength and my song;
He has become my salvation.
> PSALM 118:14 HCSB

See, the Lord GOD comes with strength,
and His power establishes His rule.
His reward is with Him,
and His gifts accompany Him.
> ISAIAH 40:10 HCSB

"He energizes those who get tired,
gives fresh strength to dropouts.
For even young people tire and drop out,
young folk in their prime stumble and fall."
    ISAIAH 40:29-30 MSG

"I am the LORD, and there is no other;
apart from me there is no God.
I will strengthen you,
though you have not acknowledged me."
    ISAIAH 45:5 NIV

The LORD God is my strength;
He will make my feet like deer's feet,
And He will make me walk on my high hills.
    HABAKKUK 3:19 NKJV

Then he said to me, "This is what the LORD says to Zerubbabel: It is not by force nor by strength, but by my Spirit, says the LORD of Heaven's Armies."
    ZECHARIAH 4:6 NLT

But my people—oh, I'll make them strong, GOD strong!
and they'll live my way. GOD says so!
    ZECHARIAH 10:12 MSG

Now it is God who strengthens us, with you, in Christ and has anointed us.
    2 CORINTHIANS 1:21 HCSB

I take pleasure in weaknesses, insults, catastrophes, persecutions, and in pressures, because of Christ. For when I am weak, then I am strong.
    2 CORINTHIANS 12:10 HCSB

I know what it is to be in need, and I know what it is to have plenty. I have learned the secret of being content in any and every situation, whether well fed or hungry, whether living in plenty or in want. I can do all this through him who gives me strength.

PHILIPPIANS 4:12-13 NIV

I have written to you who are God's children
because you know the Father.
I have written to you who are mature in the faith
because you know Christ, who existed from the beginning.
I have written to you who are young in the faith
because you are strong.
God's word lives in your hearts,
and you have won your battle with the evil one.

1 JOHN 2:14 NLT

Success

"Be strong and very courageous. Be careful to obey all the law my servant Moses gave you; do not turn from it to the right or to the left, that you may be successful wherever you go."

JOSHUA 1:7 NIV

"Observe the requirements of the LORD your God, and follow all his ways. Keep the decrees, commands, regulations, and laws written in the Law of Moses so that you will be successful in all you do and wherever you go."

1 KINGS 2:3 NLT

"But have you not heard?
I decided this long ago.
Long ago I planned it,
and now I am making it happen.
I planned for you to crush fortified cities
into heaps of rubble."

2 KINGS 19:25 NLT

"Listen to me, Judah and people of Jerusalem! Have faith in the LORD your God and you will be upheld; have faith in his prophets and you will be successful."

2 CHRONICLES 20:20 NIV

Keep protecting and cherishing your chosen ones;
in you they will never fall.
Like a Shepherd going before us, keep leading us forward,
forever carrying us in your arms!

PSALM 28:9 TPT

My child, only when you treasure my wisdom
will you acquire it.
And only if you accept my advice and hide it within
will you succeed.
> PROVERBS 2:1 TPT

Seek good and not evil,
That you may live;
> AMOS 5:14 NKJV

Suffering

"Go, assemble the elders of Israel and say to them, 'The LORD, the God of your fathers—the God of Abraham, Isaac and Jacob—appeared to me and said: I have watched over you and have seen what has been done to you in Egypt. And I have promised to bring you up out of your misery in Egypt into the land of the Canaanites, Hittites, Amorites, Perizzites, Hivites and Jebusites—a land flowing with milk and honey.'"
    EXODUS 3:16-17 NIV

"He gives prosperity to the poor
and protects those who suffer."
    JOB 5:11 NLT

"But He knows the way that I take;
When He has tested me, I shall come forth as gold."
    JOB 23:10 NKJV

For he who avenges murder cares for the helpless.
He does not ignore the cries of those who suffer.
    PSALM 9:12 NLT

But you, God, see the trouble of the afflicted;
you consider their grief and take it in hand.
    PSALM 10:14A NIV

Even though I walk
through the darkest valley,
I will fear no evil,
for you are with me;
    PSALM 23:4 NIV

You have allowed me to suffer much hardship,
but you will restore me to life again
and lift me up from the depths of the earth.
    PSALM 71:20 NLT

Your promise revives me;
it comforts me in all my troubles.
>   PSALM 119:50 NLT

My suffering was good for me,
for it taught me to pay attention to your decrees.
>   PSALM 119:71 NLT

When times are good, be happy;
but when times are bad, consider this:
God has made the one
as well as the other.
>   ECCLESIASTES 7:14 NIV

Shout for joy, you heavens;
rejoice, you earth;
burst into song, you mountains!
For the LORD comforts his people
and will have compassion on his afflicted ones.
>   ISAIAH 49:13 NIV

In all their suffering he also suffered,
and he personally rescued them.
In his love and mercy he redeemed them.
He lifted them up and carried them
through all the years.
>   ISAIAH 63:9 NLT

Even in times of trouble we have a joyful confidence, knowing that our pressures will develop in us patient endurance. And patient endurance will refine our character, and proven character leads us back to hope.
>   ROMANS 5:3–4 TPT

For I consider that the sufferings of this present time are not worth comparing with the glory that is going to be revealed to us.
>   ROMANS 8:18 HCSB

He comforts us in all our affliction, so that we may be able to comfort those who are in any kind of affliction, through the comfort we ourselves receive from God. For as the sufferings of Christ overflow to us, so through Christ our comfort also overflows.
2 CORINTHIANS 1:4-5 HCSB

For our momentary light affliction is producing for us an absolutely incomparable eternal weight of glory.
2 CORINTHIANS 4:17 HCSB

Consider it a great joy, my brothers, whenever you experience various trials, knowing that the testing of your faith produces endurance.
JAMES 1:2-3 HCSB

In all this you greatly rejoice, though now for a little while you may have had to suffer grief in all kinds of trials. These have come so that the proven genuineness of your faith—of greater worth than gold, which perishes even though refined by fire— may result in praise, glory and honor when Jesus Christ is revealed.
1 PETER 1:6-7 NIV

For what credit is it if, when you are beaten for your faults, you take it patiently? But when you do good and suffer, if you take it patiently, this is commendable before God. For to this you were called, because Christ also suffered for us, leaving us an example, that you should follow His steps.
1 PETER 2:20-21 NKJV

For it is better, if it is God's will, to suffer for doing good than for doing evil.
1 PETER 3:17 NIV

Stay alert! Watch out for your great enemy, the devil. He prowls around like a roaring lion, looking for someone to devour. Stand firm against him, and be strong in your faith. Remember that your Christian brothers and sisters all over the world are going through the same kind of suffering you are.
1 PETER 5:8-10 NLT

Support

"Be strong and courageous. Do not fear or be in dread of them, for it is the LORD your God who goes with you."
>
> DEUTERONOMY 31:6A ESV

The little that the righteous man has is better
than the abundance of many wicked people.
For the arms of the wicked will be broken,
but the LORD supports the righteous.
>
> PSALM 37:16-17 HCSB

The steps of the God-pursuing ones
follow firmly in the footsteps of the Lord.
And God delights in every step they take to follow him.
If they stumble badly they will still survive,
for the Lord lifts them up with his hands.
>
> PSALM 37:23-24 TPT

Cast your cares on the LORD
and he will sustain you;
he will never let
the righteous be shaken.
>
> PSALM 55:22 NIV

Temptation

"If your right eye causes you to stumble, gouge it out and throw it away. It is better for you to lose one part of your body than for your whole body to be thrown into hell. And if your right hand causes you to stumble, cut it off and throw it away. It is better for you to lose one part of your body than for your whole body to go into hell."
MATTHEW 5:29-30 NIV

But those who want to be rich fall into temptation, a trap, and many foolish and harmful desires, which plunge people into ruin and destruction. For the love of money is a root of all kinds of evil, and by craving it, some have wandered away from the faith and pierced themselves with many pains.
1 TIMOTHY 6:9-10 HCSB

Blessed is the man who endures temptation; for when he has been approved, he will receive the crown of life which the Lord has promised to those who love Him.
JAMES 1:12 NKJV

When you are tempted don't ever say, "God is tempting me," for God is incapable of being tempted by evil and he is never the source of temptation.
JAMES 1:13 TPT

Submit yourselves, then, to God. Resist the devil, and he will flee from you.
JAMES 4:7 NIV

Testing

GOD said to Moses, "I'm going to rain bread down from the skies for you. The people will go out and gather each day's ration. I'm going to test them to see if they'll live according to my Teaching or not. On the sixth day, when they prepare what they have gathered, it will turn out to be twice as much as their daily ration."

EXODUS 16:4-5 MSG

"I will put this third through the fire;
I will refine them as silver is refined
and test them as gold is tested."

ZECHARIAH 13:9 HCSB

No test or temptation that comes your way is beyond the course of what others have had to face. All you need to remember is that God will never let you down; he'll never let you be pushed past your limit; he'll always be there to help you come through it.

1 CORINTHIANS 10:13 MSG

He suffered and endured every test and temptation, so that he can help us every time we pass through the ordeals of life.

HEBREWS 2:18 TPT

So then, since we have a great High Priest who has entered heaven, Jesus the Son of God, let us hold firmly to what we believe. This High Priest of ours understands our weaknesses, for he faced all of the same testings we do, yet he did not sin.

HEBREWS 4:14-14 NLT

The Law

Therefore no one will be declared righteous in God's sight by the works of the law; rather, through the law we become conscious of our sin.

ROMANS 3:20 NIV

What the law could not do since it was limited by the flesh, God did. He condemned sin in the flesh by sending His own Son in flesh like ours under sin's domain, and as a sin offering, in order that the law's requirement would be accomplished in us who do not walk according to the flesh but according to the Spirit.

ROMANS 8:3-4 HCSB

Let me put it another way. The law was our guardian until Christ came; it protected us until we could be made right with God through faith. And now that the way of faith has come, we no longer need the law as our guardian.

GALATIANS 3:24-25 NLT

Transformation

"See, I will make you into a sharp threshing board,
new, with many teeth.
You will thresh mountains and pulverize them
and make hills into chaff.
You will winnow them
and a wind will carry them away,
a gale will scatter them.
But you will rejoice in the LORD;
you will boast in the Holy One of Israel."

ISAIAH 41:15-16 HCSB

"I will give you a new heart and put a new spirit within you; I will remove your heart of stone and give you a heart of flesh."

EZEKIEL 36:26 HCSB

This is what the Lord GOD says: "I will respond to the house of Israel and do this for them: I will multiply them in number like a flock. So the ruined cities will be filled with a flock of people, just as the flock of sheep for sacrifice is filled in Jerusalem during its appointed festivals. Then they will know that I am Yahweh."

EZEKIEL 36:37-38 HCSB

You are not a Jew if it's only superficial—for it's more than the surgical cut of a knife that makes you Jewish. But you are Jewish because of the inward act of spiritual circumcision—a radical change that lays bare your heart. It's not by the principle of law, but by power of the Holy Spirit. For then your praise will not come from people, but from God himself!

ROMANS 2:28-29 TPT

For when we were in the flesh, the sinful passions operated through the law in every part of us and bore fruit for death. But now we have been released from the law, since we have died to what held us, so that we may serve in the new way of the Spirit and not in the old letter of the law.

ROMANS 7:5-6 HCSB

Stop imitating the ideals and opinions of the culture around you, but be inwardly transformed by the Holy Spirit through a total reformation of how you think. This will empower you to discern God's will as you live a beautiful life, satisfying and perfect in his eyes.
ROMANS 12:2 TPT

For "who has known the Lord's mind,
that he may instruct Him?"
But we have the mind of Christ.
1 CORINTHIANS 2:16 HCSB

Just as we are now like the earthly man, we will someday be like the heavenly man.
1 CORINTHIANS 15:49 NLT

All of us! Nothing between us and God, our faces shining with the brightness of his face. And so we are transfigured much like the Messiah, our lives gradually becoming brighter and more beautiful as God enters our lives and we become like him.
2 CORINTHIANS 3:18 MSG

Therefore, if anyone is in Christ, he is a new creation; old things have passed away, and look, new things have come.
2 CORINTHIANS 5:17 HCSB

For as many of you as have been baptized into Christ have put on Christ like a garment.
GALATIANS 3:27 HCSB

For once you were full of darkness, but now you have light from the Lord. So live as people of light!
EPHESIANS 5:8 NLT

Let us draw near with a true heart in full assurance of faith, our hearts sprinkled clean from an evil conscience and our bodies washed in pure water.
HEBREWS 10:22 HCSB

For you have been born again, not of perishable seed, but of imperishable, through the living and enduring word of God.
1 PETER 1:23 NIV

But friends, that's exactly who we are: children of God. And that's only the beginning. Who knows how we'll end up! What we know is that when Christ is openly revealed, we'll see him—and in seeing him, become like him.
1 JOHN 3:2 MSG

Trust

But the LORD said to Moses and Aaron, "Because you did not trust me enough to demonstrate my holiness to the people of Israel, you will not lead them into the land I am giving them!"

NUMBERS 20:12 NLT

I waited patiently for the LORD,
and He turned to me and heard my cry for help.
He brought me up from a desolate pit,
out of the muddy clay,
and set my feet on a rock,
making my steps secure.
He put a new song in my mouth,
a hymn of praise to our God.
Many will see and fear
and put their trust in the LORD.

PSALM 40:1 HCSB

All you who fear the LORD, trust the LORD!
He is your helper and your shield.

PSALM 115:11 NLT

The decrees You issue are righteous
and altogether trustworthy.

PSALM 119:138 HCSB

You keep all your promises.
You are the Creator of heaven's glory,
earth's grandeur, and ocean's greatness.

PSALM 146:6 TPT

Depend on GOD and keep at it
because in the LORD GOD you have a sure thing.
ISAIAH 26:4 MSG

To all the rich of this world, I command you not to be wrapped in thoughts of pride over your prosperity, or rely on your wealth, for your riches are unreliable and nothing compared to the Living God. Trust instead in the one who has lavished upon us all good things, fulfilling our every need.
1 TIMOTHY 6:17 TPT

Truth

The sum total of all your words adds up to absolute truth,
and every one of your righteous decrees is everlasting.
> PSALM 119:160 TPT

Every word of God proves true.
> PROVERBS 30:5A NLT

Understanding

How sweet Your word is to my taste—
sweeter than honey in my mouth.
I gain understanding from Your precepts;
therefore I hate every false way.

PSALM 119:103-104 HCSB

"To those who listen to my teaching, more understanding will be given, and they will have an abundance of knowledge. But for those who are not listening, even what little understanding they have will be taken away from them."

MATTHEW 13:12 NLT

"So pay attention to how you hear. To those who listen to my teaching, more understanding will be given. But for those who are not listening, even what they think they understand will be taken away from them."

LUKE 8:18 NLT

Now we have not received the spirit of the world, but the Spirit who comes from God, so that we may understand what has been freely given to us by God.

1 CORINTHIANS 2:12 HCSB

Unity

In the human body there are many parts and organs, each with a unique function. And so it is in the body of Christ. For though we are many, we've all been mingled into one body in Christ. This means that we are all vitally joined to one another, with each contributing to the others.

ROMANS 12:4-5 TPT

The human body has many parts, but the many parts make up one whole body. So it is with the body of Christ. Some of us are Jews, some are Gentiles, some are slaves, and some are free. But we have all been baptized into one body by one Spirit, and we all share the same Spirit.

1 CORINTHIANS 12:12-13 NLT

There is neither Jew nor Greek, there is neither slave nor free, there is neither male nor female; for you are all one in Christ Jesus.

GALATIANS 3:28 NKJV

Together, we are his house, built on the foundation of the apostles and the prophets. And the cornerstone is Christ Jesus himself. We are carefully joined together in him, becoming a holy temple for the Lord. Through him you Gentiles are also being made part of this dwelling where God lives by his Spirit.

EPHESIANS 2:20-22 NLT

This mystery is that through the gospel the Gentiles are heirs together with Israel, members together of one body, and sharers together in the promise in Christ Jesus.

EPHESIANS 3:6 NIV

For there is one body and one Spirit, just as you have been called to one glorious hope for the future.

EPHESIANS 4:4 NLT

Victory

I see him, but not now;
I perceive him, but not near.
A star will come from Jacob,
and a scepter will arise from Israel.
He will smash the forehead of Moab
and strike down all the Shethites.
Edom will become a possession;
Seir will become a possession of its enemies,
but Israel will be triumphant.
One who comes from Jacob will rule;
he will destroy the city's survivors.

NUMBERS 24:17-19 HCSB

"That's right. If you diligently keep all this commandment that I command you to obey—love GOD, your God, do what he tells you, stick close to him—No one will be able to stand in your way. Everywhere you go, GOD sent fear and trembling will precede you, just as he promised."

DEUTERONOMY 11:22, 25 MSG

"How blessed you are, O Israel!
Who else is like you, a people saved by the LORD?
He is your protecting shield
and your triumphant sword!
Your enemies will cringe before you,
and you will stomp on their backs!"

DEUTERONOMY 33:29 NLT

"After the death of Joshua, the Israelites asked the LORD, Which tribe should go first to attack the Canaanites?" The LORD answered, "Judah, for I have given them victory over the land."

JUDGES 1:1-2 NLT

One day she sent for Barak son of Abinoam, who lived in Kedesh in the land of Naphtali. She said to him, This is what the LORD, the God of Israel, commands you: "Call out 10,000 warriors from the tribes of Naphtali and Zebulun at Mount Tabor. And I will call out Sisera, commander of Jabin's army, along with his chariots and warriors, to the Kishon River. There I will give you victory over him."
JUDGES 4:6-7 NLT

The LORD told Gideon, "With these 300 men I will rescue you and give you victory over the Midianites. Send all the others home."
JUDGES 7:7 NLT

That night the LORD said, "Get up! Go down into the Midianite camp, for I have given you victory over them!"
JUDGES 7:9 NLT

"Is this the right time to attack the Philistines? Will you give me the victory?" GOD answered, "Attack; I'll give you the victory."
1 CHRONICLES 14:10 MSG

But you will not even need to fight. Take your positions; then stand still and watch the LORD's victory. He is with you, O people of Judah and Jerusalem. Do not be afraid or discouraged. Go out against them tomorrow, for the LORD is with you!
2 CHRONICLES 20:17 NLT

Now this I know:
The LORD gives victory to his anointed.
He answers him from his heavenly sanctuary
with the victorious power of his right hand.
PSALM 20:6 NIV

For I do not trust in my bow,
and my sword does not bring me victory.
But You give us victory over our foes
and let those who hate us be disgraced.
PSALM 44:6-7 HCSB

Give us a Father's help when we face our enemies.
For to trust in any man is an empty hope.
With God's help we will fight like heroes,
and trample down our every foe!
PSALM 60:11-12 TPT

I wait quietly before God,
for my victory comes from him.
PSALM 62:1 NLT

For the LORD delights in his people;
he crowns the humble with victory.
PSALM 149:4 NLT

"See, God has come to save me.
I will trust in him and not be afraid.
The LORD GOD is my strength and my song;
he has given me victory."
ISAIAH 12:2 NLT

Your hand will be lifted up in triumph over your enemies,
and all your foes will be destroyed.
MICAH 5:9 NIV

What, then, shall we say in response to these things? If God is for us, who can be against us?
ROMANS 8:31 NIV

The sting of death is sin, and the power of sin is the law. But thanks be to God! He gives us the victory through our Lord Jesus Christ.
1 CORINTHIANS 15:56-57 NIV

If we are joined with him in his sufferings, then we will reign together with him in his triumph. But if we disregard him, then he will also disregard us.
2 TIMOTHY 2:12 TPT

I am writing to you, fathers,
because you have come to know
the One who is from the beginning.
I am writing to you, young men,
because you have had victory over the evil one.

1 JOHN 2:13 HCSB

My dear children, you come from God and belong to God. You have already won a big victory over those false teachers, for the Spirit in you is far stronger than anything in the world.

1 JOHN 4:4 MSG

For every child of God defeats this evil world, and we achieve this victory through our faith. And who can win this battle against the world? Only those who believe that Jesus is the Son of God.

1 JOHN 5:4-5 NLT

He said to me: It is done. I am the Alpha and the Omega, the Beginning and the End. To the thirsty I will give water without cost from the spring of the water of life. Those who are victorious will inherit all this, and I will be their God and they will be my children.

REVELATION 21:6-7 NIV

Weariness

Those who wait on the LORD
Shall renew their strength;
They shall mount up with wings like eagles,
They shall run and not be weary,
They shall walk and not faint.
　　ISAIAH 40:31 NKJV

"People will live together in Judah and all its towns—farmers and those who move about with their flocks. I will refresh the weary and satisfy the faint."
　　JEREMIAH 31:24–25 NIV

"Come to Me, all of you who are weary and burdened, and I will give you rest."
　　MATTHEW 11:28 HCSB

Wickedness

Then the Lord said, "I will wipe off from the face of the earth mankind, whom I created, together with the animals, creatures that crawl, and birds of the sky—for I regret that I made them." Noah, however, found favor in the sight of the Lord.
GENESIS 6:7-8 HCSB

"And I will require the blood of anyone who takes another person's life. If a wild animal kills a person, it must die. And anyone who murders a fellow human must die. If anyone takes a human life, that person's life will also be taken by human hands. For God made human beings in his own image."
GENESIS 9:5-6 NLT

"The wicked are denied their light,
and their upraised arm is broken."
JOB 38:15 NIV

The wicked conceive evil;
they are pregnant with trouble
and give birth to lies.
They dig a deep pit to trap others,
then fall into it themselves.
The trouble they make for others backfires on them.
The violence they plan falls on their own heads.
PSALM 7:14-16 NLT

He will rain down blazing coals and burning sulfur on the wicked,
punishing them with scorching winds.
PSALM 11:6 NLT

A little while, and the wicked will be no more;
though you look for them, they will not be found.
PSALM 37:10 NIV

"I will punish the world for its evil,
And the wicked for their iniquity;
I will halt the arrogance of the proud,
And will lay low the haughtiness of the terrible."
    ISAIAH 13:11 NKJV

"For out of the heart come evil thoughts—murder, adultery, sexual immorality, theft, false testimony, slander. These are what defile a person; but eating with unwashed hands does not defile them."
    MATHEW 15:19-20 NIV

Wisdom

"With God are wisdom and might;
he has counsel and understanding.
If he tears down, none can rebuild;
if he shuts a man in, none can open."

JOB 12:13-14 ESV

And this is what he says to all humanity: "The fear of the Lord is true wisdom;
to forsake evil is real understanding."

JOB 28:28 NLT

God's Word is perfect in every way.
How it revives our souls!
His laws lead us to truth,
and his ways change the simple into wise.

PSALM 19:7 TPT

The fear of the LORD is the beginning of wisdom;
all who follow his precepts have good understanding.
To him belongs eternal praise.

PSALM 111:10 NIV

How then does a man gain the essence of wisdom?
We cross the threshold of true knowledge
when we live in complete awe and adoration of God.
Stubborn know-it-alls will never stop to do this,
for they scorn true wisdom and knowledge.

PROVERBS 1:7 TPT

Yes, if you cry out for discernment,
And lift up your voice for understanding,
If you seek her as silver,
And search for her as for hidden treasures;
Then you will understand the fear of the LORD,
And find the knowledge of God.
> PROVERBS 2:3-5 NKJV

For the Lord has a hidden storehouse of wisdom
made accessible to his godly lovers.
He becomes your personal bodyguard as you follow his ways,
protecting and guarding you as you choose what is right.
> PROVERBS 2:7-8 TPT

For wisdom is more profitable than silver,
and her wages are better than gold.
Wisdom is more precious than rubies;
nothing you desire can compare with her.
> PROVERBS 3:14-15 NLT

Getting wisdom is the wisest thing you can do!
And whatever else you do, develop good judgment.
> PROVERBS 4:7 NLT

Wisdom will exalt you when you exalt her truth.
She will lead you to honor and favor
when you live your life by her insights.
> PROVERBS 4:8 TPT

You will find true success when you find me,
for I have insight into wise plans,
that are designed just for you!
> PROVERBS 8:14 TPT

I lead you into the ways of righteousness
to discover the paths of true justice.
Those who love me gain great wealth and a glorious inheritance,
and I will fill their lives with treasures.
PROVERBS 8:20-21 TPT

If you wait at wisdom's doorway, longing to hear a word for every day,
joy will break forth within you as you listen for what I'll say.
For the fountain of life pours into you every time that you find me,
and this is the secret of growing in the delight and the favor of the Lord.
PROVERBS 8:34-35 TPT

Fear of the LORD is the foundation of wisdom.
Knowledge of the Holy One results in good judgment.
PROVERBS 9:10 NLT

Fear of the LORD teaches wisdom;
humility precedes honor.
PROVERBS 15:33 NLT

For to the man who is pleasing in His sight, He gives wisdom, knowledge, and joy, but to the sinner He gives the task of gathering and accumulating in order to give to the one who is pleasing in God's sight.
ECCLESIASTES 2:26 HCSB

"Men and women who have lived wisely and well will shine brilliantly, like the cloudless, star-strewn night skies. And those who put others on the right path to life will glow like stars forever."
DANIEL 12:3 MSG

Where is the wise person? Where is the teacher of the law? Where is the philosopher of this age? Has not God made foolish the wisdom of the world?
1 CORINTHIANS 1:20 NIV

Remember what you were taught from your childhood from the Holy Scrolls, which can impart to you wisdom to experience everlasting life through the faith of Jesus, the Anointed One!
2 TIMOTHY 3:15 TPT

If any of you lacks wisdom, you should ask God, who gives generously to all without finding fault, and it will be given to you.
JAMES 1:5 NIV

But the wisdom from above is always pure, filled with peace, considerate and teachable. It is filled with love and never displays prejudice or hypocrisy in any form and it always bears the beautiful harvest of righteousness! Good seeds of wisdom's fruit will be planted with peaceful acts by those who cherish making peace.
JAMES 3:17-18 TPT

Wonders

"I will display wonders
in the heavens and on the earth:
blood, fire, and columns of smoke.
The sun will be turned to darkness
and the moon to blood
before the great and awe-inspiring Day of the LORD comes."
    JOEL 2:30-31 HCSB

"As in the days when you came out of Egypt,
I will show them my wonders."
    MICAH 7:15 NIV

Work

And to Adam he said,
"Because you have listened to the voice of your wife
and have eaten of the tree
of which I commanded you,
'You shall not eat of it,'
cursed is the ground because of you;
in pain you shall eat of it all the days of your life;
thorns and thistles it shall bring forth for you;
and you shall eat the plants of the field.
By the sweat of your face
you shall eat bread,
till you return to the ground,
for out of it you were taken;
for you are dust,
and to dust you shall return."
> GENESIS 3:17–19 ESV

"So now you are cursed, alienated, from the ground that opened its mouth to receive your brother's blood you have shed. If you work the ground, it will never again give you its yield. You will be a restless wanderer on the earth."
> GENESIS 4:11–12 HCSB

"They shall not labor in vain,
Nor bring forth children for trouble;
For they shall be the descendants of the blessed of the LORD,
And their offspring with them."
> ISAIAH 65:23 NKJV

Worry

"Blessed is the man who trusts in the LORD,
whose trust is the LORD.
He is like a tree planted by water,
that sends out its roots by the stream,
and does not fear when heat comes,
for its leaves remain green,
and is not anxious in the year of drought,
for it does not cease to bear fruit."

JEREMIAH 17:7-8 ESV

"You're blessed when you're at the end of your rope. With less of you there is more of God and his rule."

MATTHEW 5:3 MSG

"This is why I tell you: Don't worry about your life, what you will eat or what you will drink; or about your body, what you will wear. Isn't life more than food and the body more than clothing? Look at the birds of the sky: They don't sow or reap or gather into barns, yet your heavenly Father feeds them. Aren't you worth more than they?"

MATTHEW 6:25-26 HCSB

Worship

My heart, O God, is steadfast,
my heart is steadfast;
I will sing and make music.
Awake, my soul!
Awake, harp and lyre!
I will awaken the dawn.
I will praise you, Lord, among the nations;
I will sing of you among the peoples.

PSALM 57:7-10 NIV

"All mankind will come to worship Me
from one New Moon to another
and from one Sabbath to another,"
says the LORD.

ISAIAH 66:23 HCSB

"The day will come when watchmen will shout
from the hill country of Ephraim,
'Come, let us go up to Jerusalem
to worship the LORD our God.'"

JEREMIAH 31:7 NLT

In the last days, the mountain of the LORD's house
will be the highest of all—
the most important place on earth.
It will be raised above the other hills,
and people from all over the world will stream there to worship.

MICAH 4:1 NLT

"A time is coming and has now come when the true worshipers will worship the Father in the Spirit and in truth, for they are the kind of worshipers the Father seeks. God is spirit, and his worshipers must worship in the Spirit and in truth."

JOHN 4:23-24 NIV

Beloved friends, what should be our proper response to God's marvelous mercies? I encourage you to surrender yourselves to be his sacred, living sacrifices, as those offered to God. And yet live in holiness, experiencing all that delights his heart. For this becomes your genuine expression of worship.
ROMANS 12:1 TPT

When we worship the right way, God doesn't stir us up into confusion; he brings us into harmony. This goes for all the churches—no exceptions.
1 CORINTHIANS 14:33 MSG

"Mighty your acts and marvelous,
O God, the Sovereign-Strong!
Righteous your ways and true,
King of the nations!
Who can fail to fear you, God,
give glory to your Name?
Because you and you only are holy,
all nations will come and worship you,
because they see your judgments are right."
REVELATION 15:3-4 MSG